PRAISE FOR THIS BOOK

"This is the best book on Catholic Social Teaching I have
ever read! Not only does Dr. Kwasniewski give a true
account of the Church's perennial teaching on a range of
central questions, he helps readers identify and skewer
counterfeit versions of the Faith. A powerful antidote to
the dreary liberalism which has held Catholics captive
for far too long."

—DR. C.C. PECKNOLD, Associate Professor of Theology, The Catholic University of America

"Catholic Social Teaching has a simple premise from
which its content flows: just as the individual person
must become a disciple of Jesus Christ if he is to have
any hope of the healing and transformation that we call
redemption, so too must the corporate person of the
polity. That is indeed exactly what Scripture teaches us
in Matthew 28:19 and Apocalypse 7:9. Unfortunately, the
meaning of Catholic Social Teaching has changed in the
minds of many, at worst being presented as a kind of
clericalized Marxism. Dr. Kwasniewski, with characteristic clarity, reminds us what the mission to establish a
Christian social order *really* means. Whether it is the issue
of property rights, or freedom of speech, or democratic
processes and the rule of law, or any other issue that
plagues contemporary political discourse, Kwasniewski
demonstrates that the Lord's Kingship is the ultimate
answer, and that outside His Kingdom there is only chaos
and confusion."

—DR. SEBASTIAN MORELLO, Wolfgang Smith Chair
in Philosophy at St Mary's University, London

"Peter Kwasniewski's *His Reign Shall Have No End* is
a work of superlative clarity. With a steady hand, he
retrieves the Church's perennial wisdom on the Kingship
of Christ, carefully engaging with Scripture, Tradition,
and Magisterial teaching while confronting the errors of
secular liberalism. This book is at once historically rooted

and urgently relevant, a vital contribution to Catholic political thought that will serve both scholars and lay readers seeking to understand how Christ's reign shapes every dimension of life."

—FR. WILLIAM J. SLATTERY, author of *Enchanted by Eternity: Recapturing the Wonder of the Catholic Worldview*

"The line between rupture and continuity in the post-conciliar ecclesiastical landscape is a subtle one and and it undoubtedly cuts through the merely authentic magisterium while leaving inviolate the territory of both the extraordinary and the ordinary-and-universal magisterium. Few scholars have the courage not only to penetrate these regions but also to attempt the necessary demarcation, especially when it comes to the most contested area of all: Catholic Social Teaching. Peter Kwasniewski is a meticulous cartographer and a bold explorer who is equally contemptuous toward claims of El Dorado and of dragon infestation. We should be grateful for his labours."

—ALAN FIMISTER, co-author of *Integralism: A Manual of Political Philosophy*

"What does the social and political world look like to a Catholic who accepts the Faith as the most adequate expression of the truth about God, man, and the world? *His Reign Shall Have No End* tries to answer that question. This book is especially good on the great encyclicals of Leo XIII and kindred popes, on how these classical principles are reflected in the Church's traditional life of prayer, and on the radical oppositions between Catholic social teaching and every current political movement."

—JAMES KALB, author of *The Tyranny of Liberalism* and *The Decomposition of Man*

HIS REIGN SHALL HAVE NO END

His Reign Shall Have No End

Catholic Social Teaching
for the Lionhearted

PETER A. KWASNIEWSKI

XIII Books
An Imprint of Arouca Press
PO Box 55003
Bridgeport PO
Waterloo, ON N2J 0A5
Canada
www.aroucapress.com

Send inquiries to info@aroucapress.com

ISBN: 978-1-998492-64-0 (paperback)
ISBN: 978-1-998492-65-7 (hardcover)
ISBN: 978-1-998492-66-4 (ebook)

Book design by Michael Schrauzer

For J. B.,
who introduced me to political philosophy

For M. M.,
who guided me into the papal encyclicals

For M.W.,
who opened my mind to the common good

For J. H.,
whose friendship is beyond price

The kings of the earth stood up, and the princes met together, against the Lord and against his Christ. "Let us break their bonds asunder: and let us cast away their yoke from us."...O ye kings, understand: receive instruction, you that judge the earth. Serve ye the Lord with fear: and rejoice unto him with trembling. Embrace discipline, lest at any time the Lord be angry, and you perish from the just way.

Psalm 2:2–3, 10–12

When the Christianity of a country is reduced to the bare proportions of life at home, when Christianity is no longer the soul of public life, of public power, of public institutions, then Jesus Christ deals with this country in the manner he is there dealt with. He continues to give his grace and his blessings to the individuals who serve him, but he abandons the institutions, the powers which do not serve him; and the institutions, the kings, the nations become like shifting sand in the desert, they fall away like the autumn leaves which are gone with the wind.

Cardinal Louis-Édouard-
François-Desiré Pie

The City cannot be built otherwise than as God has built it; society cannot be set up unless the Church lays the foundations and supervises the work. Civilization is not something yet to be found, nor is the New City to be built on hazy notions; it has been in existence and still is: it is Christian civilization, it is the Catholic city. It has only to be set up and restored continually against the unremitting attacks of insane dreamers, rebels, and miscreants.

Pius X, *Notre Charge Apostolique*

CONTENTS

PREFACE

THE ARCHANGEL GABRIEL SAYS TO THE Blessed Virgin Mary, concerning the Son to be born of her virginal womb: "He shall reign over the house of Jacob for ever; and of his kingdom there shall be no end" (Lk 1:33). The Mass for the Feast of Christ the King, established one hundred years ago by Pope Pius XI, emphasizes this truth again and again. The Collect and the Preface alike call Jesus Christ "King of the whole world," *Rex universorum*. The Epistle from Colossians reminds us that "in all things he holds the primacy" (Col 1:18). The Gradual states: "He shall rule from sea to sea, and from the river unto the ends of the earth. And all kings of the earth shall adore Him: all nations shall serve Him" (Ps 71:8, 11). The Offertory antiphon echoes it: "Ask of Me and I will give Thee the nations for Thine inheritance, and the ends of the earth for Thy possession" (Ps 2:8).

When we hear the expression "shall have no end," we usually think of temporal duration: it may have had a beginning but it will never come to an end, it will endure forever, for all eternity. But the phrase can also mean "shall have no limit," as in, no temporal, spatial, or existential limitation. Christ is King over the whole of reality; He is King of all angels and men, whether in their merciful glorification or in their just condemnation. No one can dictate terms to Him, no one can prevent Him from reigning or set boundaries to His Kingdom. He may permit moral evils and refrain from intervention in a certain time or place, but that is a decision of His wisdom, made in sovereign freedom.

The purpose of this book is not to cover the entirety of Catholic Social Teaching (CST), much less to offer an encyclopedic prospectus of popes, encyclicals, movements, controversies, and the like. There are many books, some of them quite hefty, that go into every detail with which CST concerns itself. Some of these volumes are very handy and insightful; the "Further Reading" at the end lists the best among them, for those who wish to delve deeper. Here, my purpose is more focused: I want to present fundamental principles of CST that are often neglected in recent presentations because they are frankly embarrassing to a modern secular democratic and pluralistic outlook; they are considered old-fashioned, irrelevant, superseded by the "march of events" or "progress." Yet without these foundations, CST lacks coherence; its hundreds of particular recommendations disintegrate as a body begins to do at the soul's departure.

For this reason, my book will seem provocative to some who have reduced CST to a grab-bag of catechetical truisms and social welfare policies. Instead, I emphasize the *traditional* stance of the Church on the pivotal difference that the Incarnation of the Son of God makes to the whole of human history and human society. God has always been the great King, metaphorically speaking, regardless of whether or not His rule was acknowledged; but when God became man, *man became God's*, in the sense that Christ is metaphysically the King of all individuals, all societies, and all nations, which therefore have a solemn obligation to recognize Him as their King and to serve Him as members of the Church He founded.

To the extent that individuals, societies, and nations fail to recognize Christ as King, and still worse, to the extent that they take steps to throw off His reign where it had previously been acknowledged, to just that extent will they know restlessness, confusion, perversion, and dissolution. History tells many stories, it can be and often is a confusing mess, but it does not lie: good and evil trees manifest themselves in the good and evil fruits they produce. We can see all around us in the "new world order" a compelling demonstration—if only, alas, in the form of an accelerating *reductio ad absurdum*—that Christ's divine claims over the human race are true.

Today's *soi-disant* democratic governments are all about limits: speed limits, age limits, smoking bans, zoning laws, the list goes on and on. Yet they allow (and sometimes encourage) their citizens to maim or even destroy themselves and their dependents in the name of freedom from the law of God. Such is the revolutionary inhumanity of the secular humanism enshrined in the laws, customs, and education of most modern nations, a system of "practical atheism" that has become a religion, or rather, a death cult that undermines itself over time as it wears away the foundations of sanity and fellowship.

In the decades I have been teaching and writing about CST, one of the most common objections I hear is: "Why should we take seriously a doctrine that, at this point, is rejected by nearly everyone in the world? Is this not a flight into utopia, a self-indulgent escapism?" But this objection misses what is primary and most important, namely, *each believer*'s embracing the kingship of Christ *in full*, together with all its ramifications—whether they are actualized in the wide world around us or not; and this for two reasons. First, it was because Christ was accepted as king of souls that He, in due course, came to be recognized as king of families, cities, and empires. Second, in Christianity, unlike in Marxism, truth precedes, defines, and actuates praxis. It is by holding fast to the full truth of the cosmic, universal, all-encompassing rulership of the God-man and striving to live it in all the ways open to us that we ourselves become His loyal subjects, prepared for eternal life in His kingdom. The Lord Himself promises that we may join Him on His throne, if we are but faithful to Him in life and death: "To him that shall overcome, I will give to sit with me in my throne: as I also have overcome, and am set down with my Father in his throne" (Rev 3:21).

The Roman Rite, in the Hour of Prime, puts the following prayer on the lips of those who pray the Divine Office:

> *Dirigire et sanctificare, regere et gubernare dignare, Domine Deus, Rex caeli et terrae, hodie corda et corpora nostra, sensus, sermones et actus nostros in lege tua et in operibus mandatorum tuorum; ut hic et in aeternum, te auxiliante, salvi et liberi esse mereamur, Salvator mundi: Qui vivis et regnas in saecula saeculorum. Amen.*

> O Lord God, King of heaven and earth, may it please Thee this day to order and to hallow, to rule and to govern our hearts and our bodies, our thoughts, our words and our works, according to Thy law and in the doing of Thy commandments, that we, being helped by Thee, may here and hereafter merit to be saved and delivered by Thee, O Savior of the world, who livest and reignest for ever and ever. Amen.

It is precisely by having this mentality, this intention, this earnest petition, that Christ will come to reign in the world by first reigning in your heart and mine. The fact that the Hour of Prime was abolished in the new Liturgy of the Hours and this once-daily prayer was relegated to one day a month[1] shows what we are up against: a Church that does not even *ask* Christ to rule over us day by day. No Christendom will ever emerge out of that kind of religion. I am interested in presenting a coherent doctrine, not a lightweight mishmash leavened by modern Western liberalism.[2]

---

[1] Monday of the Third Week.

[2] Some people who study or write about CST are preoccupied with questions of "development of doctrine," which they usually understand in the sense of "evolution of doctrine," later iterations

What I mean by the latter can be gleaned from the Second Vatican Council's Pastoral Constitution on the Church in the Modern World, *Gaudium et Spes*, which claims in no. 63: "*Man* is the source, the center, and the purpose of all economic and social life."[3] It may have been possible to speak like this in a hypothetical universe where the Son of God did not become man (although one might still have a doubt, inasmuch as the Word of God is the exemplar of all creation and therefore remains central to any and all endeavors of the rational creature); but in the *real* universe of which the incarnate Word is the head, the source, and the center of creation, the purpose of all economic and social life is and cannot be other than the Son of God made flesh, Christ the King, and, consequently, it must aim at the realization of *His* Kingdom. Anything other than that is a distortion and a deviation.[4]

This, indeed, is why I have chosen to lean so heavily on the teaching of Pope Leo XIII, who deserves to be called "the pope of the political question" no less than "the pope of the social question." This great pontiff, after whom the imprint "XIII Books" is named, will

---

correcting and replacing earlier ones (and, specifically, Vatican II or post-Vatican II supplanting much of what came before it). While there are doubtless tensions and differences in emphasis between this or that period of time, I think that the remarkable coherence of CST greatly outweighs whatever disputed questions there may be, and that the massive pillars established by Pope Leo XIII have not been shaken; on the contrary, they are absolutely necessary for the structural soundness of the magisterial building erected upon them. For this reason, my book is unapologetically "Leonine" in character, which best suits its purpose as a primer and not an academic monograph.

[3] The same idea emerges in Paul VI's final message at the closing of the Council: "The old story of the Samaritan has been the model of the Council's spirituality. A sympathy without limits has entirely invaded it.... We also, We more than anyone, We hold the cult of man." See Chiron, *Paul VI*, 214.

[4] The fact that the same document says elsewhere that God is the ultimate end of man (e.g., *Gaudium et Spes* 13) does not erase the difficulty in no. 63, which is false *as stated*.

be our guide throughout: hence the subtitle to this book, "Catholic Social Teaching for the Lionhearted." He himself had the heart of a lion, and those who would follow him today must be no different, as they will find themselves resisting not only the unbelieving world but also the misbelieving and misbehaving world within the Church.

The year of publication, 2025, marks the centenary of Pope Pius XI's great encyclical *Quas Primas*,[5] by which the beloved feast of the Kingship of Our Lord Jesus Christ was established. The fate of this feast itself is highly illuminating, inasmuch as its original form proclaimed the full truth of CST, while the retooled feast that replaced it under Paul VI subverted that full truth.[6] As with the benighted liturgical reform in general, so with this deconstructed feast in particular: the postconciliar changes sought a *modus vivendi* with a modern West that was already tottering on the edge of its final rebellion against all order, divine and human. It can therefore be no surprise that vitality will be found in the Catholic Church today above all where the traditional rites of divine worship have been recovered, nor is it surprising that the *original* feast of Christ the King, placed at the end of October just before the feast of All Saints, has become the titular feast (as it were) of the cultural and political Reconquista now in its infancy.

The chapters that make up this book were reworked from a large variety of previous publications. I wish to express my thanks to the editors of the print and online journals that published my work in this area: *Catholicism.org, Catholic Family News, Catholic Men's Quarterly, Homiletic & Pastoral Review, The Josias, Lay Witness, LifeSiteNews, New Liturgical Movement, OnePeterFive, The Remnant*, and *The Social Justice Review*. A good

---

[5] Promulgated on December 11, 1925.
[6] I will return to this point in chapters 17 and 18.

deal of rewriting was done, and new writing added, as I developed the pieces into a single manuscript.

For simplicity's sake, citations of papal or conciliar documents are accompanied simply by the paragraph or section number as found in the standard Vatican editions. Quotations from more recent popes are by no means intended as a blanket endorsement of all that they said and did; rather, the teaching of these popes should be valued whenever it is in manifest continuity with Tradition and offers new insights into it.[7]

Quotations from Scripture follow the Douay-Rheims version and, occasionally, the Revised Standard Version.

Readers may be surprised not to find, among the many topics taken up in this book, an extensive treatment of marriage and the family. Be assured, the reason is not that I disagree with the oft-repeated claim that the family is the most basic society, in some sense *prior* to the state and determining its purposes, and that, in the words of John Paul II, "as the family goes, so goes the nation, and so goes the whole world in which we live."[8] On the contrary, I believe it so fervently that I have dedicated a separate book to the subject: *Treasuring the Goods of Marriage in a Throwaway Society* (Sophia Institute Press, 2023). I would commend that book to the reader as a companion to the present one.

Peter A. Kwasniewski
October 26, 2025
Feast of Christ the King

---

[7] Regarding Pope Francis, my views align, in the main, with those expressed in the anthology *Defending the Faith Against Present Heresies*, edited by Lamont and Pierantoni.

[8] John Paul II, Homily in Perth, Australia, November 30, 1986.

I

LIFE IN ABUNDANCE

WHY DOES CATHOLIC
SOCIAL TEACHING EXIST?

I N THE YEARS WHEN I TAUGHT
Catholic Social Teaching (in what follows, "CST")
to college students, one thing always struck me:
my students wanted to hear, at the very beginning,
an explanation of why such a thing *even exists*. They
wanted to know where it came from—or, to put it more
bluntly, why a religion centered on eternal life, obtained
through supernatural faith and divinely-empowered
sacraments, should be interested in questions of constitutions and laws, labor and wages, ownership and
management, and so forth. It's a valid question. Why,
indeed, should the Church take an interest in man's
social life, including politics and economics?

Thanks to the theoreticians and social engineers of
the ineptly-named Enlightenment, and as a result of
Protestant errors about the visibility of the Church as
a society, moderns are especially prone to think about
religion as a "private" affair, something "between God
and the soul." In this way of looking at things, the
Church has but the business of helping each soul to
find its way toward God, the true eternal good, rising
above a world of deceptive promises.

In one sense, this is true: it is God who creates each
individual soul with an immortal destiny, and Jesus
Christ, the Son of God, died for the redemption of that
soul. As the priest Caecilius in John Henry Newman's
novel *Callista* beautifully says:

> There is but one Lover of souls...and He
> loves each one of us, as if there were no one

else to love. He died for each one of us, as
if there were no one else to die for.... The
nearer we draw to Him, the more triumphantly
does He enter into us; the longer He dwells
in us, the more intimately have we possession
of Him. It is an espousal for eternity.[1]

But in another sense, the question posed is odd, if
one appreciates the truth first formulated by the
pagan philosopher Aristotle in the second chapter of
his *Politics*: man is a social and political animal, one
who is born into, grows up with, and matures only
in, communities—first and most naturally the family,
but also the city or state comprising many families in
one place that can assist one another in living well. In
fact, Aristotle claimed that being social and political
was so connected to the nature of man that someone
who did not live in society must be either a beast
or a god. The Church takes an interest in social life
because the human person she teaches, rules, and sanctifies is *social by nature*, and Christ, true God and true
man, came to save the *whole* man *in his totality*. Unlike
the Enlightenment, Catholics do not bifurcate man
into a private religious soul and a public secular body.
Man is a unified entity: his social life surrounds and
impinges on his interior life, and his interior life seeks
expression and support in relationships and institutions
outside of him.

More than that, Christ came to bring about an eternal and perfect society, the Kingdom of God, which
would be as much greater than human society as the
divine is greater than the human. The preparation of
man for this eternal polity—we may call it the City
of God or the heavenly Jerusalem—involves his living
a good and holy life here below, in the earthly city,
along the ways of this world. There is no salvation that

---

[1] Newman, *Callista*, 222.

bypasses our treatment of neighbor, family, coworker, or fellow citizen. Ethics is not merely an individual science but a social one, with questions of moral good and evil at stake, questions of virtue and vice, actions pleasing and displeasing to God. Man's social life is not only *not* irrelevant to his salvation, it is deeply bound up with it.

Hence, CST belongs to *moral theology*: it belongs to that exercise of the Church's teaching office or magisterium that concerns matters of behavior, as distinct from that which concerns truths to be believed, though inevitably these areas are interconnected. In addition, the Church is the guardian of the natural law, which contains the precepts of justice (the virtue most directly exercised in social interactions). Thus, the Church is divinely authorized to address what the natural law requires men to do for the preservation of justice in society. A merely "natural" or "scientific" perspective would inevitably be a darkened perspective, without the illumination of divine revelation and Catholic tradition.

NATURAL AND SUPERNATURAL LIFE

Jesus Christ came that men might have life, and have it *abundantly*.[2] Our Lord does not save *every* good thing for Heaven, even if He does reserve the best. The family, friendships, neighborhoods, cultures, even states — all these things can be *more or less* sanctified, more or less imbued with divine truth, goodness, and beauty, since they already have God as their author, and should have His kingdom and the benefit of immortal souls as their conscious purpose. This will make them more or less perfect occasions for experiencing the Lord's joy and peace.

To put the same truth negatively, man cannot develop well as a child of God if his social nature is handicapped, or his social life is poisoned or paralyzed. Pope John Paul II wrote:

---

[2] Cf. Jn 10:10

When, under the influence of the Paraclete,
people discover this divine dimension of their
being and life, both as individuals and as a
community, they are able to free themselves
from the various determinisms which derive
mainly from the materialistic bases of thought,
practice, and related modes of action. In our
age these factors have succeeded in penetrating into man's inmost being, into that sanctuary of the conscience where the Holy Spirit
continuously radiates the light and strength
of new life in the "freedom of the children
of God." Man's growth in this life is hindered
by the conditionings and pressures exerted
upon him by dominating structures and
mechanisms in the various spheres of society. It can be said that in many cases social
factors, instead of fostering the development
and expansion of the human spirit, ultimately
deprive the human spirit of the genuine truth
of its being and life — over which the Holy
Spirit keeps vigil — in order to subject it to
the "prince of this world."[3]

On the other hand, the Catholic Faith always rightly
relativizes earthly happiness. We must never be allowed
to forget that this world is not our intended permanent
home and that we are created for the face-to-face vision
of God, the Most Holy Trinity, Father, Son, and Holy
Ghost, in festal communion with the saints and angels,
in a "new heavens and a new earth according to His
promises, in which justice dwelleth."[4] Our Lady said
to St. Bernadette Soubirous: "I do not promise you
happiness in this life, only in the next." As the book-
mark that St. Teresa of Avila herself penned and kept
in her breviary read:

---

[3] John Paul II, *Dominum et Vivificantem* 60, with references to
Rom 8:21 and Jn 12:31, 14:30, 16:11.
[4] 2 Pet 3:13.

> Let nothing disturb you,
> Let nothing frighten you,
> All things pass away:
> God never changes.
> Patience obtains all things.
> He who has God
> finds he lacks nothing;
> God alone suffices.

Man cannot be and was not meant to be perfectly happy in this life, in this world; yet he *is* called to share, even now, in the superabundant life, yes, the *joy*, of Jesus Christ, through belonging ever more intimately to His Mystical Body. Because the mystery of Christ is truly present in this world in His Church, she has the permanent mission and imperative to make of human life *in all of its dimensions* a gift that is worthy of God, and to foster a human environment that promotes in every way this gift of self to God and to one's fellow man. Society of all kinds — the family, the clan or tribe or ethnic community, the nation — is the ground in which the individual's response is rooted. This ground can be more or less rich, moist, and fertile. The individual can transcend the "social garden" in which he has been placed, but he has a certain dependency on it and a responsibility for cultivating it.

DEFENDING THE CHURCH'S INVOLVEMENT IN SOCIETY

There are many superficial notions of what CST means. For some, it means vague sentiments in support of mutual goodwill among classes and nations; for others, it spells out dreamy ideals about economic prosperity for all. But such views are too narrow. As Pope Leo XIII said in 1901:

> We have designedly made mention here of virtue and religion. For, it is the opinion of some, and the error is already very common,

that the social question is merely an economic one, whereas in point of fact it is, *above all, a moral and religious matter*, and for that reason must be settled by the principles of morality and according to the dictates of religion. For, even though wages are doubled and the hours of labor are shortened and food is cheapened, yet, if the working man hearkens to the doctrines that are [typically] taught on this subject, as he is prone to do, and is prompted by the examples set before him to throw off respect for God and to enter upon a life of immorality, his labors and his gain will avail him nothing.[5]

The same pope wrote in 1895 that "the social question"

cannot be regarded from one standpoint only. It is indeed concerned with external goods, but it is preeminently concerned with religion and morals. It is also directly connected with the civil constitution of the laws, so that in the last analysis, it has a broad reference to the rights and duties of all classes.[6]

St. Pius X commented on the above idea in an encyclical to the German bishops in 1912:

These are fundamental principles: No matter what the Christian does, even in the realm of temporal goods, he cannot ignore the supernatural good. Rather, according to the dictates of Christian philosophy, he must order all things to the ultimate end, namely, the Highest Good. All his actions, insofar as they are morally either good or bad (that is to say, whether they agree or disagree with the natural and divine law), are subject to the judgment and judicial office of the Church. All who glory

---

[5] Leo XIII, *Graves de Communi Re* 11, emphasis added.
[6] Leo XIII, *Permoti Nos* 5.

in the name of Christian, either individually
or collectively, if they wish to remain true to
their vocation, may not foster enmities and
dissensions between the classes of civil society.
On the contrary, they must promote mutual
concord and charity. The social question and
its associated controversies, such as the nature
and duration of labor, the wages to be paid,
and workingmen's strikes, are not simply economic in character. Therefore, they cannot be
numbered among those which can be settled
apart from ecclesiastical authority.[7]

The Church's traditional corpus of social teaching
addresses every fundamental question of social significance, both political (the origin, nature, and purpose
of civil government; its relationship to the Church and
her mission; its role in protecting persons, ensuring
rights, fostering virtue) and economic (the generation
of property, its ownership and distribution, the rightful
place of material goods, international trade, monetary
issues, and so on).

In the final analysis, CST is the articulation of what
consistent Christian witness to the gospel and social
action on its basis must be, with the goal of reforming
the social order according to Catholic truth. It recognizes that, without grace, the life of societies, as of
individuals, is, and cannot but be, deeply disordered,
lacking mutual harmony, peace, joy, festivity, and meaning. It is a vision of reality emanating from Christ the
King and embracing all human reality in communion
with the Triune God.

WHO INAUGURATED CHRISTIAN SOCIAL ETHICS?

Some would claim that the Church had no social
doctrine prior to recent centuries. Others might push
the line back a few centuries. But the Fathers of

---

[7] Pius X, *Singulari Quadam* 3.

the Church, such as St. Basil the Great and St. John
Chrysostom, already discuss the essential social questions in the early centuries of Christianity and trace
them back to Our Lord, the Apostles, and the Old
Testament Law and Prophets. The medieval schoolmen
such as St. Thomas Aquinas and the broad Thomistic tradition, especially in Renaissance Spain, dedicate
many important discussions to economic and political
matters. Catholic theologians and philosophers in the
modern period have contributed in major ways, as well;
one thinks of such authors as Joseph de Maistre, Juan
Donoso Cortés, and Louis Billot.

Most of the famous papal documents on social questions are from the "modern" period, which might be
dated from the Enlightenment that gave rise to the
Age of Revolutions (realized or threatened) against
ecclesiastical and civil authority. During the eighteenth
century the Church was forced, by attacks against her
and for the good of souls, to speak out against new
errors that had never been entertained before, such
as the total derivation of political authority from "the
consent of the governed" or "the will of the people," as
in the social contract theory in its various permutations.

A certain amount of historical background is helpful
here. For well over 1,000 years, the basic social reality of
the Christian world, the foundation of the social order
including its political elements, was the visible Catholic Church—what Cardinal Charles Journet dubbed
"consecrational Christendom": a body of peoples, cities,
states, united into an international federation by a common faith in Christ and obedience to the hierarchical
Church.[8] An enormously complex and diversified net-
work of "intermediate" institutions having genuine social
power and position, such as guilds, religious orders,
principalities, feudal domains, and universities, ensured

---

[8] See Journet, *The Church of the Word Incarnate*, 1:220–24, 241–44,
et passim.

a densely textured and locally-based civic and cultural life, in which the individual was not left standing in isolation over against an all-powerful state or at the mercy of an economy dominated by giant corporations. It was a world in which to be a citizen and to be a Catholic were one and the same in practice, although not necessarily in theory.

As this order was challenged or repudiated in the revolutions of the late eighteenth century and their aftermath, we find a surge of papal interventions for particular circumstances, but nothing that would deserve to be called a systematic response to Enlightenment political theory until the early part of the nineteenth century, about forty years after the French Revolution, with Pope Gregory XVI's encyclical *Mirari Vos* of 1832. We might date the modern social magisterium from the reign of this pope (1831–1846) for two reasons: first, he attempted a refutation, *on doctrinal grounds*, of certain trends of modern liberalism; second, his positions were adopted and built upon by subsequent popes.

In a message for Italian Catholic Action Family Day on March 23, 1952, Pope Pius XII adverted to the "new needs" of modernity:

> The divine assistance, which is intended to preserve Revelation from error and deformation, was promised to the Church and not to individuals. This also was a wise provision, because the Church, as a living organism, can thus with certainty and ease either explain or examine deeply into moral truths along with others; or, while maintaining their substance intact, can apply them to the changing conditions of places and times. As an example, we might cite the social doctrine of the Church which, having arisen in answer to new needs, is basically nothing more than the application of undying Christian morality to present-day economic and social circumstances.

Pope Leo XIII enjoys a place of special honor within the tradition, for he towers above all other pontiffs in the breadth and depth of his contributions to social doctrine. For this reason, his encyclicals—rich in wisdom, rigorous in logic, sparkling with insight, flowing with unction—deserve pride of place.[9] In the opinion of many, he is the greatest teacher of the fundamentals of social ethics. A sign of this fact is the frequency with which his encyclicals are quoted by his successors. Pope John XXIII testifies to the *deep roots* of the social teaching as well as the *special position* of Leo XIII as an exponent thereof:

> Small wonder, then, that the Catholic Church, in imitation of Christ and in fulfillment of His commandment, relies not merely upon her teaching to hold aloft the torch of charity, but also upon her own widespread example. This has been her course now for nigh on two thousand years, from the early ministrations of her deacons right down to the present time. It is a charity which combines the precepts and practice of mutual love. It holds fast to the twofold aspect [viz., spiritual and temporal] of Christ's command to give, and summarizes the whole of the Church's social teaching and activity.
>
> An outstanding instance of this social teaching and action carried on by the Church throughout the ages is undoubtedly that magnificent encyclical on the christianizing of the conditions of the working classes, *Rerum Novarum*, published seventy years ago by Our Predecessor, Leo XIII.
>
> Seldom have the words of a Pontiff met with such universal acclaim. In the weight and scope of his arguments, and in the forcefulness of their expression, Pope Leo XIII can have but few rivals. Beyond any shadow of doubt,

---

[9] See Appendix 1 for an overview of his life and work.

> his directives and appeals have established for
> themselves a position of such high importance
> that they will never, surely, sink into oblivion.[10]

Unfortunately, apart from *Rerum Novarum*—and even
then, in a somewhat one-sided way—the directives and
appeals of Leo have indeed sunk into oblivion. It is
part of our task as faithful Catholics in the third mil-
lennium of Christianity to recover his teaching, which,
far from being antiquated or irrelevant, is more timely
and urgent than ever.

WHERE DO WE FIND CATHOLIC SOCIAL TEACHING?

The main concentration of CST is to be found in
papal documents, especially the type of universal letters
called encyclicals. Although these documents are available in more than one place online, the online texts are
riddled with typographical errors and sometimes even
omissions and mistranslations. Moreover, I noticed as
a teacher (and, I'll admit, a lover of physical books)
that no single published volume contained a judicious
selection of texts, with an emphasis on the older and
stronger documents.

For this reason, I produced one myself: *A Reader in
Catholic Social Teaching: From* Syllabus Errorum *to* Deus
Caritas Est (Cluny Media, 2017), which contains Leo
XIII's greatest social encyclicals, including *Diuturnum
Illud* (1881) on the origin of civil power, *Immortale Dei*
(1885) on the Christian constitution of states, *Libertas
Praestantissimum* (1888) on the nature of human freedom,
Sapientiae Christianae (1890) on the duties of Christians
as citizens, and *Rerum Novarum* (1891) on capital and
labor, as well as Pius XI's *Quas Primas* (1925) on the
Kingship of Christ, *Casti Connubii* (1930) on marriage,
and *Quadragesimo Anno* (1931) on the reconstruction of

---

[10] John XXIII, *Mater et Magistra* 6–8.

the social order, joined by Pius XII's address "On Religious Tolerance" (*Ci Riesce*, 1953) and the best writing of John Paul II on moral theology and the family[11]—with all of the texts having been liberated from typos and poor translations, to the extent I detected them.

I am pleased to be able to report that this anthology has been widely taken up in university courses, adult Catholic education courses, and book clubs. It provides a possible syllabus at the start that one could follow as a self-study. Take the encyclicals one at a time, and you will soon discover that they make for extremely rewarding reading and provide plenty of kindling for prayer and action. The Catholic Church alone has presented to the world a coherent, complete, and compelling Christian vision of society, the state, and culture, rooted in Sacred Scripture and Sacred Tradition, and refined over twenty centuries of meditation and engagement. It is a body of wisdom we ignore at our peril.

---

[11] In an interview with P. J. Smith, I talk about why I included certain things and left out others: "The Possibility of a Catholic Social Order," *First Things*, December 18, 2017.

A SYLLABUS WE SHOULD
ALL BE STUDYING

NOT MANY CATHOLICS TODAY know about the *Syllabus of Errors*—but they should. Mocked (as one might expect) by the fashionable at the time of its issuance in 1864, Pius IX's thundering condemnation of modern errors has demonstrated prescient accuracy as the world around us, embracing these errors to the full, races heedlessly to its own destruction. I begin with this document because the *Syllabus* is like a gauntlet thrown down to Modernity, and thus well conveys the militant, reformatory, counterrevolutionary spirit of the *traditional* Catholic Social Teaching to which this volume is devoted.

The history of the compilation and promulgation of the *Syllabus of Errors* is quite complex[1] but the central motivation behind it is easy to grasp:

> All this alarming news [of revolution and rebellion] succeeded in convincing Pius IX that liberalism, the synthesis of the eighteenth-century Encyclopedists' philosophy, recast in a political form by the French revolutionaries, was truly "the error of the century," an error he was duty-bound to condemn once again by drawing the attention of Catholics to all the forms—sometimes subtle ones—that this tendency could assume in the concrete.[2]

---

[1] See Hales, *Pio Nono*, 255–90; Holmes, *The Triumph of the Holy See*, 145–51.
[2] Aubert, "Religious Liberty," 97.

After a lengthy gestation, the *Syllabus* and the encyclical to which it was appended, *Quanta Cura*, were issued on December 8, 1864, accompanied by a letter from the Secretary of State, Cardinal Antonelli. Intended for bishops who had the training required to read it carefully, the *Syllabus* quickly fell into the hands of simple-minded journalists who, like their counterparts a hundred years later at the time of the Second Vatican Council, reveled in superficial exaggerations, making the document and its promulgator the subject of front-page controversy.

Quanta Cura and the *Syllabus* are presented as a summary of teaching already set forth by the pope in allocutions and other documents going back to his inaugural encyclical *Qui Pluribus* of 1846. *Quanta Cura* denounced views typical of the Enlightenment, honing in on its definitive idea: the "impious and absurd principle of naturalism," which teaches that

> the best constitution of public society and [also] civil progress altogether require that human society be conducted and governed without regard being had to religion any more than if it did not exist; or, at least, without any distinction being made between the true religion and false ones. (*Quanta Cura* 3)

The banishment of religion from civil society and government cannot but darken and eventually extinguish justice and rights, replacing them with egoism, avarice, and violence (4). The pope states that the modern opinions mentioned in the encyclical—and, implicitly, those catalogued in the *Syllabus*—are to be held "reprobated, proscribed, and condemned by all children of the Catholic Church" (6).

What, specifically, were these opinions? *The Syllabus of the Principal Errors of Our Time*, to give the document its full title, consists of eighty propositions, divided into ten categories. The first three ("Pantheism, naturalism, and absolute rationalism"; "Moderate rationalism"; "Indifferentism, latitudinarianism") are predominantly speculative in content, regarding errors about the existence of God and His providence, the divinity of Christ and the truth of Christian revelation, the relationship of faith and reason, and the necessity of the Church for salvation. The seven remaining categories concern chiefly social errors.

It will suffice here to cite a few representative condemned propositions:

• The Church is not a true and perfect society divinely endowed with proper and perpetual rights, but rather an organization under the power of civil law (19), whose immunity of personnel and property derive from civil law (30).
• In case of conflict, civil law prevails over canon law (42).
• The education of children belongs by right to the state, not to parents or to the Church (45 and others).
• Church and state *ought* to be separated (55).
• Rights are nothing other than accomplished facts (59).
• "Authority is nothing else but numbers and the sum total of material forces" (60).
• The marriage contract is not indissoluble by the law of nature, and divorce may therefore be permitted (67).

The final category, "Errors having reference to contemporary liberalism [*liberalismum hodiernum*]," gained special notoriety at the time of promulgation. Here, the pope condemns four propositions:

• "In the present day it is no longer expedient that the Catholic religion should be held as the only religion of the state, to the exclusion of all other forms of worship" (77).
• It is wise to pass laws allowing non-Catholic immigrants the public exercise of their religion (78).

• It is false that liberty of public worship and freedom of speech conduce more easily to corruption of morals and religious indifferentism (79).

• "The Roman Pontiff can and should reconcile and harmonize himself with progress, liberalism and modern [*recenti*] civilization" (80).

The internal structure of the *Syllabus* dictates its correct interpretation. Each of the eighty propositions is followed by a citation of papal document(s) in which this particular error had already been discussed and censured by the pope. Antonelli's letter instructed the reader to gauge the tenor and scope of condemned propositions from their source documents.

Take, for example, the last proposition (80), where it may seem that the pope is repudiating modern civilization *tout court*. A glance at the source proves otherwise. In an allocution of March 18, 1861, Pius IX had railed against those who expected him to surrender to "what *they* call modern civilization and liberalism," which amounted to shutting down monasteries, secularizing schools, harassing priests, supporting anarchists and communists, etc. He concluded: "If by the word 'civilization' must be understood a system invented on purpose to weaken, and perhaps to overthrow, the Church, never can the Holy See and the Roman Pontiff be allied with such a civilization!"—hardly a surprising conclusion. It is to this allocution that no. 80 of the *Syllabus* directs us.[3]

At the time of promulgation, well-trained clerics were aware of "the classical rule that when we are faced with a proposition censured by the Church's teaching authority, in order to know the positive teaching of the Church in the matter, we must take the *contradictory* of the proposition and not its contrary, as one is naturally tempted to do."[4] In other words, if the Church were

---

[3] See Aubert, "Religious Liberty," 101–2; Hales, *Pio Nono*, 258.
[4] Aubert, 101.

to condemn the proposition that democracy is the only legitimate form of government, one may conclude positively *only* that democracy is *not* the only legitimate form of government—not that democracy is an *illegitimate* form of government. Or if she rejects the statement that "Every man is free to embrace and profess that religion which, guided by the light of reason, he shall consider true" (15), positively this means the light of reason is *not* the only guide as regards religious truth—not that one should *not* be guided by the light of reason as regards religious truth. (The documentary source of no. 15 is again illuminating: the pope is there condemning the rationalist view that human reason is the sole measure of truth and right, and thus the sole means for learning or handing down what is true and right.[5]) One may derive the contradictory proposition by adding to each condemned proposition the words: "It is not the case that…" This negation leaves untouched a considerable realm of possibilities beyond what is specifically rejected.

It is also important to interpret the censured propositions in light of the concrete historical situation. Pius IX's predecessor, Gregory XVI, a fierce opponent of liberalism, was prepared to accept compromises in practice—such as the new Belgian constitution of 1831 which endorsed separation of Church and state—while maintaining that, in principle, such arrangements were imperfect and could never be held up as ideal. Pius IX was no different, nor was his successor Leo XIII. We might be tempted to view this kind of pragmatism as a hypocritical double-standard, but that would be unjust. The popes never failed to proclaim the fullness of the truth even when they were willing to collaborate with less-than-perfect governments in order to minister to the Catholic faithful throughout the world. No one

---

[5] See Kwasniewski, "What Is the Catholic Intellectual Tradition?"

can fail to see the difference between this approach and the Second Vatican Council's eternally confusing Declaration on Religious Freedom *Dignitatis Humanae*,[6] which led to the abolition of Catholic privileges in most states where they still existed, undermined the coherent witness of the preceding magisterium, and supplied low-cost energy to the factory of fictitious rights.

As its language and the frequent repetition of its doctrine make clear, Pius IX's *Syllabus of Errors* unquestionably represents a solemn act of the papal magisterium that requires our assent. As a matter of fact, it enjoys a high status due to its propositional structure, its copious cross-referencing, its precise teaching as established by its sources, and the tenor of its language. Its content is perennial: though summoned by immediate and local threats, such content is no more time-conditioned than any statement of dogmatic or moral truth (e.g., 1–14 on God, 56–64 on ethics, 65–74 on marriage).[7]

The *Syllabus* with its companion encyclical cannot be set aside as if they had lost their relevance, belonging to a now-superseded "Constantinian" or "integrist" phase.[8] The *Syllabus* continues to serve the purpose

---

[6] A sign of its confusing doctrine is the large number of incompatible interpretations offered of it, some celebrating or condemning its rupture from prior doctrine, and some attempting elaborate proofs of its continuity therewith. See, *inter alia*, Marshner, "*Dignitatis humanae* and Traditional Teaching on Church and State"; Harrison, *Religious Liberty and Contraception*, esp. 31–61; Davies, *The Second Vatican Council and Religious Liberty*, 56–62, 267–74; Storck, *Foundations of a Catholic Political Order*, 27–49; *Dignitatis Humanae Colloquium*; Lucien, *Religious Liberty: Continuity or Contradiction?*

[7] One does find some mention of issues and policies which, being bound up with the particularities of a given society, unavoidably involve prudential judgment on the part of authorities. For example, a Catholic regime in a predominantly Catholic society *should* privilege the Church, but it would make little sense to say that special favor should be shown to the Church by a non-Catholic government in a pluralistic society, a scenario not envisioned in the documentary sources of the *Syllabus*.

[8] See Storck, *Foundations*, 27–49 and 109–21.

for which it was promulgated in 1864: putting the Catholic world on its guard against the profane, materialistic, libertine axioms of the new world order that was inaugurated with the French Revolution and soon became the political program of anticlericals and anarchists, soft or hard, throughout the world. It requires no special acumen to trace lines of direct causality from the archetypal errors collected in the *Syllabus* to the widespread errors—if anything, more perverse and destructive—targeted over a century later in the encyclicals of John Paul II and Benedict XVI.

Far from being an antique curiosity, Pius IX's *Syllabus of Errors* is a prophetic document of major importance in the early stages of modern Catholic social teaching—one that will outlive many of the wordier and woolier publications from the century and a half that followed it.

II

HIERARCHY, EQUALITY, AND FREEDOM

HIERARCHY VERSUS EGALITARIANISM

THE POLITICAL REVOLUTIONS OF modernity have tended to waffle between the exaltation of unrestricted liberty (more properly termed *license*) and the enforcement of a kind of social equality that is contrary to the plan of the Creator and the good of the body politic. These two aspirations are in permanent tension: an increase of liberty necessarily increases inequality, while enforcement of equality necessarily limits liberty. In the next three chapters (3–5), my attention will be focused on the Church's understanding of equality, which has gained a new timeliness in view of the tireless efforts of political liberals to push through "equality acts" of various sorts. This part of the book will conclude with a chapter (6) on the Catholic conception of liberty and how it differs from license.

TRUE NOTION OF EQUALITY

As with most aspects of CST, it was Pope Leo XIII who offered the most thorough analysis of the topic at hand, as he strove to give guidance to a world seduced by liberalism and at constant risk of revolutionary discord. Whereas socialists "proclaim the absolute equality of all men in rights and duties," the Christian tradition teaches that

> the equality of men consists in this: that all, having inherited the same nature, are called to the same most high dignity of the sons of God, and that, as one and the same end

is set before all, each one is to be judged by
the same law and will receive punishment or
reward according to his deserts. The inequality
of rights and of power proceeds from the very
Author of nature, "from whom all paternity in
heaven and earth is named."[1]

Drawing upon the ancient theme of the "body politic" and the cosmic organism which, in modified form,
was also a central image of St. Paul's when speaking of
the Church as "body of Christ,"[2] Leo XIII's encyclical
Humanum Genus elaborates further:

No one doubts that all men are equal one to
another, so far as regards their common origin
and nature, or the last end which each one has
to attain, or the rights and duties which are
thence derived. But, as the abilities of all are
not equal, as one differs from another in the
powers of mind or body, and as there are very
many dissimilarities of manner, disposition, and
character, it is most repugnant to reason to
endeavor to confine all within the same measure, and to extend complete equality to the
institutions of civil life. Just as a perfect condition of the body results from the conjunction
and composition of its various members, which,
though differing in form and purpose, make, by
their union and the distribution of each one
to its proper place, a combination beautiful to
behold, firm in strength, and necessary for use;
so, in the commonwealth, there is an almost
infinite dissimilarity of men, as parts of the
whole. If they are to be all equal, and each is
to follow his own will, the state will appear
most deformed; but if, with a distinction of
degrees of dignity, of pursuits and employments,

---

[1] Leo XIII, *Quod Apostolici Muneris* 1 and 5, citing Eph 3:15.
[2] See, e.g., Rom 12:4–5; 1 Cor 12:12–27; Eph 1:22–23; Eph 4:1–16;
Eph 5:23, 30; Col 1:18, 24.

all aptly conspire for the common good, they
will present the image of a state both well
constituted and conformable to nature.[3]

At the end of *Humanum Genus*, Leo XIII takes occasion to commend the *Christian* understanding of the famous slogan of the French Revolution—*liberté, égalité, fraternité*:

> not such as the Freemasons absurdly imagine
> [these three], but such as Jesus Christ obtained
> for the human race and St. Francis [of Assisi]
> aspired to: the liberty, we mean, of sons of
> God, through which we may be free from slavery to Satan or to our passions, both of them
> most wicked masters; the fraternity whose
> origin is in God, the common Creator and
> Father of all; the equality which, founded on
> justice and charity, does not take away all distinctions among men, but, out of the varieties
> of life, of duties, and of pursuits, forms that
> union and that harmony which naturally tend
> to the benefit and dignity of society.[4]

In *Rerum Novarum*, Leo XIII judged the socialist utopia of communal property a recipe for disaster: "that ideal equality about which they entertain pleasant dreams would be in reality the leveling down of all to a like condition of misery and degradation"[5]—prophetic words in 1891, with the subsequent century's numerous failed experiments in Marxist "liberation" and "empowerment," although, truth be told, it cannot be said that capitalism, burdened with its own vices, has proved itself *morally* superior.[6]

---

[3] Leo XIII, *Humanum Genus* 26. This argument, incidentally, is nicely developed in Pius XII's Christmas Message of 1944, on true and false democracy.
[4] *Humanum Genus* 34.
[5] Leo XIII, *Rerum Novarum* 15.
[6] See Pius XI, *Quadragesimo Anno*.

AUTHENTIC SOLIDARITY

Building on Leo XIII's heritage, Pius XII offers a profound treatment of the subject in his inaugural encyclical *Summi Pontificatus*, written as the shadows of World War II descended over Europe in 1939. Pius XII laments a growing forgetfulness of

> that law of human solidarity and charity which is dictated and imposed by our common origin and by the equality of rational nature in all men, to whatever people they belong, and by the redeeming sacrifice offered by Jesus Christ on the altar of the Cross to His heavenly Father on behalf of sinful mankind.[7]

From its first page Scripture teaches us that God created mankind, male and female, in His own image and for the sake of eternal beatitude, and that all generations are descended from the same first couple; thus, all men are *truly* brothers.[8] Scripture puts before us "a marvelous vision" of manifold sources of unity: we are given to see

> the human race in the unity of one common origin in God...; in the unity of nature which in every man is equally composed of material body and spiritual, immortal soul; in the unity of his immediate end and mission in the world; in the unity of dwelling place, the earth, of whose resources all men can by natural right avail themselves, to sustain and develop life; in the unity of his supernatural end, God Himself, to whom all should tend; in the unity of means to secure that end. It is the same Apostle who portrays for us mankind in the unity of its relations with the Son of God, image of the invisible God...; in the unity of its ransom, effected for all by Christ, Who, through His holy and most bitter Passion, restored the

---

[7] Pius XII, *Summi Pontificatus* 35.
[8] *Summi Pontificatus* 36–37.

original friendship with God which had been broken, making Himself the Mediator between God and men.[9]

Having reviewed the ultimate foundations of human solidarity, Pius XII can conclude:

> In the light of this unity of all mankind, which exists in law and in fact, individuals do not feel themselves isolated units, like grains of sand, but united, by the very force of their nature and by their internal destiny, into an organic, harmonious mutual relationship.[10]

The pope goes on to apply these truths to international relations and membership in the Church.[11]

Put into systematic terms, the Catholic teaching can be presented thus: human beings — men, women, and children, without any exceptions — are equal in regard to their possession of a human nature that is rational and free, their *inherent* (but not their *actualized*) capacity for truth and moral goodness, their natural rights and the duties corresponding thereto,[12] their need for and obligations toward human society and its governing authorities of all kinds. All of these points rest upon their possession of human nature, by which they are constituted as *persons*. It is never permissible to treat a person as a non-person, as a mere means to some further end for the sake of which he or she can be trampled upon.

Moreover, human beings are equal in regard to their vocation to the supernatural life, the life of participating in divine grace: God wishes all to be saved and to come to the knowledge of His saving truth.[13] In this regard, they are equal in the rights and duties

---

[9] *Summi Pontificatus* 38–39.
[10] *Summi Pontificatus* 42.
[11] See nos. 43–50, and Appendix 2 below.
[12] On this point, see John XXIII, *Pacem in Terris* 8–45.
[13] Cf. 1 Tim 2:4.

that belong *essentially* to the Christian vocation, which
would include, for example, seeking and adhering to the
truth about God, receiving baptism or any sacrament
if properly disposed for it, embracing the religious life,
and so on. No power on earth can legitimately stand
in the way of the pursuit of any of these goods.

At the same time, Catholic tradition appreciates the
subtle relationship that obtains between the person
and the societies to which he belongs, between individual dignity and social solidarity. No man is an island,
but all men are, in varying ways, responsible for and
accountable to others, in the service of that genuine
common good that is more truly mine and yours than
any purely private good.[14] In this way, both the common
good and the civil law, its support, place limits on an
individual's freedom and rights, precisely to allow and
to foster the best development of each and of all.

Human dignity is not an immutable, one-dimensional
property, but, having its enduring foundation in the

---

[14] CST frequently invokes "the common good" but it is to be
regretted that many attempts at defining it in the literature remain
rather superficial, looking to externals, incidentals, or epiphenom-
ena rather than the essence of the reality. Here is an attempt at
that essence: "The good that relates people to one another is a
common good, one that is good for many people at the same time
without being diminished or divided. Private goods get used up
or removed from circulation when they are possessed.... A truly
common good, on the other hand, can be shared simultaneously
by many, perfecting them all. The peace of a family and the just
ordering of a society are goods like this, since the more such a
good exists, the more we all share in it, without its diminish-
ment.... For these reasons, the common good is better than the
private good—that is to say, it is better even for the individual
than his merely individual good. This is important because it
means that it will always be unreasonable to choose the merely
individual good to the detriment of the common good. If the two
come into conflict, the only reasonable thing to do is to choose the
common good" (Kwasniewski, *True Obedience*, 19–20). For deeper
analysis, see De Koninck's *On the Primacy of the Common Good*, the
thrust of which is summarized in Kwasniewski and Waldstein, eds.,
Integralism and the Common Good, vol. 1, 7–48; see also Kwasniewski,
Bound by Truth, 54–81. Cf. Pius XI, *Divini Redemptoris*, nos. 25–38.

rational nature of man, admits of an increase in intensity as man draws nearer to his ultimate end, which is objectively God and subjectively the happiness of union with God.[15] Man's *actual* dignity increases or decreases in proportion to his actual stance vis-à-vis the human good, though he cannot fall so far that he lacks dignity altogether, nor can he rise so high that he possesses a dignity equal to that of his uncreated Lord. The Christian tradition is not, in this sense, egalitarian, but considers men to be ranked objectively—though invisibly to our eyes—by the fire of charity that burns in their hearts, and the clarity of vision through which they are united to the First Truth, imaging His light.[16]

ERRORS OF EXTREMES

The errors that have arisen in regard to equality are errors of extremes: on the one side, an egalitarianism that either denies *in principle* humanly significant differences, dismissing all such evaluations as "subjective" judgments, or admits their reality but views them as evils to be overcome by legislation aiming at maximal leveling-out; on the other side, the extreme of a rigid hierarchicalism that amounts to a denial, implicit or explicit, of the essential sameness of human nature in all individuals and the resultant rights and duties, as can be seen in the caste system in India or in the quondam slaveries of the New World. In the modern West, there seems to be a strange temptation to deny outright, or to downplay the significance of, the most fundamental *natural* difference, namely, that between the sexes.[17] There is also a sinister tendency to deny to whole classes of human beings (e.g., the unborn or

---

[15] See chapter 4.

[16] See St. Thomas Aquinas, *Summa theologiae* I, Q. 93; cf. Journet, *The Theology of the Church*, 104–5, 166–67.

[17] See the judicious commentary in Cahill, *Framework of a Christian State*, 422–50. For an up-to-date account, see Finley, *Sexual Identity*.

the unconscious in a "vegetative state") the status of "persons" before the law in order to avoid acknowledging them to be equal possessors of the natural rights that belong to man as man.

The first thing to clear away is the false assumption that the Christian tradition is anti-hierarchical, that it promotes a utopia where everyone is equal in every respect, endowed with the same rights and privileges. The New Testament makes it plain that the overriding concern of early Christians was liberation from the slavery of sin and the conquest of personal pride. St. Paul rejoices in the paradoxes of the gospel: "He who was called in the Lord as a slave is a freedman of the Lord; likewise he who was free when called is a slave of Christ.... So, brethren, in whatever state each was called, there let him remain with God."[18] The Apostle's perspective was that social distinctions, though they may in some cases arise from sins, are not the spiritual context within which the Christian must learn to live and move and have his being, nor are they shackles that must be thrown off at any cost. When he says, "There is neither Jew nor Greek, there is neither slave nor free, there is neither male nor female; for you are all one in Christ Jesus,"[19] he is not uttering a slogan of communist revolution, but exulting in the unspeakable mystery of communion with the risen Savior.

For St. Paul, as for the other witnesses of the New Testament, there will *always* be both the rich and the poor,[20] the powerful and the powerless,[21] the famous and the obscure, the cultured and the coarse. The decisive question, in a way the *only* question, is: Where is your *heart*?[22] Undoubtedly the more a man turns

---

[18] 1 Cor 7:22.
[19] Gal 3:28.
[20] See Mk 14:7; Rom 15:26; 2 Cor 8.
[21] See Mt 20:25; Rom 13:1-7; 1 Pet 2:13.
[22] See Mt 6:21.

toward the Lord, the further he will move away from earthly weights and measures, and the more he will think with the mind of Christ.[23] Hence, although Christianity is not egalitarianism—for it is no abstract theory, but a life of friendship with Jesus—it fosters a radical re-evaluation of worldly rank and privilege, leading the disciple ever more deeply into the self-abnegation of the Crucified King.

A BALANCED VIEW OF ARISTOCRACY

We can take our analysis further by delving into the phenomenon of aristocracy. The term "aristocracy" can be used in two senses. In a narrower sense, it refers to a form of government or regime in which the people are ruled by the *aristoi*, the "best." In a broader sense, it refers to the presence within a society of a class, an elite, distinguished by birth, wealth, education, or unusual prowess in the defense of their fatherland (at times, all four together). If, with Aristotle, one understands "the best" as those who are noble in spirit, outstanding in virtue, paragons of practical wisdom, such a class may or may not exist, depending on the social structures that favor or militate against its formation and perdurance. Moreover, a social class is a mutable, variable thing; the passage of time can have as downward an effect on class as it can have on individuals. Just as democracy can degenerate into ochlocracy or mob rule, so aristocracy can degenerate into oligarchy or the rule of the wealthy for their own sakes.

It may come as a surprise that the Church's magisterium contains official teaching directed to aristocrats, detailing their rights and duties. The main source of this teaching was Pope Pius XII, himself a Roman aristocrat, who combined a profound grasp of political history with a clear-sighted awareness of the problems

---

[23] See 1 Cor 2:16; Rom 8:6–9, 12:2; Phil 2:1–5.

of modernity. "A careful reading of the documents of
the pontiffs prior and subsequent to Pius XII reveals
that he alone treated the issue of nobility methodically,
explaining its nature and its past and present mission."[24]
Pope Benedict XV's stirring allocution of January 1920
to the Roman patriciate and nobility goes so far as to
speak of the "priesthood of the nobility," exhorting
nobles throughout the world to set a worthy example
in speech, dress, and manners, to preserve and promote
"the intellectual patrimony" of Christendom, and to
practice their holy faith fearlessly and fervently.[25]

While people often speak as if aristocratic regimes
perished with the advent of modern democracy, one
may doubt whether any people or *civitas* has ever been
ruled by anything *other* than an aristocracy, whether
its members be the "best" in reality or only in name.
There will always be a privileged elite even in societies
supposedly democratic or socialistic; one need only
think of the *nomenklatura* of the former Soviet Union,
who enjoyed the best apartments, cars, and food, or
the Kennedys of the United States.

Americans tend to believe that the USA is a democracy offering freedom on all sides to whomever wishes
to seize it, a republic "with liberty and justice for all,"
and that we have to look to the Old World of yore, to
the once-decadent societies and once-bejeweled courts
of Europe, to find examples of aristocracy twisted
into oligarchy. The reality of the situation is quite
different. Americans seldom see how deeply oligarchic
their own society has always been—and is likely ever
to remain. There is always a clique of the powerful
who wield the lion's share of influence and hold the

---

[24] Raymond E. Drake, in Corrêa de Oliveira, *Nobility and Analogous
Traditional Elites*, xviii. The fascinating allocutions of this pope
to the Roman patriciate and nobility from 1940 to 1958 may be
found in this book on pp. 431–61.
[25] de Oliveira, 463–65.

purse strings. It is one of the more curious illusions of modern times that the average citizen can think himself free, when he is often being manipulated by a small class of men and women who move in and out of political offices with a naturalness that befits their status and connections. The fine words uttered by oligarchs on behalf of the poor cannot hide the fact that they emerge from wealth, seek to sustain and augment their wealth, and, in the end, retain their exalted positions vis-à-vis inferiors who receive their handouts. This exalted position translates to cultural lordship, for it is the rich whose decisions and laws, customs and mechanisms, shape the fate, fortunes, and freedom of the poor.

In many ways, France, the "eldest daughter of the Church," offers to the historian the perfect spectacle of the virtues and vices of aristocracy. In no other country did refinement of manners, propriety of speech, tastefulness of dress, elegance in music and dancing, even piety, reach such a great height; yet side by side there was almost unimaginable vanity, luxury, wasteful-ness, negligence, and social irresponsibility. With the contemporary tendency of Catholics and Protestants to praise the religiosity of the American Republic, the modesty and piety of her great heartlands, and the vast "charitable" activity of her citizens on behalf of the needy, we are in danger of turning a blind eye to the same vices (or worse ones): the figures strutting about on the stage of world politics like vain peacocks; disproportionate salaries, exorbitant profit margins, and profligate spending habits, undergirded by an uncon-trollable national debt; the environmental devastation caused by technologically-augmented consumerism; the preferential option for comfort in the face of odious destitution throughout the Third World. Our textbooks have been written to make Europe, its princes, courts, patrons, and big men look egotistical and grasping.

What we need is the realism, or humility, to see all this in ourselves, embedded in our social structures, transmitted through the wiring of the system under which we live. And what's worse, we generally don't have a sliver of the good taste that the aristocrats of old had.

We must have the humility to see where we are going astray and to ask the Lord to make us no part of it, or rather, to make us part of a truly Catholic countermovement. Romanticized tales of the French Revolution burned into our imaginations that no lordly family has a "right" to ride horses through a peasant's field regardless of the damage it causes; no one has a right to the comforts of a grand château while villagers are starving due to a poor harvest. Where are the conscience-needling tales we should be crafting for ourselves? No one has a right to flex its military muscle across the globe at a cost of billions of dollars that our government does not have, at an incalculable cost to future Americans and to innumerable civilians right now whose only crime is that they are associated, by race or religion or geography, with our strategic enemies; no one has a right to impose the theory and praxis of an all-consuming and culture-eviscerating consumerism on other peoples and cultures. Just as historical hindsight permits us to say that the French Revolution was fueled by an iniquitous concentration of wealth and power (even if, in the end, the attempted cure proved worse than the disease), so too I believe it is obvious that a similar revolution in the First World is long overdue, although it is anyone's guess as to what form the comeuppance will take. There is an increasing artificiality, an alarming unrealism, about the way modern politics and economics continue to go their merry way, apparently blind to their own destructive logic, heedless of the laws of nature or of God. These laws do not go away; their consequences grow worse the more they are spurned.

There is no need to hide the fact that "upper" classes have perpetrated outrageous crimes against "lower" classes, as when the *de facto* aristocracy constituted by Spaniards in South America or by the English in North America treated indigenous Americans with such callous brutality that passionate protests were raised in the name of basic human rights (the great Dominicans Francesco de Vitoria and Bartholomé de Las Casas come to mind). Grievous exploitation of the poor has been all too familiar a feature of the relationship between "upper" and "lower" classes in Western history, and there can be no denying that this scandal and suffering played an enormous part in the violent upheavals of modernity. In the political sphere especially, authority has too often not been directed to the common good of the ruled but to the private good of the ruler or of special interest groups; something similar can be seen in the manner in which bishops, religious superiors, or husbands and fathers have ruled, at times, more for their own comfort and convenience than for the genuine good of their charges. The rise of liberalism (including feminism) is, at least in part, a reaction against real abuses, even as Protestantism, the progenitor of modern liberalism, gained plausibility for its dissent in light of the laxity and confusion of the late medieval Church.

It has been a temptation throughout the Christian centuries to consider any privileged class to be, *ipso facto*, an embodiment of injustice toward the underprivileged. The propaganda machine of the French Revolution was particularly successful in projecting a purely negative image of the *ancien régime* and its nobility. Yet one ought neither to exaggerate the vices of the aristocracy nor overlook their conspicuous virtues. What is certain is that elite classes of all ages have been responsible for great good *and* for great evil, in accordance with the ancient principle *corruptio optimi pessima*: the corruption of the best is the worse.

THE TRUE ARISTOCRATS

Just as the only legitimate aim of political action is the common good, the leading of the many to the most noble goods, so the only legitimate aim of "the best" (*ho aristoi*), whoever they may be in a given situation, is a social order in which the Church freely reigns and the people increasingly enjoy the self-transcending freedom of virtue, instead of being enslaved to their vices. Who, in the end, *are* "the best"—the true aristocrats in the eyes of God and God's favorites, the poor? They are the saints. We see it again and again in the annals of holy men and women: those who started out their lives wealthy nearly all ended up embracing voluntary poverty, and those who were taught, by birth or education, to place a premium on worldly accomplishments made themselves fools for Christ, persons who, like St. Paul, "knew nothing but Jesus Christ and Him crucified."[26] Yet we must also hold in remembrance and hold up for imitation the saints who lived as kings and queens, princes and powerful men—Clotilde, Edward the Confessor, Stephen of Hungary, Margaret of Scotland, Louis IX, Elizabeth of Portugal, Hedwig, Casimir, and so many more, until we come to that most noble of modern rulers, Karl of Austria (1887–1922), last reigning monarch of the Habsburg dynasty. Many who were born and bred aristocrats attained their sanctity within that social sphere—well-known examples being Elizabeth of Hungary, Thomas More, and Francis Borgia (or more correctly, Francisco de Borja y Aragon).[27] Many of the saints discussed in Ferdinand Holböck's *Married Saints and Blesseds Through the Centuries* belonged to the nobility of their age.

It bears noting that, without exception, these saintly individuals practiced asceticism, suffered misunder-

---

[26] 1 Cor 2:2.
[27] See chapter 18 for many more examples.

standing and at times persecution from others in their class, and, when they did not actually renounce position and power, distributed their wealth lavishly to the needy. In every case, these men and women, who could have transgressed but did not transgress, did everything within their power to promote the common good of their societies; they emptied out their pockets for the poor, lived austere lives, supported the Church in legislation as in benefactions, endowed monasteries and promoted Catholic education. In short, they were rich and powerful, yet lived as if poor and lowly, not lording it over their people but serving them tirelessly and winning their grateful affection.

Such models show us what our Lord Jesus Christ expects of politics among Christians. This what most of our contemporary politicians, helped along by a fusion of crony capitalism and hereditary democracy that privileges the handsome, ruthless, and monied, do not want to do. Whether we can do anything to change our political situation at this time or not, it is important that we who have been liberated by the Redeemer of Mankind know where we stand and what we stand for. Otherwise, our liberation, begun in baptism, will turn to our shame when we discover on judgment day that we have been slaves to our age and its false philosophies. The way to escape this doom and enter into life is to sit, again and always, at Our Lord's feet, drinking in His life-creating wisdom, letting our minds be shaped by His genuinely *good news*.

For God alone is good,[28] God is the best—and God is paradoxically poor in His infinite riches, since He *has* nothing, but *is* everything, and gives it away to His beloveds while they rest, leaning against His breast.[29] We learn spiritual aristocracy from Him, and we try to bring something of the best into a fallen world

[28] Cf. Lk 18:19.
[29] Cf. Ps 127:2; Jn 21:20.

where the worst holds sway. We will not, at least, fall for the textbook illusion that aristocrats are a thing of the past; they or their simulacra have always been and will always be the steersmen of our societies. The only question for us is this: Will we do everything in our power, relying on God's grace, to live in communion with the King of Kings, Jesus Christ, the Son of God, the Savior of the World, and to lead souls and social bodies to Him? If we try to do this consistently, starting over again whenever we fail and never giving up, we will find, in the end, that we have joined the only lasting upper class there is: the saints and angels in heaven.

CONCLUSION

With arguments from reason and from Scripture, the Catholic Church has always supported the "both/and" of social ethics: the overarching equality of human nature and of the baptismal vocation of the Christian, which allows no cancellation or abrogation; the justice of social stratification, that is, inequality based on virtue, effort, and position. These two truths are tightly bound by the principle that hierarchy is for the sake of the common good, and the common good is most of all attained in the Beatific Vision, where all the blessed are fully happy in the possession of the sovereign good, while enjoying God in different degrees based on their charity in this life. The cardinal principle here on earth, therefore, is this: that which is higher or better or stronger is for the sake of service to that which is lowlier, needier, and weaker, for the building up of the entire social organism in justice and in bonds of friendship. The old axiom is forever true: *servire est regnare*, to serve is to reign.

4

MAN'S DIGNITY IS NOT INFINITE

NOTHING CREATED CAN BE INFINITE

WHEN THE INSTRUCTION *DIG-nitas Infinita* from the Dicastery for the Doctrine of the Faith was released in 2024, many commentators seized immediately on the breathtaking claim of its opening lines:

> Every human person possesses an infinite dignity, inalienably grounded in his or her very being, which prevails in and beyond every circumstance, state, or situation the person may ever encounter.

But no creature has an infinite dignity; that's sheer balderdash. Only God has, or rather *is*, infinite dignity; and those who participate in Christ share, finitely, in His dignity as Son of God. Those who rebel against God lose the moral-spiritual dignity He intended to give them, and, while they retain their (again finite) metaphysical dignity as rational animals, they lack the dignity for which they were created.[1]

That which is "infinite" is that which has no limits or definition or end outside itself (that's why *God* is rightly called infinite, and He alone). Man's dignity is very much tied to his nature and his end. If his dignity were infinite, then he would stand in no need of God or of redemption/salvation. Indeed, he would be his own god.

---

[1] No. 7 in the document spells out a distinction between "ontological" and "moral" dignity, but it's not very clear. My critique of the opening line stands: it should *not* have said, without qualification, "man possesses infinite dignity," for this is true neither of ontological nor of moral dignity.

The only human person to whom one could (with any plausibility) attribute an infinite dignity would be Our Lady, on account of the grace and privilege of the Divine Maternity—a grace and privilege with which her Immaculate Conception and her Assumption are intimately bound up. She is without blemish, without sin, without disorder: the new creation in Christ, participating in His redemption in the highest conceivable manner, holding the highest rank among all creatures (which is why we call her Queen of Heaven: *Regina coeli, laetare!*).[2] Even here, however, the term "infinite" would be out of place, for it is impossible to say of *any* creature that it is infinitely X, or has an infinite X [whatever X may signify]. Examples: "This creature is infinitely wise." "This creature has infinite life." "This creature is infinitely happy." "This creature has infinite glory."

Some might bandy about the term "divinization" (or if they want to be especially cool, *theosis*) as if it refutes this point. But it does not. God is infinite (and He is infinitely whatever he is: good, wise, holy...) *by nature*. The creature—angel or man—is whatever he is (good, wise, holy...) *by participation*, which always means a finite share in what is infinite in God. Divinization does not mean becoming God simply; it means receiving, by grace, a participation in what God is by nature, the way iron can "receive the form of fire" by being heated red-hot, yet the iron does not become fire.

The proposition "man is infinitely X" or "man has infinite X" elides the creator/creature distinction, which is itself infinite. The only one whose human dignity would be literally infinite is Christ's on account of the

---

[2] St. Thomas Aquinas writes: "The Humanity of Christ since it is united to God, the beatitude of the elect since it is the possession of God, the Blessed Virgin Mary since she is the Mother of God—all these have a certain infinite dignity from their relation to God Himself, and under that respect there can be nothing more perfect than them since there can be nothing more perfect than God." *Summa theologiae* I, Q. 25, art. 6, ad 4.

hypostatic union with the Word. And even there, it's the divine Person that endows the Son of God's human nature with its infinite dignity, not anything caused by or contained in the created nature itself.

The Fourth Lateran Council taught: "Between Creator and creature there can be noted no similarity so great that a greater dissimilarity cannot be seen between them." Whatever similarity or analogy there is between God and man, *the dissimilarity is greater*. This would make any absolute way of speaking (e.g., "man has infinite dignity") not just false, but an inversion of the way things really are. If dignity belongs both to God and to man, the dissimilarity between God's dignity and man's dignity is greater than the similarity between them. It is necessary to use more precise and relative language, such as "man's metaphysical dignity is inherent / permanent / immense / irreducible / inalienable, but his moral dignity can be lost by sin and regained by penance."

CONTRASTING FERNÁNDEZ AND AQUINAS

Here's a contrast to consider. First, a quotation from the DDF document:

> By uniting himself with every human being through his Incarnation, Jesus Christ confirmed that each person possesses an immeasurable dignity simply by belonging to the human community; moreover, he affirmed that *this dignity can never be lost*.[3]

Then, a passage from St. Thomas Aquinas:

> By sinning man departs from the order of reason, and consequently falls away from the dignity of his manhood, in so far as he is naturally free and exists for himself, and he falls into the slavish state of the beasts, by being disposed

---

[3] Dicastery for the Doctrine of the Faith, Declaration *Dignitas Infinita* 19.

of according as he is useful to others. This is
expressed in Psalm 48:21: "Man, when he was
in honor, did not understand; he hath been
compared to senseless beasts, and made like to
them," and Proverbs 11:29: "The fool shall serve
the wise." Hence, although it be evil in itself to
kill a man so long as he preserve his dignity, yet
it may be good to kill a man who has sinned,
even as it is to kill a beast. For a bad man is
worse than a beast, and is more harmful, as the
Philosopher states (*Polit.* i, 1 and *Ethic.* vii, 6).[4]

You see, whenever the wiggly term "dignity" comes up,
there's room for a *lot* of equivocation. But what about
the following text, in which Aquinas seems to attribute
infinity to a creature?

Every creature is simply finite, inasmuch as
its existence is not absolutely subsisting, but
is limited to some nature to which it belongs.
But there is nothing against a creature being
considered relatively infinite. Material creatures
are infinite on the part of matter, but finite
in their form, which is limited by the matter
which receives it. But immaterial created sub-
stances are finite in their being; whereas they
are infinite in the sense that their forms are not
received in anything else; as if we were to say,
for example, that whiteness existing separate
is infinite as regards the nature of whiteness,
forasmuch as it is not contracted to any one
subject; while its "being" is finite as determined to some one special nature. Whence it
is said (*De Causis*, prop. 16) that "intelligence
is finite from above," as receiving its being
from above itself, and is "infinite from below,"
as not received in any matter.[5]

---

[4] *Summa theologiae* II-II, Q. 64, art. 2, ad 3.
[5] *Summa theologiae* I, Q. 50, art. 2, ad 4. "Infinite on the part of
matter" simply means that the matter of which they are composed,

Here we see St. Thomas, as usual, brilliantly making distinctions all along the way.

We can see the same points if we turn from the order of being to the order of knowledge. An immaterial creature is infinite *with respect to* what is beneath it, namely, the forms of material things that it knows in a higher, spiritual, universal way; but it is finite *with respect to* what is superior to it, and above all, to God, who is the only actually infinite being in the universe. When Aristotle says "the soul is, in a way, all things," he means that the intellect is open to the totality of being; anything that is, can be known. Again, this does not mean, even in the beatific vision, that the creature in itself has any actual infinity of any quality. At most, you could say the creature is in relation to the infinite, and that relationship gives it a quasi-infinite dignity. Aquinas would *never* say any human attribute is "infinite," simply or absolutely speaking.

As an example of the kind of nonsense that now occupies the heads of Catholics, a certain commenter online wrote: "Human dignity comes from God, God is infinity, thus human dignity is infinite. It's not difficult." This is known as the Fallacy of Composition: "Everything is from God; God is infinity; ergo, everything is infinite"—reminiscent of the medieval philosophaster David of Dinant, who, says St. Thomas, "most stupidly" identified God with prime matter![6]

WHY DOES THIS SENTENCE EVEN MATTER?

While defenders of the audacious opening line of *Dignitas Infinita* immediately pulled out their Thomistic distinctions like so many loaded pistols they had never learned how to use, the critics' whole point was that the

---

called *prima materia*, is capable of being anything else—in that sense, an infinite potency, though actualized under one form at any given time.
[6] *Summa theologiae* I, Q. 3, art. 8.

document's opening sentence makes its assertion *in an absolute manner*, without qualification or distinction, and, absolutely speaking, the assertion is not only false, but notoriously and dangerously false. *That* is a problem for any supposedly magisterial document. It is only a matter of time before this opening line will be quoted whenever someone wishes to argue that the death penalty is per se immoral, or, for that matter, that laws against sodomy are per se immoral because they violate man's (you guessed it) "infinite dignity." Indeed, Fernández hinted as much by leaving homosexuality conspicuously out of this document, in spite of the obvious ways in which sodomy grievously harms the human dignity of millions of people, and by saying that the *Catechism's* formulation of "intrinsically disordered" ought to be changed.[7]

What is wrong with this document is what is wrong with many postconciliar documents: they are sloppy in ways that can backfire.[8] Someone online said: "The pope has given us a good tool to work with; let's not complain about it." Yet if you start with a broken tool, don't be surprised if it injures the user or botches the result! For example, if you start by taking human dignity as infinite, of course the conclusion will be drawn that the death penalty is always wrong.[9] And, right on cue, that is what the document says—now utterly removing the ground from under the feet of

---

[7] See Haynes, "Cardinal Fernández calls for change to Catholic condemnation of homosexuality."

[8] Further reading on the problems in this document: Feser, "Two problems with *Dignitas Infinita*"; Flanders, "*Dignitas Infinita*: the Good, the Bad, and the Ugly"; Voice of the Family, "*Dignitas infinita*: Rethinking Human Dignity"; Tate, "*Dignitas Infinita*: Lowering the Bar"; Smits, "*Dignitas Infinita* as a Naturalistic Vision of Mankind."

[9] The document in effect advances the "seamless garment" theory of (homosexual predator modernist) Cardinal Bernardin, equating the death penalty with abortion as violations of human dignity. This has conveniently allowed the Left to deflect attention towards migrants, criminals, the poor, etc., and away from the monstrous holocaust of the human race *in utero*.

those who claimed that the pope's change to the catechism was meant only as a *prudential* judgment: "The death penalty...violates the inalienable dignity of every person, regardless of the circumstances."[10]

But one could also derive the conclusion that damnation is per se immoral, because it violates the infinite dignity of the rational creature. Indeed, why not simply say all human persons are already actually ordered to the beatific vision and will obtain it? If there were more room for them to grow in dignity (supernaturally), then their dignity wouldn't already be infinite, would it?

The reason we should care about the first line is that its assertion gives *Dignitas Infinita* its name and entire orientation. Words matter, because the Word, the Logos, matters. We should hardly need to be reminded of this, but providentially the feast of the Word made flesh — the Annunciation, observed the day this document was released — puts us in mind of that truth. Let's not forget that every great error in theology hinges on one or two words, e.g., *homoousion* vs. *homoiousion*, *eikon* vs. *eidos*, faith vs. faith alone, transubstantiation vs. consubstantiation.

The twentieth-century translator of Aristotle, Hippocrates Apostle, once said: "I read a modern philosopher until I reach a major error, and then I put the book aside. That means I haven't had to waste a lot of time on Kant or Hegel." One is justified in doing the same with a document if its first sentence, giving the premise of the whole, is false.[11]

---

[10] *Dignitas Infinita* 34. I will address the death penalty issue in the next chapter.

[11] I'm not saying there's no value in studying Kant or Hegel. Obviously one can learn much from the errors made by intelligent people. However, so huge a swath of post-Cartesian philosophy is founded on such fundamental errors about epistemology and metaphysics that one need not feel guilty about not having studied the entire rogues' gallery to the nth degree, using up time better spent on Plato, Aristotle, Augustine, Aquinas, and others in their league.

To arrive at a more reliable exposition of human dignity, let us take the sacred liturgy as our point of departure and Bishop Athanasius Schneider as our guide.

INITIAL ORIENTATION

A splendid prayer in the Roman Rite tells us:

> *Deus, qui humanae substantiae dignitatem mira-*
> *biliter condidisti, et mirabilius reformasti: da*
> *nobis per huius aquae et vini mysterium, eius*
> *divinitatis esse consortes, qui humanitatis nostrae*
> *fieri dignatus est particeps, Jesus Christus, Filius*
> *tuus, Dominus noster, qui tecum vivit et regnat in*
> *unitate Spiritus Sancti, Deus per omnia saecula*
> *saeculorum. Amen.*

> O God, who hast wonderfully established the dignity of human nature and still more wonderfully hast restored it: grant us, by the mystery of this water and wine, that we may be partakers of His divinity, who deigned to become a partaker of our humanity, Jesus Christ, Thy Son, our Lord, who with Thee liveth and reigneth in the unity of the Holy Ghost, God unto ages of ages, Amen.

The original creation of man was a creation *in sanctifying grace*. Man was never intended to be a merely natural creature, although it is possible and indeed important to be able to discuss philosophically what pertains simply to his nature according to its own powers. God created Adam to be His adopted son, in the image of His natural Son. When this grace was lost for all mankind, the Son of God, unto whose image Adam had been fashioned, took on human nature, becoming the New Adam in whom, by baptism, that original supernatural sonship could be regained.

Thus Bishop Schneider writes on the first page of his catechism *Credo*:

4. **Does this gift bestow upon us a great dignity?** Yes. By the wondrous gift of sanctifying grace, we become adopted children of God the Father, brethren of the Eternal Son, and living temples of the Holy Spirit.

Simply speaking, the dignity of man consists in his being a son of God by grace: that is his high calling, that is the conformity to the Logos for which he was created and into which he is inserted by the Christian sacramental economy. Man also has a certain dignity from his rational nature in and of itself, yet there is a kind of abstraction involved in prescinding from his supernatural end. After all, the souls of the damned, too, possess the dignity of their nature, but they lack the original and intended dignity of the sons of God. In fact, their metaphysical dignity is the reason they are deserving of punishment—as opposed, say, to a wild animal that cannot incur guilt for abusing a freedom it does not possess.

This double meaning of dignity is somewhat like the distinction between the *being* of a thing, and the *well-being* of it. Man has dignity in virtue of existing, but he has his fullest dignity as a reflection of the Logos when he exists *well*, that is, by divine grace. Nevertheless, if one were to ask, without qualification, "What does the worthiness (*dignitas*) of man consist in?," the correct answer would be: "In his actual conformity to God by grace." If one were to ask: "What makes that conformity *possible*?," the answer would be: "Man's rational nature."

THE ANGELIC DOCTOR WEIGHS IN

St. Thomas Aquinas teaches a more subtle doctrine of human dignity than might be apparent from the internet's self-appointed theological watchdogs. A look at Question 93 of the Prima Pars in the *Summa theologiae* shows how Aquinas builds up his doctrine of the *imago Dei* by starting with the image as found in an essence (whether man's or angel's), then looking at the image as found *more perfectly* in states, habits, and acts. At the end we learn that the image of God is more like a "sliding scale": the angel or saint in heaven is *more fully* "to the image and likeness of God" than the mortal sinner or the demon.

The longstanding distinction between *image* and *likeness* is useful in this regard. Why does Genesis mention both: "made to the image *and* likeness..."?[12] According to St. Thomas, the "image" refers to a man's rational nature (or to an angel's intellectual nature), which always abides, on earth, in heaven, or in hell; but "likeness" refers to that person's assimilation to God by grace, and this obviously varies from person to person.

Thus, the unbaptized sinner isn't *at all* "like God" in terms of being His willing subject and His son. The lukewarm Christian is more like God, but still very remote, so much so that unless he changes, he will be vomited forth (cf. Rev 3:16). The devout Christian is more like Him, and pleasing to Him. The angels and saints in heaven are *most like* God, being divinized to the full capacity of their nature. But all these spiritual creatures are still made "to the image of God," as is Satan and the other fallen angels. The foregoing doctrine is thoroughly traditional.

Incidentally, St. Thomas also probes why the text of Genesis says that man is made *to* the image of God. Why this preposition "to"? His answer: because only God the Son *is* the Image of God, wholly and perfectly;[13] and any creature that bears the image of the Image is made *to* that Image and approaches it more or less closely, as an icon points to an original. The word "to" implies standing in relation to a goal as well as the possibility of motion toward it or away from it.

Dignitas, then, concerns both metaphysical and moral-spiritual standing. The metaphysical worth of a thing is

---

[12] Gen 1:26.
[13] See Col 1:15 and Heb 1:3; *Summa theologiae* I, Q. 93, art. 1, ad 2.

connected to its ontological rank. Man has objectively the rank of a rational being made to the image of God. No other material being enjoys this dignity. However, when a man is endowed with the good habits known as virtues, and even more when he is in a state of sanctifying grace, he has an added and decisive worth in God's eyes—namely, that of a proper likeness to Him who is all-worthy, in whom (one might say) all dignity subsists.

BISHOP SCHNEIDER'S FORMULATION

Turning once more to Bishop Schneider's catechism, *Credo*, we read:

> 224. Is the *dignity of the human person* rooted in his creation in God's image and likeness? This was true for Adam, but with original sin the human person lost this resemblance and dignity in the eyes of God. He recovers this dignity through baptism, and keeps it as long as he does not sin mortally.

> 225. Then human dignity is not the same in all persons? No. The human person loses his dignity in proportion to his free choice of error or evil; e.g., the dignity of Adolph Hitler and St. Francis of Assisi are not the same.

The catechism's phrase "*this* resemblance and dignity in the eyes of God" clearly refers to the original state of Adam just mentioned, which means Bishop Schneider is talking about the supernatural rank of divine sonship—which is obvious when he immediately says that "*this* dignity" is "recovered through baptism."

For the reasons given above, dignity *without qualification* should be named from the ultimate end, and in this sense, a man who fails to achieve divine likeness and the beatific vision has lost his dignity—the dignity that counts "in the eyes of God" and for a creature's own well-being. The dignity of man as God intended it is revealed in his high calling to heaven and in his glorification in heaven; the rational nature of the damned is more a source of their punishment than a dignity of which they or anyone could boast.

My reading of the foregoing paragraphs in *Credo* is confirmed when we look a bit further on, at no. 228: "*Perfect* human dignity and fraternity for all human beings can only have one source: Jesus Christ, since it is only through the Incarnate Son of God that human dignity has been *restored* even more admirably than it was created" (emphasis added). Here, *perfect* dignity refers to Christian dignity; logically, *imperfect* dignity exists but is ordered to that final end.

What, then, of the human race as it is born into the world? Does each man have "dignity"? Can we say this? We *can* and *do* speak this way—and so does Bishop Schneider, in no. 504, where he quotes Pope John Paul II's encyclical *Evangelium Vitae*: "The use of human embryos or fetuses as an object of experimentation constitutes *a crime against their dignity as human beings* who have a right to the same respect owed to a child once born, just as to every person."[14]

It is therefore in thoroughly bad faith for Bishop Schneider's opponents to accuse him of undermining the right to life (etc.), when *Credo* so clearly teaches those things elsewhere.[15] All the same, the attentive

---

[14] Emphasis added. In point of fact, Bishop Schneider is quite willing to talk even about "the dignity of the body" when discussing why cremation should be avoided:

> 816. Why should we bury bodies intact, and avoid cremation? 1. In imitation of Christ, who was truly buried and not cremated; 2. In witness to the bodily resurrection that will occur at the end of time; 3. In witness to the dignity of the body, made in God's image and fashioned into His temple through baptism; 4. To avoid disrespecting and desecrating the body itself, as occurs when human remains are kept in a home or scattered abroad.

[15] See nos. 488–91 *et passim*; the index to *Credo* is rather useful in this regard.

reader will notice that Bishop Schneider prefers to speak in the more traditional way about "innocent human life" that no one has the right to take, rather than resting his entire case on the Enlightenment's nebulous and often self-contradictory concept of "human dignity," from which churchmen in recent decades have been known to extrapolate many dubious conclusions.[16] It is enough to say that no one has the right to take human life outside of carefully delimited situations of legitimate individual or communal self-defense, or as punishment for the worst crimes; that is enough to serve as the foundation for both the possibility of a just war and the admissibility of the death penalty.

AVOIDING THE ERROR OF NATURALISM

Let us consider why Bishop Schneider prefers the older way of speaking, and reconnects worthiness with grace while defending the innocent lives of the unborn.

If we are not careful to specify what we mean by the "dignity of man," we will play right into the hands of the pervasive naturalism of our times, in which simply *existing as a man* is seen as endowing someone with the full panoply of human rights and, ultimately, even a right to salvation—as if simply being a man means that one is owed all good things, natural and divine. This is false for so many reasons that one could write a fat book about them. It's most obvious in the debates over the death penalty, over the welfare state, and over the so-called right to religious freedom. In regard to that last topic, Bishop Schneider again speaks with the authority of the Church of the ages:

---

[16] One thinks of the assertion found in the Second Vatican Council and in Pope Francis that "modern men are more aware of the dignity of the human person." Millions of babies savagely massacred in their mothers' wombs, offered on the altars of the seven deadly sins in numbers far exceeding the death tolls of all wars and concentration camps, cry out "False!" to this absurd claim.

> **754. What is the true dignity of the human
> person regarding religion?** The dignity of
> man consists in the right use of freedom. There-
> fore, no true and proper right can be given to
> the human person that contradicts divine truth
> in the natural or positive law of God.

Modern Catholics are in grave danger of forgetting,
downplaying, or even undermining the supernatural
domain by a false exaltation of the domain of nature —
not as a foundation of grace but in and of itself, a
tendency that was once again brashly on display in
the document *Laudate Deum.*[17] The irony, of course,
is that many of the "heroes" of the Vatican II period,
especially Henri de Lubac, were praised for having
overcome a supposed divorcement of nature from grace;
but an attentive observer of today's ecclesiastical scene
cannot help noticing that the bifurcation is alive and
well, and deeper than ever.[18]

One can see, in studying *Credo*, how consistently
Bishop Schneider deploys the fuller and richer Christian conception of dignity. For example, he asks, in no.
526, "Is chastity an obligatory virtue?," and answers:

> Yes. As a natural virtue, it fosters self-mastery
> and subjects the passions to our reason and
> will, which is necessary for being a mature,
> integrated, selfless, happy person, and for the
> prosperity of the family and peace in society.
> As a supernatural virtue, it maintains our dig-
> nity as adopted children of God, members of
> Jesus Christ, and temples of the Holy Spirit.

It is, moreover, *because* of the dignity of man as God
intends it that the death penalty is in accord with, and
underlines, human dignity, by calling the criminal to

---

[17] See Adolphe, "Reading *Laudate Deum* through the Lens of the
World Economic Forum in Light of the Synod on Synodality."
[18] See Kwasniewski, "How a False Unification of Nature and
Grace Led to Their Divorce."

account for his abuse of God's gift of freedom and calling him to repentance. Thus Bishop Schneider writes:

> **514. When does society have the right to inflict the death penalty?** The lawfully constituted public authority may put proven criminals to death for the most serious crimes when this is necessary to maintain social order in repairing injustice, protecting the innocent, deterring further crime, and summoning the criminal to true repentance and atonement.

The stark confrontation of the criminal with the life-and-death gravity of his own actions is perfectly in accord with the drama of salvation, which is the *ultimate* life-and-death affair.[19] Naturalism, as we saw with the Branch Covidian religion, elevates the good of physical health and life over all other goods, and in this way strikes at the root of revealed religion and rejects God's providential plan for the human race.

Whatever weaknesses of formulation may be found in *Credo* (and there is no such thing as a "perfect catechism" to which no improvement could be made—there are only better and worse catechisms, both as to content and as to intended uses), at least it does not contain the glaring error on the death penalty that Pope Francis audaciously introduced into the *Catechism of the Catholic Church*, to the deception and detriment of souls.

THE GOOD BISHOP'S CORRECT

With this observation, we come full circle to no. 224 of *Credo*. Its question can be taken in two ways

---

[19] There is legitimate room for disagreement on whether capital punishment is rooted principally in self-defense or in the duty to apply retributive justice for grave crimes against the common good. An argument in favor of the latter view is that even a serious criminal who converts to Christ and is arguably no longer a threat to society may still be justly put to death. For historic examples, see Kwasniewski "These condemned criminals accepted 'inadmissible' death penalty and became saints."

(depending on what phrase is emphasized), and taken either way, Bishop Schneider gives the correct answer. I will use italics to bring out the two ways the question could be asked.

"Is the dignity of the human person *rooted in* his creation in God's image and likeness?" Most people would understand this question to be asking if the root or source of human dignity as God wills it is simply *man's creation* — his having been created as a rational being. The answer is no. The root of his dignity is the divine calling to divinization in Christ, to which his nature is ordered by the plan of Divine Providence.

Alternatively, the question could be asking: "Is the dignity of the human person rooted in his creation *in God's image and likeness*?" In other words: Is man always created in God's image and likeness in such a way as to have his dignity as God intended it? The answer here, too, is negative, because after the fall of Adam, while every man is made "to the image" of God by his rationality, no human being is created "in the *likeness* of God" (as we explained earlier from St. Thomas) — that is, clothed in the grace of divine sonship. Put simply, the image in fallen, unbaptized man is dimmed and dark, and in need of a radical healing and elevation. (I am bracketing here the singular case of Our Lady, immaculately conceived and full of grace; and needless to say, Our Lord is not a human person but a divine Person, so the human nature that was hypostatically united to Him in the womb of the Blessed Virgin was supernaturally perfect, with the beatific vision, all gifts and fruits of the Spirit, and all possible virtues.)

To have the dignity of being sons of God, it is not enough to be born; one must be born again of water and the Holy Spirit, as Christ our Savior teaches.[20]

---

[20] Jn 3:5.

And in the same Teacher's haunting words about Judas: "It were better for that man never to have been born,"[21] precisely because he has lost the dignity of being a child of God and has become a child of wrath.[22]

Again and again, we must be grateful to Bishop Schneider for his willingness to confront questions no one else wishes to tackle head-on, for reminding us of truths in danger of being eclipsed, for exposing the flaws in ways of speaking and thinking that moderns take for granted, and for reconnecting us with a deeper, stronger tradition.

---

[21] Mt 26:24.
[22] Cf. Eph 2:1–3. See Kwasniewski, "Damned Lies: On the Destiny of Judas Iscariot."

5

THE HORNS OF THE DEATH PENALTY DILEMMA

I N HIS ANNUAL MEETING WITH THE
diplomatic corps of ambassadors accredited to the
Holy See on January 9, 2023, Pope Francis doubled
down on his novel teaching on the death penalty:

> The death penalty cannot be employed for
> a purported state justice, since it does not
> constitute a deterrent nor render justice to
> victims, but only fuels the thirst for vengeance.
> I appeal, then, for an end to the death penalty,
> which is always inadmissible since it attacks the
> inviolability and the dignity of the person, in
> the legislation of all the countries of the world.[1]

As discussed in the last chapter, *Dignitas Infinita* subsequently repeated the same assertion.

This chapter will not be yet another attempt to
prove that the Catholic Church has always (and indeed
infallibly) taught the permissibility of the death penalty.
That project has already been done many times,[2] and
I have written about it at length elsewhere.[3] Rather, I
would like to focus on the dilemma into which those
who attempt to defend Pope Francis's novel teaching

---

[1] Francis, Udienza al Corpo Diplomatico, January 9, 2023.
[2] Trabbic makes several good points in his "Some Responses to
Pope Francis's Revision of CCC 2267." For the definitive treatment,
see Feser and Bessette, *By Man Shall His Blood Be Shed.*
[3] See Kwasniewski, "What Good is a Changing Catechism?
Revisiting the Purpose and Limits of a Book," in *The Road from
Hyperpapalism to Catholicism*, 2:137–55; the same volume has a
number of relevant chapters on the subject; see, e.g., 44–51,
58–59, 75–77, 88–91, 156–59, 246–49, 298–99.

on the death penalty—reflected in an official change to the *Catechism*—necessarily fall. The pro-Francis apologists can't possibly "win" in this scenario.

For either:

(A) Pope Francis attempted to change the constant teaching of the Church—or, more precisely, of Scripture and Tradition—that the death penalty is *not* intrinsically immoral and indeed is justifiable and justified under certain circumstances; *or* (B) he is "merely" stating that there is no longer any possible prudential situation in the entire world in which the death penalty may be justified in order to defend the common good of society from malefactors.[4]

If (A) is the case, the pope is at least materially heretical.

However, if (B) is the correct interpretation, he is equally in error, because not even the most extreme ultramontanist imaginable ever maintained that the papacy is endowed with a political prudence superior to and inclusive of the political prudence of all princes, presidents, prime ministers, parliaments, legislatures, and courts of the entire world, such that he is capable of knowing, in detail, what is right and just in every possible and actual social circumstance. (During the era of the Papal States no one ever said that the pope was guaranteed to know what is politically expedient *even for the Papal States*, let alone for the rest of the globe!) Moral actions are, after all, always about the particular: one can act only in the *hic et nunc*, with all of its circumstances. It would be nonsense to say "generally speaking, the death penalty is never admissible in any case, but there might be exceptions."

In short, if someone believes the death penalty to be prudentially inadvisable *in given circumstances*, then he

---

[4] That would be the necessary set of conditions required to declare that it is "inadmissible" in every case.

can never hold it to be "inadmissible" simply speaking;
while if he believes the death penalty is intrinsically
immoral, he is no longer a Catholic. Thus, either Pope
Francis unjustly absorbed and arrogated to himself all
secular power, with all the practical knowledge and
political prudence on which it rests; or he abrogated
Divine Law and Natural Law.

Gravely wrong, and harmfully wrong, either way.

The Church has taught, from the New Testament
and Pope Gelasius through Pope Leo XIII and the
Second Vatican Council, that God has instituted two
powers: the sacred and the temporal, or, in shorthand, the Church and the state. They have separate
spheres of authority, albeit with overlapping terrain
(e.g., marriage is rightly a concern of both Church
and state). Now, when the Church teaches authorita-
tively about moral universals (e.g., that abortion and
euthanasia are intrinsically evil), the state is obliged to
accept her determinations—if perchance the light of
reason in its rulers is not strong enough to arrive at
them independently. The fact that most states ignore
or contradict the Church's moral teaching will redound
to their harm and eventual dissolution.[5]

However, this moral teaching must be about things
that can be *universalized*, i.e., it is *always* right or
wrong to do such-and-such. Once one enters into
matters where prudential determinations concerning
the political common good must be made on the
basis of local circumstances (e.g., how good prisons
are, how reliable the police are, how well the penal
process works, etc.), the state has the primary and
direct responsibility, and it would be contrary to the
nature of the Church and her authority—and this,
according to the magisterium itself!—for a pope or
bishop to arrogate to himself this prudential domain.

---

[5] On these points, see Waldstein, ed., *Integralism and the Common
Good: Selected Essays from "The Josias,"* vol. 2: *The Two Powers.*

It would be pure theocracy at that point, which has never been the Church's teaching.[6]

The only rare exception would be when a particular political entity happens to be run by the pope (as were the Papal States and as is the current Vatican City) or by a bishop (as in the archepiscopal principalities formerly found in Europe, e.g., in Salzburg, whose Prince-Archbishop once had Mozart thrown down the stairs). There and there alone, the Church and state authorities are fused; yet this is a *de facto* fusion, not one that is demanded by the nature of things. Obviously in 99% of cases, the Church and state authorities are distinct—and this, moreover, by the wisdom of Divine Providence, as so clearly laid out in Catholic teaching from Pope Gelasius I's *Duo Sunt* to Pope Leo XIII's *Immortale Dei*.

So, once again, if Francis meant to teach universally about the evil of the death penalty, we are dealing *either* with a claim about its intrinsic evil—which cannot be sustained against 2,000 years of Catholic teaching on the subject, not to mention the witness of Divine Revelation—*or* with a claim about its being always-and-everywhere imprudent, which is simply not the pope's judgment to make without seizing all actual civil authority and political prudence into his own hands, in a theocratic monism that would make even Innocent III or Boniface VIII blush.

The question may be raised: "Does Church teaching say anything about the circumstances under which the death penalty is justifiable? Or are those circumstances left entirely to the reasoning of the lawgiver?" One can find indications in magisterial texts of *how* capital punishment should be regulated and administered, and

---

[6] The single best source is Leo XIII's encyclical on the two powers, *Immortale Dei*, but the doctrine, often called that of the "Two Swords," is enunciated by Pope Gelasius (*Famuli Vestrae Pietatis* or *Duo Sunt* of 494), Gregory VII (Letter to Bishop Hermann of Metz, March 15, 1081), Boniface VIII (*Unam Sanctam* of 1302), and many others.

of course one can find indications that its use should be minimized (that was John Paul II's and Benedict XVI's line). But it still belongs to the nature of ethical reasoning that these indications would be about general circumstances, taking the form of "In such and such cases (e.g., where excellent prison systems and a reliable penal process are available), the death penalty should be avoided." Actual ethical choices are always about particulars and must be assessed according to particulars, by those divinely empowered to assess them.[7]

This is why Cardinal Ratzinger, acting as head of the Congregation for the Doctrine of the Faith, confirmed in 2004 (in the context of the US presidential election) that a Catholic can disagree with the pope (then John Paul II) about the death penalty and just war, but *not* about abortion and euthanasia.[8]

It's important to see that Francis is not only wrong but *dangerously* wrong on this subject. Popes can be and have been wrong about things that are rather minor in the larger picture, like what is the best color for a pope's shoes, or where is the best place in the Vatican for a pope to live. But when the pope is wrong about something that touches on the judicial and criminal systems of hundreds of nations and on the foundations and ramifications of their God-given authority, one is dealing with a level of wrongness that threatens the good of political society—the common good that Aristotle and Aquinas describe as something divine.[9]

Indeed, to return to our earlier either/or dilemma, it may be that the pope is culpable of heresy regardless

---

[7] I say "divinely empowered" because civil authorities do indeed receive their authority from God, not from the people (although the leader can be chosen *by* the people): see Leo XIII's *Diuturnum Illud*.

[8] See Ratzinger, "Worthiness to Receive Holy Communion: General Principles."

[9] See *Nicomachean Ethics* I.2, 1094b; Aquinas quotes this passage many times in his writings.

of which of the two alternatives we take. For (as a friend of mine put it) "if the pope thinks that his moral judgment as to the just response to any possible situation involving a potentially capital crime is superior to anyone's moral judgment in any situation now and into the future, then this would also be heretical, for he would be undermining the naturally known truth that the judgment of crime and criminals belongs by nature (i.e., in fact, by God's grant) to the civil authority: 'You would have no authority over me,' says Our Lord as He is being sent to capital punishment, 'unless it had been given to you from above' (Jn 19:11)."

Yet still the papal apologists defend the Roman Pontiff to this point of irrationality. Such apologists bend and flow with the times, throwing in their hat with the modernists' doctrinal evolutionism. As if adopting the stance of Jesus toward rabbinical customs ("You have heard it said...but I say to you"), our papal apologists have arrived at the threshold of a new dispensation: "You have heard it said in the Bible—or in the Church Fathers and Doctors, or in the universal ordinary magisterium, or in previous papal and conciliar documents, etc.—that the death penalty is permissible and admissible as a punishment for serious crime and for the protection of the civil common good, according to the judgment of civil authorities; but *I* say to you, things have changed, and now we have a different teaching for today: it is never permissible or admissible," etc. Thus is born Catholic Mormonism, except with the Book of Bergoglio as the newest testament. In this way "Catholic Answers" turns into "Vatican Views."

It is one thing for apologists who are not theologians to parrot the papal line. Yet there are even bishops of the Catholic Church who, having *admitted* they did not understand His Holiness's death penalty teaching, nevertheless proposed to alter the national catechism accordingly.[10] Imagine catechizing your child with a teaching that is literally unintelligible to the bishops!

"But what does 'inadmissible' mean, Dad?"

"Son, as Bishop Barron said, it's 'eloquent ambiguity.'"

Whatever happened to the notion that the universal ordinary magisterium, which we glimpse in the unbroken constancy of the content of hundreds of catechisms published over the past thousand years,[11] is itself infallible? Or has all infallibility been concentrated in the person of the pope and sucked out of every other lodging it enjoyed within the Catholic Church? Behold: the religion of *solo papa*, the weird counterimage of that other reductionist Christianity based on *sola Scriptura, sola fide, sola gratia*.

In reality, the *modified* new Catechism—that is, the *Catechism of the Catholic Church* with the Bergoglian replacement paragraph on the inadmissibility of capital punishment—may not and must not be used by any believing Catholic in any circumstance or for any reason. I suppose, as with the Synod on Synodality, we should be once again grateful for the rise of a Shibboleth by which we can distinguish a true Catholic from a false one.

* * *

In some ways, the worst casualty of confusion over the death penalty is the unborn. Let us first consider, without flinching, the magnitude of the evil we are talking about when it comes to abortion. No one has put it more bluntly, or more accurately, than Dr. Alan Keyes:

> Every time abortionists rip a child limb from
> limb within the womb; every time they crush
> the fragile head; every time they scorch the

---

[10] See Bourne, "US bishops follow Pope in calling death penalty 'inadmissible,' admit they don't know what it means."

[11] See www.tradivox.com.

life from its body with a death-dealing solution; every time they scrape its nascent cells
of life from the walls of a womb—Jesus is
savagely beaten again; his skull pressed down
with thorns; his limbs pulled savagely in their
sockets; his hands and feet pierced through
with nails; his breath drawn with fiery pain;
his life finally extinguished; every time.[12]

The unborn child is, indeed, a *child*, a human being.
Not only have modern embryology and genetics done
nothing to shake a truth so evident to all; on the
contrary, they support it ten-thousandfold. Eminent
geneticist Jerome Lejeune bore witness in courts all
over the world that modern science shows no fundamental biological discontinuity in the entire process
from fertilized ovum to born child and beyond. If
one invents a right to kill the former, one logically
must invent a right to kill the latter; if one can kill
the latter, there is no end to the life-extinguishing
policies governments may approve, as we already see
in the spread of euthanasia.

We now have university professors who are coldly
"rational" enough to draw the conclusion: since we have
legalized abortion, we ought to legalize the killing of
small children when they are severely disabled—or
perhaps simply unwanted. Dr. Lejeune saw that either
you must defend innocent human life from beginning
to end, *or* you have to maintain that limits on killing
are purely pragmatic and can be changed at will by
legislative fiat. In a world that prides itself on the
fragile construct of a "social contract" in which we
all belong to the state in exchange for protection of
our basic rights, this amounts to selling all your goods
in order to purchase a field of quicksand, and then
walking into it.

---

[12] See Koppelman, "Alan Keyes' letter from Notre Dame jail."

In recent years, the pro-life movement has seen heartening victories and harrowing losses; yet nothing is stranger than the ongoing subtle sabotage of pro-life efforts coming from an unexpected quarter: Pope Francis and his ideological entourage. The pope's preoccupation with abolishing capital punishment, going so far as to double down on his claim that long-standing Catholic doctrine can and should change on this matter, has reanimated an almost-defunct "seamless garment" or "consistent life ethic" that has never accomplished anything more than diffusing attention from the plight of the unborn, slaughtered in their millions.

Consider some statistics. According to the Death Penalty Information Center, 25 criminals were executed in the USA in 2024. According to the Guttmacher Institute, 1,038,100 "legal" "clinician-provided abortions" were performed in the USA in the same year.[13] For each convicted criminal whose life was required of him by justice, nearly 41,524 babies were killed for no other "crime" than that of existing. Statistical models estimate that 56 *million* babies were aborted across the Earth *per year* in 2010 to 2014;[14] in comparison, about 1,000 were sentenced to death in the year 2017. That would be a ratio of 56,000 babies per 1 execution. Another way of seeing the difference: there are 525,600 minutes in each year. Worldwide, therefore, over one hundred children are aborted *every minute*; in the USA, almost one hundred children are aborted *each hour*. In contrast, one person was executed every nine hours somewhere in the world in 2017; in the USA, it was one criminal executed every fifteen *days* on average. These comparisons are mind-boggling.

---

[13] This figure does not include the huge and ever-increasing number of "self-managed" abortions via pills, nor off-the-record provision in states that have passed legislation against abortion, nor abortifacient contraceptive methods.

[14] See Sedgh, et al., "Abortion incidence between 1990 and 2014."

By relating and comparing these statistics, I am not asserting that the lives of criminals do not matter, nor that some of the executions (especially in Islamic countries) are not unjust. I am simply trying to show the sheer *disproportion* between judicial executions, which are *in theory* defensible—in the USA, at least, we are looking at some of the most monstrous criminals ever to be held in jails—and the slaughter of the unborn, which cannot under *any* circumstances *ever* be defended, not for a single case.

The so-called "seamless garment" is a diabolic ploy to turn our gaze away from the most egregious moral evil the world has ever seen to something that is much more debatable and ambivalent. Pope Francis has created the illusion that, for the Catholic Church, the death penalty question is as big a deal as other life questions. But it is *nothing* compared to abortion (and, increasingly, euthanasia).

We saw the bitter fruits of Pope Francis's silence in the betrayal of Ireland's Catholics during the abortion referendum in 2018. The Irish received zero support from Pope Francis in defense of the unborn, in spite of his relative popularity with progressives, which *might* have made some difference. He provided no help when it was most desperately needed, and when any worthy successor of the apostles would have spoken out clearly, as Pius X did in his encyclical letter *Vehementer Nos* when protesting against the evil actions of the French government in 1905. *The Irish Times* blazed the headline: "Pope Francis's non-judgmental style influenced abortion Yes vote."[15]

The crisis of morals, nay, of intelligence, has reached such a grave point that our bishops are no longer even capable of distinguishing between different kinds of dignity that people have. Bishop Frank Dewane of Venice,

---

[15] By journalist Catherine McCann, published July 17, 2018.

Florida, stated: "All human beings are created in the image and likeness of God, and the dignity bestowed on them by the Creator cannot be extinguished, even by grave sin"—as if this has any bearing on the death penalty—and noted that Benedict XVI had urged "society's leaders...to make every effort to eliminate the death penalty."[16] The same news story quotes Msgr. Stuart Swetland: "Theologians have been arguing that we could make this next step, as a true development of doctrine: to intend the death of a human person violates their human dignity and that the death penalty is always and everywhere non-admissible."

Remarkable! A bishop cannot see that eliminating the death penalty for practical reasons is not the same as saying that the death penalty is *per se* immoral, as Pope Francis maintains. A noted monsignor cannot see that "development of doctrine" does not mean contradiction of Scripture, Tradition, and reason. Neither of them can see that the death penalty is not directed against human nature or the person as such but against the criminal *as* a criminal, which is a highly relevant aspect for the state to consider. Nothing, in fact, more emphasizes human dignity than the realization that moral actions have consequences; evil may be punished not only in the world to come, but even here and now.

Why isn't God at fault when He intends the death of a human person? Because, as the author of man, He has absolute authority over life and death. The traditional Catholic view is that the state derives its power from God and, to a certain extent, stands in His place, and therefore shares in this power. Bradley Lewis rightly commented: "If executing those guilty of capital crimes is wrong, why is this not the case with the intentional killing of enemy combatants in a

---

[16] Desmond, "Catechism's New Text on Death Penalty Draws Praise and Concern."

just war? If the protection of the common good does not authorize capital punishment, does it no longer justify killing enemy soldiers?"[17]

In spite of Pope Francis's diffusive and divisive efforts, and in spite of the left-leaning politics of too many Catholic bishops who are worse than useless when it comes to defending natural-law morality, the pro-life cause remains strong and focused on the supreme moral evil of abortion, which contradicts the most basic right of all human persons.

---

[17] Desmond, "Catechism's New Text."

6

LIBERTY VERSUS LICENSE

MODERN WESTERN PEOPLE, PER-
haps Americans above all, tend to be enam-
ored of, not to say preoccupied with, the
question of freedom—"live free or die!"—but few, if
pressed, could give anything like a coherent account
of what these words mean. The social teaching of the
Church comes to our aid on this question as on so
many others, with a teaching that is clear, profound,
and rich with practical applications.

Pope Leo XIII's 1888 encyclical *Libertas Praestantissimum* contains what is by far the most ample discussion
of human freedom in the Church's magisterium. The
encyclical may be divided into three parts (using its
section numbers): free-will (3–6), law (7–13), and the
errors of liberalism (14–46). The tone of the encyclical
is set by the first paragraph. Freedom confers on man
the dignity of being *master of his actions*, yet this very
freedom can be the means not only of his reaching
the highest good, but also of his sinking to the lowest
evil. Although Our Lord Jesus Christ has set man free
from sin and given him the gift of genuine spiritual
freedom, there are some who think the Church is an
enemy of human freedom because they have a perverse
or exaggerated notion of it (1). The remainder of the
encyclical unfolds what is sketched here: a true notion
of freedom contrasted with a false and absurd notion,
and the political implications of each.

FREEDOM AND THE NEED FOR LAW

Leo XIII begins with a philosophical analysis indebted
to St. Thomas Aquinas. Natural freedom is the "faculty

of choosing means fitted for an end proposed" (5). "The end, or object, both of the rational will and of its freedom is that good only which is in conformity with reason" (5), i.e., something that reason perceives to be good and judges to be choiceworthy. However, both reason and will are imperfect faculties and can make mistakes. Reason can take to be a good something which is, in fact, bad for a person. When the will, dependent on reason, freely acts according to this false judgment, sin is the result (6). Sin thus testifies to freedom in the same way disease testifies to health, whereas perfect freedom acting in perfect wisdom would never fail to achieve what is best. God and the Saints who cannot choose evil are not *less* free, but *more* free, while the more a sinner sins, the more he becomes a slave of sin.[1]

Being fallible, our exercise of free-will in this world needs "light and strength to direct its actions to good and restrain them from evil." In a word, we need *law*, a determination of reason prescribing to the will what it should embrace or shun in order that man's ultimate end might be attained (7). The *natural law* engraved in the mind of man is "our reason, commanding us to do right and forbidding sin" (8). This law is the rational creature's participation in the eternal law that is God Himself, infinite intelligence and goodness, Creator and Ruler of all the world.

"What reason and the natural law do for *individuals*, human law, promulgated for their good, does for the *citizens* of states" (9). Human laws do not originate in civil society alone, nor does their rightness stem from human consent; they have their origin in natural law and its eternal exemplar, and their function is to specify what citizens must do or not do in order to serve the common good, as well as to restrain those bent on harming it. Thus,

---

[1] Cf. Jn 8:34.

> the true freedom of human society does not
> consist in every man doing what he pleases, for
> this would simply end in turmoil and confusion,
> and bring on the overthrow of the state; but
> rather in this, that through the injunctions of
> the civil law all may more easily conform to
> the prescriptions of the eternal law. (10)

True, or "moral," freedom really consists in "being
free to live according to [just] law and right reason" (13).

THE ERROR OF LIBERALISM

In his transition to the topic of liberalism, Leo XIII
does not mince words: the men who, "usurping the
name of liberty, style themselves *liberals*" are imitators
of Lucifer, who "adopt as their own his rebellious cry,
'I will not serve'" (14). Liberalism is the social coun-
terpart of the twin errors of naturalism and rationalism, whereby supremacy is given to human reason and
submission is refused to the authority of God and His
Church (15; cf. 36ff.). This makes "every man a law unto
himself" and civil society the product of collective
free-will; civil authority is deemed to result from the
mere consent of the governed, and laws are held to
owe their justice solely from their having been willed
by "authorities." Such errors destroy the distinction
between good and evil, make pleasure the standard of
lawfulness, and open a way to universal corruption, "a
road leading straight to tyranny" (16). In such a society, religion is doomed to be "treated with complete
indifference"—one of the many places where this great
pope predicts the state of the world in which we now
live, where liberalism is so ubiquitous it goes unnoticed.

More controversially to Americans, Leo XIII then
frontally attacks "the *fatal theory* of the need of separation between Church and state," a position of "manifest
absurdity" which denies in practice the link between
man's temporal everyday life and his eternal destiny

(18). In language that demonstrates how "integralist" traditional Catholic doctrine actually is, Leo teaches that rulers owe it to the nation not only to provide for its worldly prosperity but even more to cultivate the spiritual good of the people. Political power is given *by* God (not by the people) in order to lead men *to* God. "Civil society must acknowledge God as its founder and parent, and must obey and reverence His power and authority. Justice therefore forbids, and reason itself forbids, the state to be godless" (21). The harmony that should exist between Church and state may be likened to the relationship of immortal soul and fleshly body. If the soul is separated from the body, the former remains alive but the latter perishes and dissolves into dust (ibid.). The state, as a creation of God redeemed by Christ, is bound by an inescapable obligation to seek out the one true religion, adhere to it, and subordinate itself to it.[2]

DESTABILIZING FREEDOMS OF MODERNITY

Having set down these principles, Pope Leo XIII considers various freedoms championed by liberalism—freedom of religion (19–22), freedom of speech (23), academic freedom (24–29), freedom of conscience (30)—and explains why *unlimited* freedom in each case is impossible in principle and massively destabilizing whenever attempted in practice. "Right [*ius*] is a moral power [*facultas moralis*] which ... it is absurd to suppose that nature has accorded indifferently to truth and falsehood, to justice and injustice" (23). "It is contrary to reason that error and truth should have equal rights" (34). As error and moral vice are directly opposed to

---

[2] The traditional teaching that the state is thus bound, generally rejected in the period after the Second Vatican Council, has been taken up anew and persuasively defended in a growing number of Catholic publications. See, for example, Crean and Fimister, *Integralism*; Storck, *Foundations*; Waldstein, *Integralism and the Common Good*, vol. 2.

the common good of civil society, they enjoy no claim
to protection by civil authority. "It is quite unlawful to
demand, or to defend, or to grant unconditional freedom of thought, of speech or writing, or of worship, as
if these were so many rights given by nature to man. For,
if nature had really granted them, it would be lawful
to refuse obedience to God" (42). I will come back to
the question of freedom of speech later in this chapter.

Can we say that *freedom of conscience* exists? Could
we give this popular term a legitimate meaning? Leo
XIII says we can do so, and that the Church always
has done so:

> Every man in the state may follow the will of
> God and, from a consciousness of duty and
> free from every obstacle, obey His commands.
> This, indeed, is true freedom, a freedom wor-
> thy of the sons of God, which nobly maintains
> the dignity of man ... This Christian freedom
> bears witness to the absolute and most just
> dominion of God over man, and to the chief
> and supreme duty of man toward God. (30)

Freedom of conscience is not only legitimate, it is one
of man's noblest freedoms, one for which countless
martyrs have laid down their lives. What is crucial
is to see that "freedom" here means the right use of
our will towards the supreme good and all that is in
harmony with that good, while "conscience" means a
well-informed faculty of practical judgment.

PRUDENTIAL TOLERATION OF EVIL

As if in response to a question on the minds of his
readers, Leo XIII joins to his critique of liberalism a
substantial coda on the necessity of a *policy of toleration*
in some states (33–35).

> The Church weighs the great burden of human
> weakness, and well knows the course down
> which the minds and actions of men are in

this our age being borne. For this reason, while
not conceding any right to anything save what
is true and honest, she does not forbid public
authority to tolerate what is at variance with
truth and justice, for the sake of avoiding some
greater evil, or of obtaining or preserving some
greater good. (33)

Even God, says the pope, permits certain evils lest
a greater good be impeded or a greater evil ensue.
Although such toleration can be justified by the exi-
gencies of the common good, the evil may never cease
to be called *evil* by those who know better, nor may
it be approved of or desired for itself, as if the best
condition for a state is one in which the errors of false
religions are tolerated or, worse, encouraged in a sort
of equal-opportunity relativism. The more a state is
compelled to tolerate evils, the further it is from perfection; hence toleration, too, must be limited to what
is strictly necessary for the circumstances, and there
are times when toleration would be wrong (34). "The
Church usually acquiesces in certain modern liberties,
not because she prefers them in themselves, but because
she judges it expedient to permit them" (ibid.). The
pope also takes pains to specify which type of liberalism
he is condemning (37–46), noting that it is possible
to uphold "some equitable adjustment consistent with
truth and justice" between the Church and "the modern
system of government," so long as one views it as an
indulgence, a less-than-ideal state of affairs (41).

Though *Libertas Praestantissimum* contains nothing
that could not be found in the pages of St. Thomas
Aquinas or the writings of prior sovereign pontiffs, its
radiant synthesis of Catholic doctrine on the subject it
treats makes it a document of outstanding worth. Routinely appealed to by the popes of the first half of the
twentieth century, *Libertas Praestantissimum* somewhat
surprisingly makes an appearance in the footnotes of

the Second Vatican Council (e.g., *Dignitatis Humanae*, *Gaudium et Spes*). It continues to be cited in the post-Conciliar magisterium (e.g., *Centesimus Annus*, *Veritatis Splendor*, *Catechism of the Catholic Church*). One has the impression that so impressive a document cannot be ignored but must somehow be engaged. We can certainly hope for a time when the rulers of the Church will subscribe wholeheartedly to its teaching.

CIVIL LIBERTIES: THE PROBLEM

A fundamental question of political philosophy and one that faces us every day is what range of freedom of behavior should be allowed to, or is inherent in, citizens of a state—hence the term "civil liberties," as distinct from other kinds of liberty (e.g., the psychological liberty identical to freedom of will, the spiritual liberty identical to holiness). Not everything is permissible, for some actions cause grave harm to social life; yet not all immoral behavior can be prohibited, lest fallen nature be unduly strained and social unrest result.

Until modern times, nearly every philosopher and theologian agreed that any significant exercise of freedom in the public forum—forming associations with others, speaking or publishing one's thoughts, undertaking communal acts of divine worship, and the like—had to be placed under certain limits if the society's common good were to be safeguarded, and that government had the power and the obligation to impose such limits. In Catholic countries, rulers were expected to defend the Faith against heresy, and the code of civil law was expected to reflect the natural law as interpreted by the Church.

The modern problem of civil liberties stems from the Enlightenment's secularist, individualist conception of social life, wherein the individual's perception of the good is accorded a theoretical primacy, a nation's government becoming essentially the citizens' mouthpiece, mirror, and policeman. In a so-called "social contract," citizens are assumed to be entitled to the exercise of all liberties compatible with "public order" understood in a positivistic sense. For example, each man is to be left entirely free to determine his own religious beliefs; to worship one God, twenty gods, or no god;[3] to defend or attack, in speech or print, whatsoever opinions he considers right or wrong.

CIVIL LIBERTIES: THE CHURCH'S RESPONSE

Pope Gregory XVI's encyclical *Mirari Vos* (1832) established the basic principle: unrestrained freedom to act, speak, or publish as one fancies is an "absurd and erroneous proposition" guaranteed to pull down the fabric of society and to occasion the loss of innumerable souls (no. 14). Pius IX affirmed this judgment in *Quanta Cura* (1864) and the *Syllabus of Errors* appended to it (see no. 79). It was not, however, until the encyclical we have been discussing, *Libertas Praestantissimum*, that the Church could be said to be in possession of a fully worked-out account. According to Leo XIII, the provision and exercise of civil liberties is intelligible only in reference to the moral perfection of the individual and the sound order of civil society—that is, in reference to the social body's attainment of genuinely common goods such as peace, justice, truth, and ultimately God. John Paul II captures well Leo's concerns:

> [*Libertas Praestantissimum*] called attention to the essential bond between human freedom and truth, so that freedom which refused to be bound to the truth would fall into arbitrariness and end up submitting itself to the vilest of passions, to the point of self-destruction.

---

[3] A reference to Thomas Jefferson: "But it does me no injury for my neighbor to say there are twenty Gods, or no God. It neither picks my pocket nor breaks my leg." *Notes on the State of Virginia*, Query XVII, p. 170.

> Indeed, what is the origin of all the evils to which *Rerum Novarum* wished to respond, if not a kind of freedom which, in the area of economic and social activity, cuts itself off from the truth about humanity?[4]

The error, he continues,

> consists in an understanding of human freedom which detaches it from obedience to the truth, and consequently from the duty to respect the rights of others. The essence of freedom then becomes self-love carried to the point of contempt for God and neighbor, a self-love which leads to an unbridled affirmation of self-interest and which refuses to be limited by any demand of justice.[5]

INHERENT LIMITS TO FREE SPEECH

The phrase "freedom of speech" is shorthand for the legal-political issue of what kind of right belongs to a person by nature or by citizenship to express his thoughts outwardly in the public forum, and what limits may or should be placed upon this activity. It makes an especially good case study for how civil liberties work (or should work), as it brings into play all the elements of CST.

The Catholic tradition begins its distinctive analysis from a fact of human nature, namely, that speech is a *rational* activity that can be done well or poorly, rightly or wrongly. Its due exercise is measured by its purpose, which is, broadly, the communication of truth, and therefore also the discovery and defense of truth — including not only speculative truths, but also advice, opinions, predictions, and the like, where one is attempting to come as near the truth as possible. From this intimate connection between the human mind and truth arises an *inalienable right* to the proper use

---

[4] John Paul II, *Centesimus Annus* 4.
[5] *Centesimus Annus* 17.

of speech in all its forms, which translates into a just claim upon others, whether private citizens or public authority, to respect this right.

By striking at the intellect's natural inclination to the truth, government prohibition of due freedom of speech is a tyrannical act pure and simple. Notorious examples of this tyranny were supplied by the twentieth century's totalitarian regimes, which idolized one or another ideology as "truth" and ostracized those who sought truth outside of it.[6] At the same time, these principles illuminate the contrary error of liberalism, which absolutizes rights by ignoring or denying definite *goods* on which they rest, i.e., by severing the exercise of an activity from its natural purpose. In liberal democracies, freedom of speech is typically understood in absolute, individualistic terms—namely, as an inherent freedom to say or write *whatever one pleases*, provided a positivistically-conceived "public order" is not disturbed,[7] a view that Gregory XVI in 1832 characterized as "that harmful and never sufficiently denounced freedom to publish any writings whatever and disseminate them to the people, which some dare to demand and promote with so great a clamor."[8]

WHAT IS THE GOOD THAT SUPPORTS FREEDOM OF EXPRESSION?

In reality, speech, like any created thing, is a finite good; like all finite goods, it is ordered to an end outside itself, and its goodness consists in its order to, and above all its attainment of, that end. Man, by nature, is neither a beast nor a god; he is a social animal who lives his life in a community of fellow citizens who share labors, pleasures, and ideas. An individual's mind is ordered

---

[6] Tellingly, the Soviet Communist Party's newspaper was named *Pravda*, "Truth."
[7] See *CCC* 2109.
[8] Gregory XVI, *Mirari Vos* 15.

to truth not simply for its own perfection, but also for
the benefit of others who may become his partners in
conversation. Because the human mind naturally *craves*
truth and nothing less is worthy of it, a speaker or writer
owes the same truth to others, and he *injures* them by
refusing to share knowledge that they have a right to
know, by disseminating errors, or by plain lying—the
most obvious case of an abuse of the faculty of speech.

As St. Augustine often says, any good thing suscep-
tible to abuse cannot be a perfect or unqualified good;
rather, it must be an imperfect, relative good, deriving
such goodness as it has strictly from the greater good
toward which it is aimed. Accordingly, no one can
have an unlimited "right" to use, or exercise, something
which is not an unlimited good, or put positively, one
may freely use a limited good only within due limits.
There are two such limits: the truth, which stands as
measure or form to the human mind (and in that sense,
"limits" it; when a certain truth perfects my mind—say,
the Pythagorean theorem—it simultaneously excludes
all opinions incompatible with it); and the good of
others in society, to whom truth is owed (this condition
limits the speaker to expressing publicly only what he
understands to be true, and not indiscriminately, but
according to the right circumstances of audience, place,
time, manner, and purpose).

Indeed, the very existence of legitimate civil authority and its boon, tranquility of order, depends upon the
non-absoluteness of individual rights and the superiority
of goods common to all—goods among which truth,
especially truth about God, stands foremost. To posit
an unlimited right is equivalent to favoring tyranny, for
on that hypothesis whoever happens to have power
may exercise his "right" as he wishes, and whoever
lacks power is trampled upon.[9]

---

[9] See Leo XIII, *Libertas Praestantissimum* 16 and 31; John Paul II,
Centesimus Annus 44ff.

This, in fact, is the hidden premise of a positivistic legal order: it is only by "common consent," always changeable and changing, that any form of behavior is to be considered offensive and punishable. Thus, over time, even the murder of unborn children and the abomination of sodomy have found their well-paid legal advocates and, in the minds of many, have been removed from the list of crimes. If a society or a regime turns its back on the natural law, all moral evaluations are reduced to positive, self-motivated acts of will; law becomes merely a reflection of *majority egoism*. This perversion of social life, incessantly critiqued by the Catholic Church, flows from a view of personal rights that cannot be sustained either on natural or supernatural criteria.

MAN HAS NO "RIGHT" TO ABUSE A GOD-GIVEN POWER

Since the God-given purpose of speech is to discover, declare, discuss, or defend the truth, the power of speech is used virtuously whenever the speaker, in good conscience, endeavors to speak truth, and thereby to lead others to knowledge of the truth or away from falsehood. When, on the other hand, it is used for deception, cruelty, perjury, moral depravity, etc., the speaker is *abusing* the power of speech, and hence forfeits the immunity of the natural law and makes himself subject to civil prosecution. Speech is a natural power and the use of speech a natural good; accordingly, the *abuse* of speech is contrary to nature and cannot be a natural *or civil* right.

Pope Pius XII reiterated the traditional teaching that "error has no rights": what is in itself false can never be a good for any intellect.[10] Even if error has no rights, however, it does not follow that an *erring person* has no rights; therefore, persons are always to be treated

---

[10] Pius XII, *Ci Riesce*, December 6, 1953.

with respect, whereas errors and other evils deserve contempt and, to the extent possible, should be eradicated. Something like pornography has no *right* to exist, nor can those who produce it have any right to do so. Many speak equivocally of such "rights," but they are pure fictions, as are so-called "rights" to abortion, sterilization, euthanasia, same-sex "marriage", and so forth.

For the benefit of society as a whole, civil authority *must* limit, and in practice has *always* limited, the exercise of natural powers. For example, just as I am forbidden to kill or maim an annoying neighbor, so I may not sound my opinions in the street with a bull horn at 3 A.M.; indeed, if my opinions are sufficiently obnoxious, I may be forbidden to sound them at *any* time of day or night. If a traveler were fool enough to kid around with a companion at an airport, "I guess those guards didn't find the machete in my bag," an officer who overheard the comment would search him in a flash. If there were no evil in the world, men could be permitted to say and do whatsoever they pleased, and all would be to the good. Freedom of speech was unlimited in the Garden of Eden before the Fall. But since there *are* miscreants who do evil, citizens need to be protected, for otherwise their own happiness will be endangered and the community cannot prosper. As Leo XIII wrote: "If unbridled license of speech and of writing be granted to all, nothing will remain sacred and inviolate; even the highest and truest mandates of nature, justly held to be the common and noblest heritage of the human race, will not be spared."[11] How true this observation is requires no demonstration today.

DISCRETIONARY PRUDENCE ABOUT EVILS

Granting, as Catholics have always done, that the state has *by its very nature* the right and the duty to forbid harmful uses of speech and even to destroy

---

[11] Leo XIII, *Libertas Praestantissimum* 23.

publications that undermine the common good of society,[12] a serious question still remains: How should the state's policy vis-à-vis abuses of speech or press be determined?

Following Aquinas, Leo XIII teaches that evils may be tolerated if, and only if, attempts at abolishing them would lead to a still greater evil or impede a greater good. Such toleration does not positively *will* the evils but merely *allows* them to remain unchecked.[13] This distinction is not merely semantic, for it stresses the truth that a ruler does not choose the ultimate *end* of government; he chooses rather the *means* by which, in his judgment, this end may best be achieved. The supreme end of political society is the attainment of the common good.[14] Thus, it is evident that any activity opposed to the common good may be legitimately restrained or proscribed by public authority.

The tightening or relaxation of civil liberties and the toleration of evils incident upon liberty are left to the discretion of the statesman's prudence, aspiring to the highest realization of the common good under the possibilities afforded by concrete circumstances.

WHY LIBERALISM SELF-DESTRUCTS

We've heard for a long time that the solution to society's problems, including the problems of Catholics in today's modern Western democracies, is that everyone should "live and let live"—that we should all be *classical* liberals who rejoice in a land where people are free to live as they choose, as long as they allow others to live as the others choose to live, and "as long as nobody hurts anybody else." There's no reason for conflict if we just follow this common-sense tolerance.

---

[12] See Leo XIII, *Immortale Dei* 32 and *Libertas Praestantissimum* 23.
[13] *Libertas Praestantissimum* 33–35.
[14] See, e.g., *Immortale Dei* 5 and *Rerum Novarum* 35; Pius XII, *Summi Pontificatus* 59.

This sounds nice in theory, but how does it work in practice?

The reality is that the practice of religion (and, *mutatis mutandis*, the violent opposition to religion that is modern atheism) is *necessarily public and political*. For example, if all Catholics are to worship on a given day, they must have part or all of the day off of work; and if there is to be a procession, a main road might need to be shut down during it. The former will make companies less efficient and less profitable; the latter will impinge on traffic, perhaps on trade, and certainly it may seem an imposition on the unbelieving or the unenthusiastic.

Modern atheism, for its part, is no less public and political: it tries to get rid of all religious symbols, like crucifixes and Christmas scenes, and if it could, it would abolish Sundays and Holy Days (indeed, this has already largely occurred). If the unbelievers had their way, there would be no room and no respect left for Christianity in the public square. In this sense, the liberal isn't one who thinks all views should be allowed to flourish; he believes that the only view that can be allowed is the one that says *no* view is sufficiently known to be true for it to have any precedence or prerogatives. By this "reasoning," atheism becomes *de facto* the public and political creed, elbowing out any other.

We can illustrate the problem with a crystal-clear example. When someone plays music in his car (especially with extra speakers and windows open, driving down Main Street) or through his leaking earbuds, he *makes* everyone around him listen to what he is listening to. His "free choice" to listen imposes on the others a situation they did not freely choose. He is forcing them to submit to his freedom. So, "giving everyone freedom" is illusory; one man's exercise of freedom may and likely will impinge on another's rights.

We see this playing out dramatically with the aggressive homosexual lobby. When "gay marriage" is legalized, what happens to the freedom of bakers, decorators, clothiers, musicians, and churches to follow their Christian (and natural law-based) conscience, whereby they would choose to be involved only in heterosexual weddings? Sorry, people, you have no freedom anymore; liberalism has taken it away. You must now do just what the state tells you—no more, no less.

The most serious instantiation of this withering of justice is the denial of the unborn baby's right to the care of a mother and father and to legal protection. Because of liberalism's intolerant creed, the woman's freedom means *everything*; the child's life, rights, and eventual freedom (and, often, the father's too) mean *nothing*. But only a demonic parody of freedom seeks to abolish and annihilate another person's freedom in order to secure its own.[15]

If the social space is not Catholic, it will be filled, over time, with pagan and anti-Catholic elements. Society, like nature, abhors a vacuum. We have seen more confirmation than we could ever have wished of the truth of what the great popes of the nineteenth century declared: there is *no such thing* as a religiously-neutral public square, a society that does not privilege a creed. The public sphere will be either religious or irreligious, either Christian or anti-Christian. Liberalism self-destructs into intolerant ideology.

---

[15] See Ratzinger, "Truth and Freedom."

MATERIAL GOODS AND
THE KINGDOM OF HEAVEN

ARE PROPERTY RIGHTS ABSOLUTE?

HAVING CONSIDERED THE INTER-
play of hierarchy and equality, the dignity
that pertains to man as created and redeemed,
and the nature of freedom as a power and a right—all
matters that concern primarily the spiritual nature of
man's soul—we now turn to goods that pertain to our
bodily life in this world, where we need food, clothing, shelter, tools, livestock, transportation—to speak
broadly, *property*.

Let's begin with the most fundamental consideration:
Do we have an absolute right to the possession of our
property? In other words, is there any limit or check to
our private possessions? From an individualistic point
of view, there would seem to be no limit. In a (more
or less) free economy, I can work hard, earn money,
and buy stuff to my heart's content. I can amass land,
houses, and clothing, businesses and stocks, technological gadgets of every description, and, provided that
I am paying my taxes and not committing criminal
offenses, no one will stop me.

But there are other lenses through which we need to
view property. First, we must consider the *social* purpose of private ownership, and the duties each citizen
has to the city or community of which he is a part. We
are not isolated monads but social animals who depend
on one another and who are required, by the virtue of
justice, to care for one another—at least to the extent
of not willfully depriving others of what they need to
live. Second, we must consider the ultimate purpose
of earthly goods, which is the attainment of our final
end in Heaven. A bad use of property, including its

unwarranted accumulation, is an impediment to virtue, to sanctity, and to salvation, as all Fathers and Doctors of the Church have taught.

UNIVERSAL DESTINATION OR COMMON USE

The doctrine I will examine in this chapter is often called "the universal destination (or purpose) of goods," which some prefer to call "the common use of all things." Either phrase has to be understood correctly or one may easily fall into error, particularly the error of social-ism, unfortunately so common in our post-Christian era because it functions as a secular substitute for the charitable habits and Christian institutions that are ever dwindling. The doctrine is expounded principally in social encyclicals ranging from Leo XIII's *Rerum Novarum* to John Paul II's *Centesimus Annus*.

"In the plan of the Creator, all of this world's goods are primarily intended for the worthy support of the entire human race," wrote John XXIII.[1] God's command, "Fill the earth and subdue it!" (Gen. 1:28), said Paul VI,

> teaches us that the whole of [material] creation is for man, that he has been charged to give it meaning by his intelligent activity, to com-plete and perfect it by his efforts and to his advantage. Now if the earth truly was created to provide man with the necessities of life and the tools for his own progress, it follows that every man has the right to glean what he needs from the earth. The recent Council reiterated this truth: "God intended the earth and every-thing in it for the use of all human beings and peoples. Thus, under the leadership of justice and in the company of charity, created goods should flow fairly to all."[2]

---

[1] John XXIII, *Mater et Magistra* 119.
[2] Paul VI, *Populorum Progressio* 22, citing *Gaudium et Spes* 69; cf. *Mater et Magistra* 43.

John Paul II expands on this point:

> The original source of all that is good is the
> very act of God, Who created both the earth
> and mankind, and Who gave the earth to man-
> kind, so that we might have dominion over it
> by our work and enjoy its fruits. God gave the
> earth to the whole human race for the suste-
> nance of all its members, without excluding
> or favoring anyone. This is the foundation of
> the universal destination of the earth's goods.[3]

"The principle of the common use of goods or, to put
it in another and still simpler way, the right to life and
subsistence"[4] can even be called, in a way, "the first
principle of the whole ethical and social order"[5] and
"the characteristic principle of Christian social doctrine."[6] It is first in a material sense: if human beings
are not capable of staying alive, they can make no
contributions as citizens of the earthly city, and they
can receive no other benefits from their membership
in human society.

How, then, should the Church's insistence on the
necessity and inviolability of private property be understood? "That God has given the earth for the use and
enjoyment of the whole human race can in no way be a
bar to the owning of private property," writes Leo XIII.

> For God has granted the earth to mankind in
> general, not in the sense that all without dis-
> tinction can deal with it as they like, but rather
> that no part of it was assigned to any one in
> particular, and that the limits of private posses-
> sion have been left to be fixed by man's own
> industry, and by the laws of individual races.
> Moreover, the earth, even though apportioned

---

[3] John Paul II, *Centesimus Annus* 31.
[4] John Paul II, *Laborem Exercens* 18.
[5] *Laborem Exercens* 19; cf. 14.
[6] John Paul II, *Sollicitudo Rei Socialis* 42.

among private owners, ceases not thereby to
minister to the needs of all.[7]

Developing Leo XIII's doctrine, Pius XI explains:

Nature, rather the Creator Himself, has given
man the right of private ownership not only
that individuals may be able to provide for
themselves and their families, but also that
the goods which the Creator destined for the
entire family of mankind may, through this
institution, truly serve this purpose. All this
can be achieved in no wise except through the
maintenance of a certain and definite order.[8]

Pius XI's words recall Leo XIII's basic argument in
Rerum Novarum: the practice of all ages has accepted
private ownership as conformable to human nature,
conducing to social peace and tranquility.[9] By a socialist transfer of property, the worker himself would be
the first to suffer; the dream of equality would be in
reality a leveling down of all to the same misery and
degradation.[10] Socialization would rob lawful possessors,
distort the state's functions, and create confusion in
the community.[11] "This great labor question cannot
be solved save by assuming as a principle that private
ownership must be held sacred and inviolable. The
law, therefore, should favor ownership, and its policy
should be to induce as many as possible of the people
to become owners."[12]

Pius XII particularly insists on this last point: "The
dignity of the human person ... requires normally as
a natural foundation of life the right to the use of
the goods of the earth. To this right corresponds the

---

[7] Leo XIII, *Rerum Novarum* 8.
[8] Pius XI, *Quadragesimo Anno* 45.
[9] Leo XIII, *Rerum Novarum* 11
[10] *Rerum Novarum* 4 and 15.
[11] *Rerum Novarum* 4.
[12] *Rerum Novarum* 46.

fundamental obligation to grant private ownership of property, if possible, to all."[13] The "moral nobility of work" demands not only "a just wage which covers the needs of the worker and his family," but also "the conservation and perfection of a social order which will make possible an assured, even if modest, private property for all classes of society."[14] As far back as Aristotle we find a convincing account of why the widespread distribution of property is both according to human nature and enormously beneficial in its ripple effects:

> It is clearly better that property should be private, but the use of it common; and the special business of the legislator is to create in men this benevolent disposition. Again, how immeasurably greater is the pleasure when a man feels a thing to be his own; for surely the love of self is a feeling implanted by nature and not given in vain, although selfishness is rightly censured; this, however, is not the mere love of self, but the love of self in excess, like the miser's love of money; for all, or almost all, men love money and other such objects in a measure. And further, there is the greatest pleasure in doing a kindness or service to friends or guests or companions, which can only be rendered when a man has private property. These advantages are lost by excessive unification of the state.[15]

The striking thing about Aristotle's defense of private property is that he frames it in reference to the common good of society, which the institution of property serves (or should serve). The legislators must aim to produce a benevolent disposition in men, so that they will share what is their own. The whole point, indeed,

---

[13] Pius XII, Christmas Message 1942, no. 28.
[14] Christmas Message 1942, no. 31.3.
[15] *Politics* II.5.

is to have things *by which to do kindnesses to others.*
Aristotle here anticipates, in a way, the Pauline and,
later, Benedictine emphasis on hospitality.[16]

SATISFACTORY AND UNSATISFACTORY
PROPERTY DISTRIBUTIONS

Catholic teaching underlines the difference between
satisfactory and unsatisfactory distributions of property.
In other words, not any old distribution is conformable
to natural and divine law, but only that which allows
all citizens access to a dignified existence. The goal
towards which society ought to be moving, under gov-
ernmental guidance, is the extension of ownership to
all members of society, an equitable division of wealth
sadly lacking in the industrial nations.[17] An economy
can be considered well-ordered only when all members
of society command the goods needed for life and well-
being.[18] In a statement utterly opposed to the modern
capitalist mentality, John XXIII notes: "The economic
prosperity of a nation is not so much its total assets in
terms of wealth and property, as the equitable division
and distribution of this wealth," i.e., equitable because
it is widespread, not amassed primarily in the hands
of a few.[19] "It is not enough to assert that the right
to own private property and the means of production
is inherent in human nature. We must also insist on
the extension of this right in practice to all classes of
citizens."[20] Hence Paul VI can declare:

> All other rights, whatever they may be, includ-
> ing the rights of property and free trade, are
> to be subordinated to this principle [i.e., the

---

[16] See Rom 12:13 and 15:17; Heb 13:1–2; 1 Tim 3:2; Tit 1:8;
cf. 1 Pet 4:8–9; and St. Benedict, *Holy Rule*, chs. 31, 53, 61.

[17] See Pius XI, *Quadragesimo Anno* 58–60.

[18] See *Quadragesimo Anno* 75.

[19] John XXIII, *Mater et Magistra* 74.

[20] *Mater et Magistra* 113.

universal destination of goods]. They should in no way hinder it; in fact, they should actively facilitate its implementation. Redirecting these rights back to their original purpose must be regarded as a grave and urgent social duty.[21]

The right to private property—no question about it—is "fundamental for the autonomy and development of the person," writes John Paul II. At the same time, "the possession of material goods is not an *absolute* right; its limits are inscribed in its very nature as a human right."[22] "The dominion granted to man by the Creator is not an absolute power, nor can one speak of a freedom to 'use and misuse,' or to dispose of things as one pleases."[23]

Striking are the words of the Angelic Doctor, St. Thomas Aquinas: "Man should not consider his material possessions as his own, but as common to all, so as to share them without hesitation when others are in need."[24] Leo XIII explains:

> Whoever has received from the divine bounty a large share of temporal blessings, whether they be external and material, or gifts of the mind, has received them for the purpose of using them for the perfecting of his own nature, and, at the same time, that he may employ them, as the steward of God's providence, for the benefit of others.[25]

Regarding the duty of the rich toward the poor, Paul VI quotes another great Father of the Church, St. Ambrose of Milan: "You are not making a gift of what is yours to the poor man, but you are giving him back what is his. You have been appropriating things that are meant

---

[21] Paul VI, *Populorum Progressio* 22.
[22] John Paul II, *Centesimus Annus* 30, emphasis added.
[23] John Paul II, *Sollicitudo Rei Socialis* 34; cf. *Rerum Novarum* 22.
[24] Cited by Leo XIII in *Rerum Novarum* 22.
[25] *Rerum Novarum* 22.

to be for the common use of everyone. The earth belongs to everyone, not to the rich." On this, the pope comments: "These words indicate that the right to private property is not absolute and unconditional. No one may appropriate surplus goods solely for his own private use when others lack the bare necessities of life," for "the right of private property may never be exercised to the detriment of the common good."[26]

According to John Paul II, "private property, in fact, is under a 'social mortgage', which means that it has an intrinsically social function, based upon and justified precisely by the principle of the universal destination of goods."[27] If it obstructs this goal, private property "has no justification, and represents an abuse in the sight of God and humanity."[28] Pius XI formulates this truth as the "twofold character of ownership, called usually individual or social as it regards either separate persons or the common good."[29] Since citizens are truly parts of a social whole and their property exercises a social function, owners must look beyond their own advantage to the community's good, and for its part, public authority "can determine more accurately upon consideration of the true requirements of the common good, what is permitted and what is not permitted to owners in the use of their property."[30]

Everything man works with, masters, and owns is first and always a gift from the Creator, to be used according to the Creator's plan.[31] By working, a worker enters into a twofold inheritance: natural resources and human artifacts. In using them, he asserts and establishes a claim to being benefited thereby. Hence,

---

[26] Paul VI, *Populorum Progressio* 23.
[27] John Paul II, *Sollicitudo Rei Socialis* 42.
[28] John Paul II, *Centesimus Annus* 43.
[29] Pius XI, *Quadragesimo Anno* 45; cf. John XXIII, *Mater et Magistra* 120.
[30] *Quadragesimo Anno* 49.
[31] See John Paul II, *Laborem Exercens* 12.

> Christian tradition has never upheld this right
> [to ownership] as absolute and untouchable.
> On the contrary, it has always understood this
> right within the broader context of the right
> common to all to use the goods of the whole
> of creation: the right to private property is
> subordinated to the right to common use, to
> the fact that goods are meant for everyone.[32]

So inherently is capital ordered to the good of workers
that there is no ground for the possession of the means
of production apart from the social benefits conferred
through them.[33] "Just as the person fully realizes himself in the free gift of self, so too ownership morally
justifies itself in the creation, at the proper time and in
the proper way, of opportunities for work and human
growth for all."[34]

HARD TRUTHS INVOLVE MORAL COSTS

There are moral costs to the acceptance of these
hard truths — hard especially for those captivated by
the siren song of "free market capitalism." If we took
seriously the natural law's demands of generosity, equitable distribution, fair wages, and thinking oriented to
the common good rather than to perpetual expansion
and enrichment, the result would undoubtedly be "sac-
rificing the positions of income and of power enjoyed
by the more developed economies"; it would require
"above all a change of lifestyles, of models of production
and consumption, and of the established structures
of power which today govern societies."[35] The "God-
given purpose" of all earthly goods[36] is the benefit of
each and every man, not any arbitrary use or endless

---

[32] *Laborem Exercens* 14.
[33] Cf. *Laborem Exercens* 14.
[34] John Paul II, *Centesimus Annus* 43.
[35] *Centesimus Annus* 52, 58.
[36] *Centesimus Annus* 37.

acquisition.[37] An economy that structurally favors an ever-widening gap between the rich and everybody else is a betrayal of this original purpose.

"But what of businesses, the profit incentive, entrepreneurship, wealth creation, and all that good stuff? Are we supposed to throw it away for a state-planned worker paradise that will end as a Soviet-era nightmare?" No, that's not at all what the Church is saying.

For John Paul II, there is no conflict between the universal destination of goods and a profitable business enterprise, provided the enterprise seeks to benefit employees by way of just policies and customers by way of useful, well-made, morally acceptable products, instead of seeking an expanding profit for a few by way of worker exploitation or the provision of useless, shoddy, or immoral products.[38] A business or market economy can be judged morally good or evil on the basis of whether or not it promotes, *in practice*, the dignity of workers, acceptable working conditions, an ever-widening distribution of property really worth having (primarily land or other real estate), a sense of moral accountability, and a capacity for self-control as seen, for example, in the setting of a reasonable ratio between the highest-paid and lowest-paid employees. A shining example would be the Mondragon corporation in Spain, founded in 1956 by Fr. José María Arizmendiarrieta in accord with the principles of CST, and still

---

[37] Here I have in mind Aristotle's statement that "the desire for artificial wealth is infinite" (*Politics* I.3, cited in *Summa theologiae* I-II, Q. 2, art. 1, ad 3) — infinite in the sense of having no limit. For food and drink, there is a limit: I get full and don't want to eat or drink anymore. But with money there is no natural limit, no moment when you "feel full" of money. And similarly, goods like clothes, furniture, houses, cars, boats, computers, etc. can be acquired endlessly — there is no reason *in the things themselves* to stop acquiring them. The only reason one would wish to stop is that one has a clear sense of the *purpose* of one's possessions and rationally judges that this purpose has been fulfilled.

[38] See John Paul II, *Centesimus Annus* 32–43.

flourishing today—a worker cooperative in which talent and longevity of service are rewarded by increasing opportunities for ownership, management, and social services. The company is profitable and competitive.

Such results can occur only within a "strong juridical framework" and under the constant vigilance of statesmen animated by love for the common good[39]—and, needless to add, only when Christians themselves live as witnesses to the gospel, fruitful in works of justice and charity. We can see two reasons, then, why the universal destination of goods is today denied in theory and in practice: (1) weakness in civil rulership, pushed about as it is by lobbies and monetary interests, and (2) the relative weakness of the Christian witness in the modern West.

CONCLUSION

Two common misunderstandings must be guarded against.

First, the universal destination of goods does not imply—in fact, it decisively repudiates—all forms of socialism or communism, for these systems are incapable of securing even a minimally just distribution of earthly goods, much less the earthly paradise promised by revolutionaries. Human dignity requires awareness of one's own responsibility as a worker, incentive to work, and a reasonable hope of stability for oneself and one's family. A modicum of property—a roof over one's head, enough food and clothing—allows freedom for what truly matters in life: fellowship with one's family and friends, leisure for prayer, worship, and festivity.

Secondly, and contrary to the caricatures promoted by opponents of distributism, the Church's proposals exclude a statist scenario in which government functionaries seize vast tracts of land or sums of wealth and

---

[39] E.g., *Centesimus Annus* 36, 40, 42, *et passim.*

redistribute them by executive fiat. This enterprise would likely end in the mere substitution of one plutocracy for another. In most cases, distribution of property is not the government's responsibility. Rather, the state must devise policies, laws, and incentives that will promote and protect a social order in which the greatest possible number of citizens become owners of stable property, shareholders, or business partners.

8

THE DISPUTE BETWEEN
DISTRIBUTISTS AND CAPITALISTS

I HAVE NOTICED THAT TWO SUB-jects cause the most immediate, most visceral debates among those who disagree: music and economics. If I offer a critique of rock, pop, rap, praise & worship, or any other type of modern music, the floodgates of wrath open and the cataracts of indignation pour out. Similarly, if I say so much as one negative word about American-style capitalism, or the Austrian fantasy of a self-regulating free market that maximizes goods and services while minimizing vice and exploitation, I can expect lightning and thunder to fall on my head.

So it has proved with writings in which I have presented various arguments against capitalism *as an ideal, a mentality, and an ideology*. Nowhere did I speak a word against initiative, profit, or investment as such. As earlier chapters have shown, the properly *political* question is always about how the exercise of individual liberty contributes to or undermines the common good of the society, which in fact is the chief good even of individuals. If we do not guard the common good, we are injuring ourselves, since we are fundamentally not atoms but social animals. If we are Christians, we have a still more compelling reason to care about the fate of our neighbor.

THE ROOT OF DISTRIBUTISM
The economic philosophy known as *distributism* — the most famous proponents of which are Hilaire Belloc (1870–1953) and G.K. Chesterton (1874–1936), with Thomas Storck and John Médaille as well-known advocates today — is named from its most essential axiom: a

society is successful in meeting the elementary needs of citizens in direct proportion to the equity and breadth of property ownership among them, and civil government is responsible for implementing policies that aim at such widespread distribution of property. In other words, it is premised on the assumption, defended in the last chapter, that the world's goods are intended by the Creator for the benefit of all men, and that this benefit is realized chiefly through the well-ordered ownership, care, and use of those goods by families. While there will always be corporate entities with considerable wealth and landlords renting to tenants, an economy is imbalanced to the extent that it is dominated by them.

Distributism is not as far-fetched as some people make it sound. For example, the incentives given in the United States to first-time homeowners, various tax breaks for larger families and for farmers, and tax write-offs for donations to charities are well-appreciated ways to encourage obtaining or preserving private property or, in complementary fashion, to see that it reaches as many of the needy as it can, without the inefficient and impersonal intervention of the state.

The most common charge made against distributists is actually a double charge: on the one hand, that they are not serious students of "scientific economics"; on the other hand, that they advocate solving the world's economic problems by socialist executive *fiat*. If ever there has been a caricature, this is it, for distributism is abundantly clear about its eternal enmity towards socialism as a system, and its solutions are far more nuanced and practical, as can be seen in the success of distributist enterprises like Mondragon. Storck and Médaille have demonstrated in many articles that economics is not a science; it is rather a set of assumptions and predictions that rest on beliefs about human nature and the human good. Far from being value-neutral, it is as biased as neo-Darwinian evolutionism.

THE CHARGE OF STATISM

The aforementioned double charge nevertheless points to a deeper source of disagreement. Distributism says, for example, that it is immoral for a CEO to be earning $35 million a year when his company is laying off workers at the same time. It will be enough if he earns, let's say, a modest $2 million.[1] Enthusiasts of free enterprise will cry out: "You'll destroy the entrepreneurial spirit! You'll gum up investments! Brilliance and risk deserve more pay!" These are the cries of men trapped in a profane market mentality who fail to acknowledge the moral devastation wrought by centuries of materialism and hedonism promoted by that very same mentality. Might it not be better *not* to have so much enterprise, investment, and technology, which is driving us into a dehumanized apocalypse?

I once heard someone blame the medieval guild system for never making men rich. Apparently this person saw it as a fault in the system that if you belonged to a guild, you were "held back" by the common standards to which the members agreed. Even as admittedly nobody would starve to death if he had lost his hands in an accident, nobody could ever rise above the ranks to dominate the field. Is this matter for critique or matter for praise? It was precisely the Catholic genius of guilds that they *ensured* their members would not become rich, at least by modern capitalist standards. Guilds were *designed* not to make anyone disproportionately wealthy over his peers. The truth of the matter is harsh

---

[1] It is no secret to anyone who keeps up on news in the world of economics that, as one article put it, "Executive Salaries Are Still Flying High," with the subtitle: "CEOs in U.S. Make 475 Times What the Average Worker Makes." Or another article: "Executive Pay: Over the Top? Debate Continues Over Lavish Salaries." What is surprising is that most Americans, even if they may feel a sense of injustice at hearing about such a thing, do not call into question the kind of economic system that produces it, or feel moved to search into its ultimate causes and remedies.

and few are willing to hear it: for most people, getting
rich would be the first step to hell. Any system that
makes people rich or even makes them *want* to get rich
is a system that paves a broad way to the underworld.
The guilds, in contrast, brought artisans *together into a
Catholic community* and kept the larger society cohesive.
Rather than competing with and fighting against one
another, artisans joined strengths and produced some
of the greatest art, both utilitarian and fine, that the
world has ever known—and they did so in an explicitly
Catholic, Eucharistic, Marian context. They supported
their sick members, buried the dead, had Masses said
for the dead, prayed to their patron saints, and went
to Mass together. It was genuinely Catholic, inherently
social, and *modestly* successful economically, which is
the most one should aim for in light of the gospel. To
go beyond that is to dance the tango with the devil.

Proponents of a "morally neutral" or even "morally
good" capitalist free-market economy seem blind to the
perils of handing over the keys to masses of citizens
driven by their selfish passions—not to mention blind
to economic reality itself, since, as Pius XI recognized
in *Quadragesimo Anno*, there has never been, nor could
there ever be, a perfectly free market; there will only
be an arena in which the strong and the weak and
their allies or enemies struggle for power. This is why
a society cannot avoid the need for a strong government that implements a system of just laws to regulate
economic life. No fence-sitting is possible; either a
system of just laws will exist to guide the economy,
or a system of unjust laws, or a confused chaos of
both kinds—but a government-free realm of economic
transactions is practically impossible, and undesirable
even if it were possible.

We do not presently have a sound framework of just
laws governing the economy because Western governments have long been puppets and playmates of private

or corporate economic interests, as Pius XI saw almost a hundred years ago.[2] In overreaction to this peculiar vice of capitalism, communist and socialist governments seek to assimilate the market to themselves and to exercise total control, which suppresses individual initiative, personal responsibility, and the development of moral and intellectual virtue in the citizenry. The dizzying pendulum swing from socialism to capitalism and back again is not an inevitable ebb and flow of contrary natural forces but the predictable result of a perverted relationship between the political and the economic domains, founded on a false understanding of each.

Supporters of free-market economics are begging the question when they invoke the so-called "science of economics." There is no such thing, nor are there economic laws in the sense in which these people seem to think there are. There are social mores and political constructs that dictate economic attitudes, and these produce patterns that are then abstracted as laws by sociologists. It's like modern Freudian psychology. You can predict what men will do in a bordello, or what a sex-obsessed novelist is going to write about, but you cannot construct a theory of human nature on that basis.

History offers a great deal more in its record than economic forces. History shows us an example of a social order, Christendom, in which, by and large, men subordinated *everything* to the Catholic faith. This catholicity of medieval society was decisively political and economic. The common good was deliberately aimed at and attained more consistently, not because "life was simpler back then" but because Europe was traditionally Catholic in theory and in practice.[3] The modern West

---

[2] See Pius XI, *Quadragesimo Anno* 109.
[3] This is not a matter of personal opinion but of historical evidence. Take, for example, Duffy's *Stripping of the Altars*, which demonstrates in some detail just how *Catholic* medieval England was before the "Reformers" destroyed this vibrant spiritual-cultural ecosystem.

is liberally Protestant in theory and in practice. This is the real difference that separates CST from all rival theories of social organization and prosperity. The vital, qualitative difference between the Middle Ages and modernity is that the former deliberately aimed at and attained a common good anchored in metaphysical and religious truth, while the latter has just as deliberately chosen to forego the universality and objectivity of the good and the reality of an ultimate end for man. In doing so, modern liberalism—the parent of all our defective political and economic theories and systems—both eviscerates the notions of right, justice, prudence, unity, and peace, and obstructs their attainment.

Thomas Storck's *Foundations of a Catholic Political Order* has a brilliant chapter on economics that punctures the balloons of our modern prejudices about money, business, and statecraft.[4] Neither Storck nor the Catholic social magisterium he argues from asserts that the government should set wages or control all aspects of the economy. In fact, the whole point of subsidiarity and of the guilds that all the popes from Leo XIII onwards have recommended is to carve out a *via media* between state autonomy and corporate hegemony. What the government cannot and must not abdicate, however, is its solemn responsibility to regulate the economy in such a fashion that the largest number of citizens may become property-owners, that the rights and duties of owners, managers, and workers may be guaranteed, and that the distribution of wealth may not be marred by enormous excesses and deficiencies.[5]

---

[4] See pp. 51–107 of that book, as well as the same author's *Economics: An Alternative Introduction* (XIII Books, 2024).
[5] Crucial to this, of course, is a perpetual ban on all forms of usury, as explained by David Hunt, *Something for Nothing? An Explanation and Defense of the Scholastic Position on Usury* (Os Justi Press, 2024). Aristotle regards hedonism as the source of avarice: "Those who do aim at [what they take to be] a good life seek the means of obtaining bodily pleasures; and, since the

The distributist knows that a just social order is possible because it once really existed, to an impressive if still imperfect extent. He also knows that our society is groaning with injustices because it refuses to abide by the natural and supernatural principles on which any sane society must be founded. He knows that the desire for, availability of, and possession of nearly unlimited material goods spells doom for the human spirit and its freedom to achieve lasting good. Our materialistic society is lacking what might be called *economic chastity*. Those who defend the present arrangements defend them much the way a sex educator defends his assumptions against a proponent of chastity: he will say, perhaps shaking his head, "It can't be done, it's unrealistic; kids will be kids, you know, and you've got to give them condoms. Your idealism is admirable but we live in a real world with real problems," etc. No. The "real world" is not whatever uncontrollable mess fallen human beings have gotten themselves into by their erroneous ideas and idiotic decisions. It is the world that God created, that Christ redeemed, that the Holy Spirit can influence, that the Church spiritually rules, and that Christians are obliged to heal and elevate: *this* is how we must

---

enjoyment of these appears to depend on property, they are absorbed in getting wealth.... As their enjoyment is in excess, they seek an art which produces the excess of enjoyment; and, if they are not able to supply their pleasures by the art of getting wealth, they try other causes, using in turn every faculty in a manner contrary to nature" (*Politics* I.9). Thus, for Aristotle, usury, gluttony, and homosexuality are analogous: the first is the art of getting more money from less, the second is getting more pleasure from food than is appropriate, and the last is using a faculty of nature contrary to nature, to satisfy excessive appetites. In all cases, there is first an excessive desire, and secondly, the discovery of means to realize these desires. It seems that the structure of the free market, from a moral perspective, is a structure by which to conceive and achieve an ever-increasing excess of desire; and this is why it tends to become, inevitably, a *structure of sin*. It could only cease to be sinful by ceasing to posit economic selfishness as its final end.

see the world. It is our failure to work from and for *this* world—the real one, in God's eyes—that explains the secularizing juggernaut's victories in recent centuries.

In his encyclical *Sollicitudo Rei Socialis*, John Paul II says that the Lord Jesus will be the judge who takes away what people have and gives it to those who have not (I thought this language was supposed to be the exclusive province of Marxists!). He believed that the nations of the West were doomed to be stripped of their glory because of their abuse of God's creation, their refusal to honor the "universal destination of material goods"—that is, the fact that God intended the goods of creation to reach and benefit everyone through well-distributed private property. John Paul II's teaching on consumerism and waste, his comments on structures of sin, his blunt statement that the roots of the problems in the modern world are political and ideological, make it obvious that he saw the modern West as a reckless experiment in hypertrophic selfishness culminating in self-destructive obsessions and cruelty to the weak, which we see above all in the sexual revolution and its inevitable consequence, the murder of millions of the unborn, propelling the world into a demographic winter. The present political-economic "order" in the United States and in many other Western nations is erected along lines that are anti-natural, anti-rational, and anti-spiritual, with built-in mechanisms to ensure that it remains on those lines and even accelerates along them.

ECONOMIC JUSTICE IS NOT UTOPIAN

Advocates of the free market accuse adherents of CST in general—and of distributism in particular—of promoting the kind of centralized statism symbolized by Sauron in *The Lord of the Rings* or The Party in George Orwell's *1984*. Even if the claim is exaggerated, it furnishes an occasion to clarify what is, and is not, held by proponents of CST.

Social ethics, which concerns the requirements of a just civil order, is truly a part of Christian doctrine, not an optional and incidental element of the Catholic tradition. Accordingly, the critique of liberalism in economics and politics is not a passing fad promoted by medievalist popes but the timely application of perennial principles. One rarely finds "conservatives" of any stripe bothering to learn what distributists actually hold; they prefer a caricature that offers an easy target of attack. They assume we stand for massive state-led redistribution, heavy taxation, fascist or communist centralization, etc. We do not. But it takes time to discover that there *are* alternatives to capitalist hegemony.

Many misinterpret CST as an unabashed exaltation of the welfare state, social democracy, or even straight socialism. This is by no means correct. One of the central pillars of CST is the principle of subsidiarity. Distributists maintain that the state must erect a framework of laws that, by their long-term operation, channel wealth in culturally healthy ways—for example, laws that support local family-run businesses while penalizing or prohibiting massive chains like McDonald's or Walmart; laws that support a mosaic of thousands of family farms instead of the enormities of agribusiness. Even one or two policies like this would radically change the urban, suburban, and rural landscape of America.

Observers frequently downplay the extent to which the modern economistic mindset privileges the amassing of wealth and property and the redefinition of the human good in terms of possessions (this was one of John Paul II's most frequent, and most warranted, criticisms of the modern West). Thus it seems to me not merely desirable but essential for human flourishing that legal structures be set up that discourage wealth multiplication and concentration while encouraging the distribution of real property. For many decades distributists have been addressing both why this is necessary for a just social order and how it is realistically achievable without constant interference from the state.

Jesus did not teach that justice on earth was completely impossible and should, as a consequence, never be the goal of our toils here (did He abolish the natural law?; did He reject the existence of such a thing? — tell that to St. Thomas Aquinas and see what he says in reply!), nor did He institute a divine law that has no relevance to daily life in the world. His followers are supposed to be the salt that flavors the food, the leaven that raises up the dough. This, too, is what the Second Vatican Council said: the laity should *transform* earthly institutions by infusing them with the principles of the gospel.

The Church has never in practice, and will never in principle, exclude the political domain from those institutions that are supposed to be oriented by and toward justice. There can be many disagreements about how this "infusion" should be done concretely, but it certainly rules out a radical separation of the public and the private spheres, which only mirrors the fateful separations of nature from grace, culture from faith, and politics from morality. It's obvious that saints do not wait for the civil authorities to solve problems; they go out into the streets and do it themselves. But it's equally obvious that Christian tradition has unanimously recognized a genuine obligation on the part of civil authorities to do everything in their power to promote the common good. This will include, of necessity, a certain amount of regulation of the economic sphere. What Jesus rejected was the kind of power *Satan* offered him. Not all earthly power is such, otherwise parental authority, for example, would be diabolical.

We are sinners, yes, and so are our rulers. Yet we still have obligations to fulfill on our own behalf and on behalf of our neighbors, and God gives us the grace to fulfill them if we do what He asks us to do: accept the faith He has revealed, receive the sacraments, seek Him in prayer. To say it is enough for men to believe privately in Christ or to fear the punishments of hell in order for them to be motivated to pursue justice is a naive position. Because man is a political animal, as Aristotle saw, he is profoundly influenced by and indebted to the social structures he grows up in and lives in. Therefore, the law is a major force for good or for evil; so has it ever been, so will it ever be.

That is why, too, there has never been nor could there ever be a "free market," strictly speaking. The only real question is: Is a given market surrounded by a wise and just framework of laws, or a stupid and wicked framework of laws? Probably a mixture; but what are the proportions? There have been more and less Christian rulers, more and less just societies. We are not doomed to the worst, nor are we guaranteed the best. Our fate is in large part left in the hands of our freedom and our counsel. This is why Scripture teaches that while it is true that God will judge all men mercifully, He will judge *rulers* with more severity, because to them was entrusted the gravest earthly responsibility.[6] The ruler's active and central role in

---

[6] Scripture is remarkably forceful on this point: "Hear therefore, ye kings, and understand: learn, ye that are judges of the ends of the earth. Give ear, you that rule the people, and that please yourselves in multitudes of nations: For power is given you by the Lord, and strength by the most High, who will examine your works, and search out your thoughts: Because being ministers of his kingdom, you have not judged rightly, nor kept the law of justice, nor walked according to the will of God. Horribly and speedily will he appear to you: for a most severe judgment shall be for them that bear rule. For to him that is little, mercy is granted: but the mighty shall be mightily tormented. For God will not except any man's person, neither will he stand in awe of any man's greatness: for he made the little and the great, and he hath equally care of all. But a greater punishment is ready for the more mighty. To you, therefore, O kings, are these my words, that you may learn wisdom, and not fall from it" (Wis 6:2–10). Would that more politicians kept these words before their eyes!

shaping society is so much a part of Christian tradition that to deny it is simply to withdraw oneself from a chorus of saints and sages and to strike off on a lonesome path.

One may object that a state could be trusted to fix the boundaries of acceptable enterprise if, and only if, God were the one who ran it. In fact, God *does* "run the state"—not directly and immediately, but through the rulers who hold their authority from Him, and in the wisdom of His doctrine concerning individual and social ethics. Over each human society stand men who are entrusted, by God, with the care of that community, who can discharge their duty well or poorly, virtuously or sinfully. This is a constant refrain in the Christian tradition, beginning with the New Testament which teaches that all earthly authority derives from God and is answerable to Him. A wicked ruler is abusing a God-given trust; a good ruler is exercising his God-given right. This is not to invoke a divine right of kings, but to accept what follows logically from the divine origin and goal of man in all his dimensions, including the social.[7]

CRIPPLED BY VAGUENESS?

Libertarians and their sympathizers will object that Pope Leo's advice in *Rerum Novarum* is vague and difficult to enforce. Concerning these lines—"The employer is bound to see that the worker has time for his religious duties; that he be not exposed to corrupting influences and dangerous occasions; and that he be not led away to neglect his home and family, or to squander his earnings. Furthermore, the employer must never tax his work people beyond their strength, or employ them in work unsuited to their sex and age" (no. 20)—they might be tempted to say: "Well, of course; but how is this vagueness to be enforced?"

---

[7] This argument is presented at length in Pope Leo XIII's encyclicals *Diuturnum Illud* and *Immortale Dei.*

I answer that it is not vague at all to say that owners or employers have to observe certain rules about their employees. The Church does not hesitate to ask states to make Sundays and holy days public days off, on which no factories should be running or shops open. Hours can be set such that men are not working through the night (which is unnatural) but only during the day, having time in the evening to be with their families. Pregnant women or women with infants should not be allowed to work; stress is dangerous to the unborn, and small children have tremendous need for their mothers' companionship if they are to develop a healthy psyche. And, since sweatshops are an abomination, they should be outlawed by any sane government. The only reason laws like this are not framed — or are deliberately removed where they once existed — is *avarice*.

The capitalist always retorts: "Before my factory, the people had no work." What he doesn't say is that before the Western nations' economic imperialism ruined traditional social structures, the people had a balanced community life in which the young, the middle-aged, and the elderly had their valuable roles to play. It was the importation of a foreign way of life that created the kind of situation to which a factory might seem a good solution. The capitalist provides "answers" to problems he (or the anti-culture he represents) have manufactured.

My conclusion? There are many obvious ways in which civil authority — and here I have in mind primarily local government, in keeping with the principle of subsidiarity — can and *should* regulate economic life. Within a framework of just laws, ample opportunity still remains for the charitable endeavors of individuals and organizations; ample opportunity still remains for businesses to make fair profits. What will *not* be possible is a CEO who earns a hundred times what his workers earn; what will *not* be possible is a company that makes its profits selling pornography or condoms.

One does not have to be a confirmed "theocrat" to recognize in these statements the constant teaching of the Church on the solemn obligations of individuals *and societies* toward the natural moral law, indeed toward the Church of Christ. Do I advocate, therefore, a "welfare state"? No, I advocate something far more radical—a state that implements a consistent, rigorous juridical and legal order inspired by Christian principles.

Thus, to the assertion that enforcement of a set of labor laws amounts to an "arbitrary exercise of force," I reply that such laws are legitimate boundaries for human activity, which *needs* boundaries if it is to remain ethical. Good laws are a way for the better side of fallen man, when soberly in charge, to restrain his worse side when it's drunk. Uncoordinated individual endeavors will never spontaneously promote the common good; they are far more likely to detract from it unless they are harnessed to that end by principles of action that can be reasonably followed by citizens.

What is needed to get to this scenario? Two things, wisdom and courage—the wisdom to craft appropriate legislation, and the courage to apply it. Such wisdom and courage have not always been as lacking as they sadly are today among politicians and political theorists.

A PARTICULAR CASE: WAGE LAWS

The principle of subsidiarity should be implemented as much as possible. Nevertheless, if each state or local government were permitted to set its own minimum wage laws in the present context, there would be massive movement of factories and other businesses to those places that have the lowest rates. If a state could prevent a corporation chartered in another state from doing business in their state, laws at the state level would suffice. But at present, since businesses can treat the entire United States as one playing field, an effective legal remedy must also encompass the entire country. For this reason, right now a national law on the subject may be necessary. Eventually, much more basic reforms are called for—everything comprised by the term "distributism"—that would take away the necessity for minimum-wage laws.

When free trade exists across fifty states and one state makes its laws more demanding, many businesses will move out. Capitalist economic degeneration has proceeded so far that businesses would uproot themselves simply to escape the local laws, so there have to be federal regulatory laws. Obviously, one should desire and aim at a social order in which the maximization of profit would not be an assumed axiom of economic planning. Imagine, in contrast, there were businesses that actually wanted to be *in a certain place*, to serve the populace *of that area*. Such businesses exist among Catholics. They would put up with all reasonable laws, even if their earnings might be greater elsewhere. A business solely interested in profit, on the other hand, will move to the cheapest place to do business. In fact, in our degenerate situation, companies commonly not only flee higher-cost areas, but engage in "bidding wars" with state and local governments, demanding favorable taxation, zoning, training, and other concessions before they will deign to defile the area with their hideous factories or warehouses. State and local governments vie with each other in offering what amounts to "corporate welfare."

Perhaps this is a way of seeing that there will *always* be a "welfare state"—in quite a different sense: the state's policies, or lack thereof, will always redound to *someone's* welfare. With a socialist regime, policies *may* redound to the material welfare of the poor, but ultimately they do nothing to restore a just social order; they are like bandages wrapped around incurable wounds. With a capitalist regime, on the other hand, policies redound to the benefit of owners, employers, pirates of profit, doing nothing to create a just social order based on the widest possible distribution of stable, beneficial, family-supportive property. Hence, I reject altogether the position that a state could be, as it were, economically neutral. Either it will craft legislation that wisely supports all social groups, aiming at a harmony of parts requiring some compromise from all sides, for the good of the whole; or it will tend to favor one part at the expense of others, demanding no serious compromise from that part, but many serious compromises from the others.

Although all should favor subsidiarity, it must be implemented fairly, i.e., restrictions on employers have to go hand-in-hand with restrictions on employees. For this reason, there is no need to be against a federal minimum wage law at present, even if one wishes to see it become unnecessary as a result of more radical and far-reaching social reforms.

The distributist is one who insists that a just social order is possible *in the present* by means of a well-regulated economy hedged about with laws favoring the broad distribution of private property across all levels of society—not an impossible dream whose fulfillment is postponed until the Second Coming.

9

SELF-ENTANGLEMENT IN RICHES

> Truly, I say to you, it will be hard for a rich
> man to enter the kingdom of heaven. Again I
> tell you, it is easier for a camel to go through
> the eye of a needle than for a rich man to
> enter the kingdom of God.[1]

> But God said to him, "Fool! This night your
> soul is required of you; and the things you
> have prepared, whose will they be?" So is he
> who lays up treasure for himself, and is not
> rich toward God.[2]

IN YEARS PAST WHEN I TAUGHT CST
at the university level, students were often shocked
to read the popes' critical evaluation of liberal
capitalism. And I'm not referring only to recent popes;
Pius XI's *Quadragesimo Anno* of 1931 is hard to sur-
pass in this regard.[3] The students wondered: How do
we respond to Christ's praise of poverty? How can
we change our attitude toward and use of material
things for the sake of the kingdom of God? *Why* is it
important for us to not seek wealth as an end? Why
should we flee from or give away material riches to the
extent that we can? Why should we work on changing
our inner attitudes about acquisition, possession, and
enjoyment?

---

[1] Mt 19:23–24.
[2] Lk 12:20–21.
[3] To head off misunderstandings, by "capitalism" I do not mean
a competitive business market that fosters employment, rewards
initiative, or allows suitable profits for owners; this, indeed, is
entire possible under distributism, which is the only viable alternative to capitalism, since socialism and communism self-destruct.

For my answer I will turn to St. Paul and St. Thomas Aquinas. In the second chapter of the Second Epistle to St. Timothy we read:

> Labor as a good soldier of Christ Jesus. No man, being a soldier to God, entangleth himself with secular businesses; that he may please him to whom he hath engaged himself. For he also that striveth for the mastery, is not crowned, except he strive lawfully.[4]

St. Thomas begins his commentary on these verses with the following perceptive remarks:

> The goal of bodily warfare is obtaining victory over the enemies of the fatherland, and so soldiers have to abstain from those things that divert them from the fight, namely, business and pleasure. "Everyone that fights in the struggle abstains from all things" (1 Cor 9:25). But the goal of spiritual warfare is to be victorious over the men who are against God, and so one must abstain from all those things that distract us from God. Now these are "secular businesses" (cf. 2 Tim 2:4), because concern for this world chokes the Word. And so he says: "No man . . . entangles himself."

Wait a minute. Can it really be true that "concern for this world chokes the Word"? It sounds terribly narrow and strict. In fact, it sounds like the very opposite of the belief and behavior of most Christians in affluent societies today. Perhaps in some sense it has always been that way, for Aquinas continues by entertaining a difficulty concerning Paul the tentmaker:

> Against this [view], someone might say that secular businesses are temporal ones, and that the Apostle did such things, when he lived by the work of his hands.

---

[4] 2 Tim 2:3-5.

No relevant detail in the text escapes the Angelic Doctor's notice! He finds the solution in St. Paul's exact choice of words:

> My reply would be that the Apostle says *entangles*, not *exercises*. Now a man is entangled in the things with which his cares and concerns are connected. Properly speaking, then, the things forbidden to the soldiers of Christ are those entanglements of the mind that are shown to be unnecessary. Likewise, he does not say "is entangled," but "entangles himself," for one entangles oneself when one takes on business without piety and necessity. However, when the necessity of the duty of piety and authority is involved, then one does not entangle oneself, but rather is entangled by such necessity. "I commend to you Phebe...that you assist her in whatsoever business [for which] she shall have need of you" (Rom 16:2). The reason why they must not entangle themselves is "that he may please Him to whom he has engaged himself" (2 Tim 2:4). "If any man love the world, the charity of the Father is not in him" (1 Jn 2: 15). For he who is a soldier of Christ has committed himself to waging war for God; and so he must try to please Him to whom he has committed himself.[5]

St. Thomas's careful analysis of self-entanglement can help one perceive the root problem with American-style capitalism. This fundamental problem is not exploitation of workers, bad though that is, or the overpayment of CEOs and CFOs, or the production of cheap, ugly, throw-away "goods" (or the patronage of Chinese manufacturing of the same), or the divorcing of fathers from families and mothers from children. These are indeed terrible things, highly typical of the modern marketplace. But the worst problem of capitalism is

---

[5] *Expositio super II Timotheum*, cap. 2, lec. 1.

that it powerfully breeds, and in turn feeds upon, a soul-dominating *love of this world*—a preoccupation with possessions, riches, status, power, so many "entanglements of the mind" as St. Thomas puts it. The other problems mentioned above flow from that love as bad fruits grow from a bad tree.

The passages of Scripture that rail against riches and the rich deserve to be brought forward again and again because they are too conveniently forgotten or written off as "applying only to manifestly unjust people—which virtuous capitalists aren't, of course." On the contrary, Christ's objection has nothing to do with virtue or vice, at least not initially. It is an objection against getting rich and being rich in this world because of how dangerous worldly wealth is for the soul's spiritual health. The love of riches turns quickly to longing for them, then lusting after them, until there is envy, rivalry, violence, selfish enjoyment and apathy, even contempt, toward other persons. By a law of fallen nature, the amassing of worldly wealth leads, in most cases, to shriveled virtues and proliferating vices. Over time, then, the richest will be among the worst people in the world—a spectacle exemplified every year in Davos at the World Economic Forum.

OVERCOMING THE SPIRIT OF POSSESSIVENESS

Our Lord's first anxiety is about the danger to salvation presented by the attachment to worldly goods that resides in every fallen human heart. The actual vices and sins come later, when the danger has been ignored and the attachments indulged. This, then, is the negative reason to keep giving away what we earn, what we have, to others who need it more (and, for fathers of families, this means, first and foremost, spending it on what is truly good for the family, rather than spending it on oneself or on things harmful to the family's good). But the positive reason for getting rid of wealth is more beautiful: "For you know the grace of our Lord Jesus Christ, that though he was rich, yet for your sake he became poor, so that through his poverty you might become rich."[6] We want to imitate our Master in His loving generosity. When God gives a person wealth, He gives it to him primarily for the sake of benefiting others and not of pleasing oneself. The ultimate Christian paradox is that whatever we keep or hold on to, we will lose, and whatever we lose or give away for God's sake, we will keep.[7] We are here to *be expended*, to burn up like candles in the worship of God and the illumination of the world.

On the one hand, therefore, distributism suggests policies that seek to foster the universal destination (or common use) of goods for the *natural* good of mankind. On the other hand, it recognizes that possessions when multiplied and coveted lead to possessiveness, which is sinful and self-destructive, contrary to both the natural and supernatural good of mankind. Christianity itself offers a strange paradox. It brought into the world a spirit of concern for the poor, of care for the newborn, the enslaved, the handicapped and the sick, which had never been seen in paganism — and which is evaporating in our neo-pagan society. Yet it simultaneously preached the relative value, indeed the comparatively minor value, of earthly goods compared to spiritual goods and our heavenly inheritance in Christ. For this reason, it required fasting and abstinence and encouraged voluntary poverty, such as became famous in the "mendicant" or begging orders, the Franciscans and Dominicans.

The fact that real voluntary poverty is extremely rare in the modern Church, comfortably settled in a Western world overrun with more material wealth and more spiritual indigence than history has ever seen, seems not to trouble the consciences of many

---

[6] 2 Cor 8:9.
[7] See Mt 10:39–42, 16:25; Lk 9:24–25; Jn 12:25; Sir 29:11–15, 32.

shepherds or religious orders, including the mendicants in their twenty-first century instantiation. It is not to our credit that a subject which troubled the medieval Church so much that it prompted mass movements of heresy and sanctity alike now scarcely elicits a yawn or a twitch.

It is very hard to become truly poor in spirit, but we must keep trying. When should you get a new pair of pants—when your old pair is fraying at the seams and no longer wearable in public, or before that stage? How many pants, shoes, shirts, ties, etc., should you have? Do you buy the best quality because you know it will last, or a cheap brand because it's a much smaller expenditure? Do you *insist* on American-made goods, although they are more expensive, versus "Made in China" or some other ignominious label? Is it even realistic to try to avoid Third-World products? When is a "structure of sin" something to accept with a shrug of the shoulders? Globalization has meant fewer and fewer choices: chances are the things I buy have been manufactured by wage slaves in sweatshops.

POSITIVE RENUNCIATION FOR THE KINGDOM

It's easy to settle down and settle for compromises, thinking all the while that we are simply being "prudent and responsible" by seeking comfort and stability in this world. It is all too easy, especially for theologians, to speak grandly of solidarity, social justice, and preferential options when we are quite comfortably ensconced in a spacious home, well dressed, well fed, and not at all desperate or denuded. Might we be tempted to forget that "we have not here a lasting city, but we seek one that is to come"?[8] As Christians, we can never put down our definitive roots here, and it is better to live in such a way that we are *conscious* of our state of alienation in and from this world, conscious of our destiny in the

---

[8] Heb 13:14.

life to come. For this reason, laity, priests, and religious should all make a point of asking regularly: Do I have things I don't really need? Can my possessions, or the things I have at my disposal, be put to a better use? How am I responding to the spiritual and physical poverty around me in the world?

Speaking of the "positive choice" that accompanies the renunciation of worldly goods among the saints, Fr. Maximilian Herraiz, OCD—an expert in the thought of St. John of the Cross and St. Teresa of Avila—observed: "It is the radical option for life, truth, freedom and, very concretely, the option for love, for God. When we opt for love, we find that there is too much extra furniture in our homes. Mysticism tells us that love is the essential dimension of life."[9] Joseph Ratzinger said something similar: "In these times we really ought to make an effort to get out of this over-furnished, crammed world into an inner freedom and vigilance. It means, too, that we need penance, without which there can be no new beginning."[10]

We tend to think in big terms, about reforming the world or the monastery or the government or the school system—or, perhaps more commonly nowadays, we focus on the seeming impossibility of ever doing so—but we don't think about what is within our power: examining, cleaning up, and uncluttering our daily lives, our rooms, the desk we work at, the closet full of stuff. It can be more painful to throw away a bunch of papers, or give away clothes or other possessions, than to write a check for a charitable organization. We fail to take note of what is around us, having grown accustomed to it; our possessions contribute to our sense of identity, well-being, and comfort. This is the "familiar," it is nicely cluttered and diversified, it is my native environment where my personality is at home.

---

[9] "Love and the Message of the Mystics."
[10] Ratzinger, *Salt of the Earth*, 281.

That can be dangerous in a small but subtle way. As we heard from the Epistle to the Hebrews, we have here no lasting home, and we should take pains to remind ourselves of that fact. We need to keep *un-domesticating* ourselves by a simplification of surroundings, by keeping alert to excessive comfort and clutter, by stirring ourselves to be more disciplined in prayer and work—in a word, by not "settling down" in spirit, even when we rightly embrace, in the flesh, a Benedictine *stabilitas loci* or stability of place. It is not a question of courting flux or rags or starvation, but a question of habituating the whole family in the freedom that comes with detachment, the power that comes from simplification and resourcefulness.

LOVE AND SOBRIETY

Let us return to St. Thomas, commenting on another passage in St. Paul's Second Letter to St. Timothy: "For God hath not given us the spirit of fear, but of power, and of love, and of sobriety."[11] Explaining the difference between the spirit of the world and the Spirit of God, he writes:

> The difference between them is as follows. "Spirit" signifies love, for the term "spirit" implies impulsion, and love impels. Now there is a twofold love, namely, the love of God, which is through the Spirit of God, and the love of the world, which is through the spirit of the world: "For we received not the spirit of this world, but the Spirit that is of God" (1 Cor 2:12).

How does Aquinas discriminate between these two spirits? His explanation hinges on our affections—how we love all that we love:

---

[11] 2 Tim 1:7.

> Now the spirit of the world makes us love the goods of this world and fear temporal ills, and so the Apostle says: "For God hath not given us the spirit of fear, but of power, and of love, and of sobriety" (2 Tim 1:7)…. There is another spirit, the spirit of the fear of the Lord, the Holy Spirit, and this makes us fear God…. We are likewise guided [by this Spirit] in the midst of good things, because, as regards affection, we are ordered through the love that is charity when we refer to God everything we love. Hence he says: "of love"…. We are likewise ordered as regards external goods, and so he says: "and of sobriety," that is, of all temperance, by observing a due mode and measure, so that we use the goods of this world in a temperate way.[12]

These comments prompt us to reflect on what it means, not just in theory but in everyday practice, to order our affections aright and thus to observe a "due mode and measure" in our use of worldly goods. We can be confident that the answer will be countercultural in a world devoted to maximizing both consumption and profit. We can also be confident that American-style capitalism—a system designed to increase our treasures here below and to multiply desires for them and access to them—is, after all, "conservative": it conserves, for the devil's profit, the selfish inclinations of fallen human nature rather than challenging and uprooting them to liberate man for the kingdom of heaven.

Every Christian must make up his mind about *whom* or *what* he will serve: "No one can serve two masters; for either he will hate the one and love the other, or he will be devoted to the one and despise the other. You cannot serve God and mammon."[13] "Sell your

---

[12] *Expositio super II Timotheum*, cap. 1, lec. 3.
[13] Mt 6:24.

possessions, and give alms; provide yourselves with purses that do not grow old, with a treasure in the heavens that does not fail, where no thief approaches and no moth destroys. For where your treasure is, there will your heart be also."[14] "Artificial wealth," says Thomas, "has the power to engender an infinite craving—and that means: an illusory specter of the desire for happiness."[15]

Christ's coming to earth in a poor stable or cave, laid in an animal's food-trough (which we politely call a "manger"), greeted initially by a congregation of shepherds who, though full of awe, were probably not clean and sweet-smelling, is a powerful reminder to us of one of the central truths of Scripture: "My thoughts are not your thoughts, neither are your ways my ways."[16] God did not enter the world as a worldly king would have chosen to enter it. He came poor and to the poor; He came in such a way that He already began to turn upside-down the logic of the world, as Our Lady had uttered a few months earlier in her Magnificat: "He hath put down the mighty from their seat, and hath exalted the humble; He hath filled the hungry with good things, and the rich he hath sent empty away."

AN EXAMINATION OF CONSCIENCE

In his commentary on Psalm 43, St. Thomas explains why God allows Christians to be overtaken with hardship, defeated, despoiled, impoverished, put to the test:

> He does this in order to draw us away from
> earthly goods, because if we always had pros-
> perity in temporal things, man would serve
> God for their sake; and if this *were* our

---

[14] Lk 12:33-34.
[15] Pieper, *Happiness and Contemplation*, 35-36, citing *Summa theologiae* I-II, Q. 2, art. 1, ad 3.
[16] Is 55:8-9.

intention, it would be frustrated by such things as defeats. In order that our love may not be mercenary, and our intention not be fixed on bodily things, He takes these goods away from His friends.

This might make a good point on which to examine our conscience. When I lose, when life is hard, when things get tough, when things get broken or lost or stolen or burnt down, when the tide turns against me, when I experience resistance, misunderstanding, even rejection—is my faith strong and mature enough that I will say: "Thank You, Lord. You have just taught me once again that my only home is in You—that I have no treasure but Your grace and Your love"? If we find we cannot say it sincerely, then we are humbled and challenged to ask for the grace to have in us the mind that was in Christ Jesus.[17] If we *can* say it to one degree or another, it is no grounds for boasting; our boast is in the Cross of Our Lord Jesus Christ.[18] He is the One Who can detach us from this passing world and glue us to eternal life, which is Himself.

Having read many popes' forceful critique of Western affluence, my students wondered again and again, both in class and outside of it: How do we respond to the Church's oft-stated demand that we *change our lives for the sake of the poor*? They were not asking in a skeptical way, as do neoconservatives who think that the papal pleas are so many grandiose platitudes, so much whistling in the wind. They asked with a genuine desire to know: How, in practice, can one live for the benefit of others, especially for the poor?

One begins with the basics: not defrauding people of what one owes them; not wasting money on useless trinkets or a daily fancy drink from Starbucks;

---

[17] Cf. Phil 2:5.
[18] Cf. Gal 6:14.

preparing one's own food rather than buying only prepackaged meals—practices that involve frugality, self-control, modesty, and personal effort. Then there are ascetical practices, including praying, fasting, abstaining, tithing, and moderating the use of technology.[19] God must have thought tithing a good idea because He was the first to propose it, in the law that He handed down to the Chosen People. Although it is ultimately inner attitudes that need to change, it would already make a huge difference if believers across the world gave a tenth of their income to the poor and to worthy non-profits.

I was disgusted to see, at one point in my life, a diocesan gift campaign that asked, with heart-wrenching pleas and rhetorical somersaults, for lay Catholics to consider *perhaps* contributing *even* as much as 1% of their income to the Church. What kind of people are we if we have to be cajoled and hornswoggled into donating $1 from every $100? I suspect that if bishops decided to throw all caution to the wind and preached a strong message about the ideal of tithing 10%, the response, over time, would be surprisingly high.[20] If we want a generous response, we have to preach a generous ideal that honors people by telling them they are called to, and capable of, real sacrifice.

One could say, universally, that a constant self-examination and simplification of life is called for. Do I really *need* all the things that I have? Can I give away (or loan, at no interest) this or that portion of my possessions or money, if it would benefit others more than it benefits me at this time? Do I really need to upgrade or to replace X, Y, or Z?

---

[19] See Marco, "'A Sign of Contradiction': Life Beyond the Smartphone—An Interview with Dr. Peter Kwasniewski."
[20] One should donate tithing money only to worthy causes. See Kwasniewski, "Five ways Catholic laity can powerfully influence Church for good from within."

For further practical advice, I recommend a prayerful reading of Fr. Thomas Dubay's book *Happy Are You Poor: The Simple Life and Spiritual Freedom.*

The Christian tradition places a strong emphasis on the value of voluntary poverty and the actual benefits of being poor or becoming poorer by giving away our material riches to the extent we can. This, in turn, is founded on the need for interior conversion in regard to our attitudes about acquisition, possession, enjoyment, and happiness. Due to the fall, we are tempted to place our happiness in creatures, and one of the most obvious manifestations of this bent inclination is avarice or the disordered desire for material goods and riches. Mother Teresa was famous for saying that the most joyful people she met were poor, and the saddest she ever met were affluent.

"BLESSED ARE THE POOR IN SPIRIT"

In case this chapter has been too abstract, here are eight things we can do to live the spirit of poverty better, according to the first of Our Lord's Beatitudes: "Blessed are the poor in spirit: for theirs is the kingdom of heaven."[21] Some of these ideas are pretty obvious, but the point of this list is not to be innovative or profound, but rather to suggest helpful and attainable means.

1. Tithe 10% of your income, prior to any further calculations or savings. Do it spontaneously and without argument, as a fundamental sign of trust in Divine Providence, and as a concrete way of thanking Him for His provision. Give this tithe to the poor, to the Church, to religious orders, to pro-life and pro-family causes, to needy individuals, to families in distress, to traditional seminarians, etc. Although tithing is no longer a matter of divine precept, it is a powerful symbol and practice of economic discipleship. It is a way of confessing that the good of building up my

---

[21] Mt 5:3.

own little domain does not exempt me from the obligation to give aid to God's people and to build up His kingdom on a larger scale. The only situation in which tithing would be inappropriate is if a man is receiving a wage manifestly lower than suits the local economy and/or lower than meets the realistic needs of his family (e.g., Catholic teachers are often volunteering half their time or more). In such cases, a man is already tithing his time and effort. Catholics should donate only to individuals, causes, or institutions that are traditionally Catholic.[22]

2. If you are married, talk to your wife and children on a regular basis about what poverty (spiritual and material) is, why Jesus asks us to practice it, and how we can practice it according to our state in life. Dare to ask their advice. Sometimes others in the family can see, much better than we, the clutter that we should thin out. And, although we may not think so, children need adults to help them simplify, focus, and remain above worldly things, rather than being entangled in them. The right habits have to be planted early on.

3. Firmly resolve to devote more time to prayer, and then do it. American men on average spend far too much time working and far too little time praying—or, for that matter, too little time doing anything intrinsically worthwhile. To "go to one's room, shut the door, and pray in secret"[23] is the first and most important step towards that "poverty of spirit" which is the hallmark of Christ's true disciples; it is the sovereign remedy for materialism, for preoccupation with the ephemeral.

---

[22] Sadly, at this time in Church history, this will usually mean *not* giving to diocesan appeals; and one may wish to restrict parish donations to particular causes such as sanctuary renovations, the installation of a communion rail, the sacred music program, or beautiful vestments.

[23] Cf. Mt 6:6.

4. Before any purchase, ask yourself pointedly (and answer honestly): Do I really *need* this? Do I need it *right now*? Moreover, buy things used or second-hand if possible. Practically all clothing can be found used, in a condition as good as new but at a fraction of the cost. To insist that one should only wear new things can be a form of self-indulgence.

5. Be content with less or little in areas of life where abundance is costly. Examples: cut back on alcoholic drinks and/or tobacco products, at least during Advent and Lent; avoid spending money on trifles such as prepared beverages of the Starbucks type. Pack your lunch instead of eating out at work—at least sometimes. Cut back on luxuries—cosmetics, jewelry, clothes, lattes, etc. Some Catholics would be amazed to discover how many hundreds of dollars they spend a year on such things, which from week to week seem trivial.

6. In honor of an anniversary or other special occasion, make a donation to a monastery or the pro-life cause rather than giving jewelry, taking a vacation, or going out for a fancy dinner. It is a sad manifestation of the decline of Christian charity that most people, including practicing Catholics, are totally self-centered (or family-centered) when it comes to how they spend their surplus wealth. That is, we do not spontaneously want to *give away* what remains after our necessities are taken care of; we would rather find new and more exciting ways to spend it on ourselves. And, of course, all advertising in a capitalist society is premised on this perverse desire. There is matter here for a serious examination of conscience.

7. In keeping with stewardship of the earth and of your household, buy higher quality things that will last longer; if possible, buy permanent things rather than disposable ones. When things break, try to fix them or have them fixed; do not surrender to the consumerist "throw-away" culture.

8. Grow a garden with the family; even a container garden is better than nothing. We spend gobs of money on mass-marketed, often flavorless and pesticide-coated produce, when we could grow some of it in our own backyards, with benefit to ourselves: sun and fresh air, exercise, organic food, chores for the kids, homeschooling science lessons! In general, whenever possible, "do it yourself" rather than buying ready-made or paying other people to do it for you. This often requires a subtle sacrifice of self-will: I may not *feel* like repairing something, even if I can do it. Yet this is exactly when poverty of spirit enters in: you are beginning to be poor when you do not think yourself too important or busy to take care of little things. Distributism takes small things seriously: the dignity of the individual; the family as the basic unit of society; the centrality of the local economy; the value of the here and now over bloodless concepts or global causes. In this respect, it is profoundly Christian. We could call it "economic incarnationalism," or "incarnational economics." For this very reason, it is something we can all begin practicing immediately, and with excellent results—not just tastier tomatoes at the dinner table, but a better and more consistent welcome in our lives for the many goods that are intangible.

WHY DOES THE CHURCH CONDEMN COMMUNISM?

P OPE PIUS XI'S ENCYCLICAL ON atheistic communism, *Divini Redemptoris*, was promulgated on March 19, 1937, the feast of St. Joseph, patron of the universal Church and patron of workers. Almost ninety years later, his analysis, so far from being outdated, holds disturbing relevance for our own times, in which many of the errors he identifies as communist are now widely believed, taught, and implemented.

Divini Redemptoris—like its "sister" encyclicals *Mit Brennender Sorge* condemning the National Socialists in Germany and *Nos Es Muy Conocida* on the continuing persecution of the Church in Mexico, all three issued in the same month: March 14, March 19, and March 28—is an impassioned outcry full of indignation, this time addressed not to the episcopate of Germany or of Mexico but to the entire Catholic episcopacy on earth.[1] Unlike Vatican II, where a petition signed by hundreds of bishops for the explicit condemnation of Soviet Communism was literally shoved into a drawer lest the *Ostpolitik* bargain struck with Moscow be diverted, Pius XI enjoyed the capacity to see the truth and fearlessly proclaimed it.[2]

---

[1] For translations of and commentaries on *Mit Brennender Sorge*, *Divini Redemptoris*, and *Nos Es Muy Conocida*, see Ehler and Morrall, eds., *Church and State Through the Centuries*, 516–92.
[2] See the following eye-opening articles: Hoffman, "Vatican II's Lost Condemnations of Communism"; Kengor, "Vatican II's Unpublished Condemnations of Communism"; and Pentin, "Why Did Vatican II Ignore Communism?"

Pius XI's principal accusation is that by denying God, the source and goal of all things and especially of the human person, and by denying Christ, Redeemer of mankind, communism robs man of the consciousness of his dignity as image of God and child of the Father.[3] Poor and powerless workers suffer the most from this robbery. The blessings poured out upon us by Christ through His Church are traded, in Bolshevist ideology, for a sinister social dream, "an arrogant attempt to free civilization from the bonds of morality and religion" (4). Since the Church is the embodiment of all that the revolution hates, its violence is unleashed against her with peculiar savagery. For this reason, she turns in prayer to "St. Joseph, her mighty protector," to whom "was entrusted the divine Child when Herod loosed his assassins against him" (81).

THE CHURCH'S ATTITUDE TOWARD COMMUNISM

In Part I (4–7), Pius XI recalls multiple condemnations of communism by his predecessors and himself, and declares his intention: since "the bitter fruits of subversive ideas...are multiplying fearfully" (6), "we wish to expose once more in a brief synthesis the principles of atheistic communism...[as] also to indicate its method of action and to contrast with its false principles the clear doctrine of the Church, in order to inculcate anew and with greater insistence the means by which the Christian civilization, the true *civitas humana*, can be saved from the Satanic scourge" (7).

In part II, a critique of communism in theory and in practice (8–24), the pope explains that communism should be regarded not merely as an economic or political theory, but as a metaphysical and even "religious" system that lives by "a false messianic idea, a pseudo-ideal of justice, equality, and fraternity," "a deceptive mysticism" (7; cf. 77). While "concealed under the most

---

[3] See Charles, *Christian Social Witness and Teaching*, 2:52–100.

seductive trappings," it is "based on the principles of dialectical and historical materialism previously advocated by Marx," which lead to the doctrine of the class struggle and the annihilation of all forces opposed to the so-called emancipation of workers (9).

Owing to its materialist orientation, communism "strips man of his liberty, robs human personality of all its dignity, and removes all the moral restraints that check the eruptions of blind impulse" (10). The human person has no intrinsic rights; a specious absolute equality is proclaimed; all authority is held to be a spontaneous outgrowth of the community and not a divine bequest. It follows that private property, which gives its owner a certain power over non-owners, is illegitimate and must be abolished.

Marxism views marriage and family as culturally-conditioned institutions destined to be swept away by the revolution, which even now anticipates this "freedom" by forcing women into public life and factories under the same conditions as men, and by withdrawing children from parental authority (11). A society based on such materialism "would have only one mission: the production of material things by means of collective labor," leading to the "paradise" of "a humanity without God" (12). Finally, the state, being the last vestige of hierarchy, will itself "wither away" (13). All of this the pope calls "a system full of errors and sophisms" which ignores the true nature of the state and "denies the rights, dignity, and liberty of human personality" (14). With what we subsequently learned about communism as it operated in Russia and Eastern Europe or as it still operates in China and elsewhere, these errors and sophisms should be vastly more obvious to us than they were in 1937—yet there are still those who advocate for this "paradise"!

Pius XI then speaks of the means employed to seduce the masses, noting that communists meet with success because they agitate for "the removal of the very real abuses chargeable to the liberalistic economic order" and demand "a more equitable distribution of this world's goods—objectives entirely and undoubtedly legitimate" (15). Indeed, in a line sure to displease defenders of capitalism and libertarianism, Pius XI judges that it was "the religious and moral destitution in which wage-earners had been left by liberal economics" that smoothed a path for communism's triumph (16).[4] Its proponents use propaganda skillfully (17) while the press of the "free" world remains culpably silent, due to conspiratorial forces (18). Once again, here's a pope unafraid to recognize, with all good historians, the presence and operation of hidden agents.[5]

The communists have recourse to murder and pillage when it will advance their cause. "Tear the very idea of God from the hearts of men, and they are necessarily urged by their passions to the most atrocious barbarity" (20)—words that have a chilling relevance in the Western world of 2025, which floats on an ocean of infant blood. The pope observes that in the long run communism is doomed to failure by its own denial of morality, because without a clear and broadly accepted public code of morals, the conditions for ethical responsibility do not exist, and no one can be trusted by anyone else. "Terrorism is the only possible substitute [for morality], and it is terrorism that reigns today in Russia" (23).

THE CATHOLIC VISION OF CIVIL SOCIETY

Part III outlines the Catholic vision of civil society and the place of the person in it, based on the findings of reason and the teaching of divine revelation (25–38). Both society and the individual have their source in God, who created man to be a social animal seeking his perfection in community. Man's spiritual and immortal

---

[4] See Cahill, *Framework of a Christian State*, 156–220.
[5] See de Mattei, *Paths of Evil.*

soul gives him a worth immeasurably greater than that of the entire universe of irrational creatures.[6] Greater still is his dignity when elevated by grace to a sharing in the divine life.

In view of such a destiny, God has endowed man "with many and varied prerogatives: the right to life, to bodily integrity, to the necessary means of existence; the right to tend toward his ultimate goal in the path marked out for him by God; the right of association and the right to possess and use property" (27). The pope explains that "society is for man and not vice versa" (29), in the sense that the happiness of the individual is attained through an "organic union with society and by mutual collaboration," *not* "in the sense of liberalistic individualism, which subordinates society to the selfish use of the individual" and which has "plunged the world of today into lamentable ruin" (cf. 32). The sum-total of goods in a society, and all the opportunities and responsibilities of social life, are at the service of the *good of persons*, instead of some individuals being subjugated to other individuals as slaves to masters. Thus, against despotic regimes, the encyclical asserts that the state exists for the good of persons, but against liberal individualism, it denies that the sole good of persons is their private good.[7]

The Church's political doctrine, continues the pope, is characterized by a "constant equilibrium": "authority is reconciled with liberty, the dignity of the individual with that of the state, the human personality of the subject with the divine delegation of the superior," a balance between solicitude for the soul's eternal welfare and promotion of sound earthly progress (34).

---

[6] One of the first principles of a genuinely Catholic environmentalism.

[7] For a fuller treatment of how the common good is most perfective of the individual, see Kwasniewski, "The Foundations of Christian Ethics and Social Order," in Kwasniewski and Waldstein, eds., *Integralism and the Common Good*, vol. 1, pp. 31–48.

Christianity is the first and only revealer of the "real and universal brotherhood of all men of whatever race and condition"; it "raised manual labor to its true dignity" and spurred the formation of charitable organizations and artisans' guilds (36–37). Christianity, in fact, is the parent and provider of the goods that communists promise in vain.

DEFENSIVE AND CONSTRUCTIVE PROGRAM

Part IV (39–59) and Part V (60–80) speak of what is to be done and who is to do it. Since communists more easily win converts where faith is lukewarm, where earthly goods are too much prized, and where Christians neglect the poor, reversing or at least resisting these trends is the first and fundamental challenge (43ff.). Serious social ills such as inadequate workers' wages require the intervention of public authorities; private charitable efforts, though obviously indispensable, are not enough. Again, for the benefit of society, a prudent regime would restrain excessive accumulation of property and business competition (49ff.; cf. 75). *Divini Redemptoris* is best understood when read in light of Pius XI's 1925 encyclical *Quas Primas* on the kingship of Christ and his 1931 encyclical *Quadragesimo Anno*, where the principles and economic structures of a just social order are expounded in detail.

The pope warns Catholics to be vigilant and not to be taken in by propaganda that reassures the world of communism's good intentions (57). No Catholic may collaborate with communists (58)—a policy that was not reversed until "good Pope John" and his Second Vatican Council.[8]

Pius XI has no illusions: "the evil which today torments humanity can be conquered only by a world-wide crusade of prayer and penance" (59). Priests should consider themselves missionaries to the working class,

---

[8] See articles listed in note 2 on page 133.

setting the example of a life that is humble, poor, and disinterested, as did St. Vincent de Paul, St. John Vianney, St. John Bosco, and others who brought so much help and consolation to the poor people they served (60ff.). Pius XI sees the world situation to be so grave that he exhorts non-Catholics and even non-Christians to lend their aid in opposing "the powers of darkness" if they wish to avoid "anarchy and terrorism" (72).

AN UNFINISHED CRUSADE

Divini Redemptoris, together with its companion encyclicals on fascism, had a worldwide effect on public opinion and left a mark on international diplomacy during the 1930s—a reminder to us that the papacy less than a century ago used its considerable moral authority to promote the truth and to expose error.[9] The encyclical gave a powerful boost to the "crusade against communism" and against all forms of totalitarianism, which became a hallmark of Catholic social theory and activism.[10] The close collaboration between Pius XI and Cardinal Eugenio Pacelli ensured that the policies of Pacelli under his papal name Pius XII would follow the same lines, doctrinally and diplomatically, during the darkest days of the Second World War and into the post-war period.[11]

As a regime, Soviet communism eventually collapsed. Yet, as Bishop Athanasius Schneider says, its fall was rather like a seedpod falling from a plant in order to release its seeds in every direction, to be carried

[9] See Holmes, *The Papacy in the Modern World*, 77–117. One wonders how popes like Leo XIII, Pius X, or Pius XI would have reacted to Paul VI's *Ostpolitik* or Francis's Sino-Vatican alliance.
[10] See Lerhinan, *Sociological Commentary on* Divini Redemptoris; Dumortier, "Totalitarianism," 955–59.
[11] On the collaboration between Pius XI and Cardinal Pacelli, see Halecki and Murray, *Pius XII*, 52–88; see also Kwasniewski, "Coincidences During the Reign of Pius XII?" and "Lights and Shadows in the Pontificate of Pius XII."

by the wind across the world. The spread of Russia's errors, a danger spoken of by Our Lady at Fatima, has transpired over the course of the many decades during which even doctrinally conservative popes like Pius XI and Pius XII refused to consecrate Russia to the Immaculate Heart in accordance with her express wishes. Their successors not only maintained this policy of disobedience to heaven's message, they went increasingly lax on the centuries-old condemnation of political liberalism, of which communism is only an aggravated extrapolation.[12] We beseech Our Lord to send us a pope who will unite, for the first time, a fearless confession of the orthodox Faith in the face of modern errors with a humble obedience to Our Lady who crushes the serpent's head.

POSTSCRIPT: A LITTLE-KNOWN SIDE OF KARL MARX

Between 1835 and 1843—that is to say, between the ages of 17 and 25—Karl Marx, the father of communism, wrote a great deal of poetry, which might be rather surprising to those who know only the "mature Marx" of *Das Kapital*, his famous critique of capitalism, which consists of hundreds of pages of ponderous and rather dull prose.

The poetry is published in the very first volume of the *Collected Works of Karl Marx and Friedrich Engels*, published by International Publishers in New York. Therein, one finds sonnets to Jenny von Westphalen, who was to become Marx's wife and the mother of seven children. A taste:

---

[12] It is quite true that Paul VI, John Paul II, and Francis all condemned economic liberalism, and, to a lesser extent, occasionally condemned political liberalism. But it is difficult to see these condemnations as more than *obiter dicta*, considering that in so many other respects they embraced the liberalism of the modern West, as seen for instance in the acceptance of *laïcité* and the corresponding repudiation of integralism.

> See! I could a thousand volumes fill,
> Writing only "Jenny" in each line,
> Still they would a world of thought conceal,
> Deed eternal and unchanging will,
> Verses sweet that yearning gently still,
> All the glow and all the aether's shine,
> Anguished sorrow's pain and joy divine,
> All of life and knowledge that is mine.
> I can read it in the stars up yonder,
> From the Zephyr it comes back to me,
> From the being of the wild waves' thunder,
> Truly, I would write it down as a refrain
> For the coming centuries to see —
> Love is Jenny, Jenny is love's name. (p. 522)

One may charitably imagine that the verses read more compellingly in their original German. One may also wish that Marx had confined himself to writing "a thousand volumes" of romantic poetry rather than *Das Kapital*, and that his Jenny had occupied so much of his time that he had none to spare for Engels.

But more volatile feelings were soon to emerge in his youthful verse, with a Luciferian twist:

> I am caught in endless strife,
> Endless ferment, endless dream;
> I cannot conform to life,
> Will not travel with the stream.
> Heaven I would comprehend,
> I would draw the world to me;
> Loving, hating, I intend
> That my star shine brilliantly. [...]
> Worlds I would destroy for ever,
> Since I can create no world,
> Since my call they notice never,
> Coursing dumb in magic whirl. [...]
> So the spirits go their way
> Till they are consumed outright,
> Till their lords and masters they
> Totally annihilate. (pp. 525-26)

These verses radiate the nihilistic force of one who would destroy if he cannot create *ex nihilo*. If creation is unavailable to men, what about manipulation by dark forces? With surprising regularity, Marx uses the language of magic and demonology. For example:

> Ha! In nerve and spirit I was stricken
> To the bottom of my soul,
> As a demon, when the high magician
> Strikes with lightning bolt and spell. (p. 524)

Or in another poem:

> With magic power and word
> I cast what spells I knew,
> But forth the waves still roared,
> Till they were gone from view. [...]
> My spirits then and there
> Soared, jubilant and gay,
> And, like a sorcerer,
> Their courses did I sway. (pp. 529–30)

Throughout his verse, Marx finds dozens of ways to depict his protagonist or himself as locked in combat with "the gods"—with theism, Christianity, natural order. (It will come as no surprise that he planned to write a thesis summarizing and comparing the natural philosophy of Democritus and Epicurus, two ancient materialists.) Here is a particularly fine example:

> So a god has snatched from me my all
> In the curse and rack of destiny.
> All his worlds are gone beyond recall!
> Nothing but revenge is left to me! [...]
> I shall build my throne high overhead,
> Cold, tremendous shall its summit be.
> For its bulwark—superstitious dread,
> For its Marshall—blackest agony. [...]
> And the Almighty's lightning shall rebound
> From that massive iron giant.
> If he bring my walls and towers down,
> Eternity shall raise them up, defiant. (pp. 563–64)

Can anyone reading these lines not be reminded of the Lucifer who says, *Non serviam* — "I will not serve!" — and who works tirelessly over the vast sweep of world history to lead astray all who are foolish enough to serve the unservant? Can anyone read these lines and not think of Stalin's Soviet empire, with its millions put to death and its Siberian gulags, ruling over men with "superstitious dread" and "blackest agony"? In the realm of fiction these lines call to mind Tolkien's Mordor, Sauron, and Melkor, or Weston as the "Unman" in Lewis's *Perelandra*.

Of Marx's early poems, the most disconcerting is one entitled "The Fiddler," written in 1837 and published in 1841:

> The Fiddler saws the strings,
> His light brown hair he tosses and flings.
> He carries a sabre at his side,
> He wears a pleated habit wide.
> "Fiddler, why that frantic sound?
> Why do you gaze so wildly round?
> Why leaps your blood, like the surging sea?
> What drives your bow so desperately?"
> "Why do I fiddle? Or the wild waves roar?
> That they might pound the rocky shore,
> That eye be blinded, that bosom swell,
> That Soul's cry carry down to Hell."
> "Fiddler, with scorn you rend your heart.
> A radiant God lent you your art,
> To dazzle with waves of melody,
> To soar to the star-dance in the sky."
> "How so! I plunge, plunge without fail
> My blood-black sabre into your soul.
> That art God neither wants nor wists,
> It leaps to the brain from Hell's black mists.
> "Till heart's bewitched, till senses reel:
> With Satan I have struck my deal.
> He chalks the signs, beats time for me,
> I play the death march fast and free." (p. 23)

The Fiddler is Marx holding a mirror up to himself: the supreme ideologue of atheistic communism, who — in spite of a boasted disbelief in the supernatural or the spiritual — struck his deal with Satan, and danced to his atonal tune, his techno beat, "an art that God neither wants nor wists."

The downfall of Soviet communism and the softening of communist regimes across the globe should not blind us to the fact that Marxist philosophy is alive, if not well. We see it lingering even in Catholic circles that tend towards socialism, progressivism, and doctrinal revisionism. We see it in the Vatican, to be sure, whose willingness to strike a deal with communist China is an insult to Almighty God and a bitter betrayal of faithful Chinese Catholics, much as was Paul VI's *Ostpolitik* decades earlier.[13]

The spirit of Marxist ideology will not be easily exorcised, as it is but one of countless manifestations of the spirit of defiance and despair that vainly but energetically contests the Kingdom of God, until the moment of the Last Judgment.

---

[13] See Weigel, "The Ostpolitik Failed. Get Over It."

IV

CONVERSION OF CULTURE

THE RESURRECTION
OF CHRISTENDOM

RELIGION AND THE PUBLIC SQUARE

IN THE FOREGOING CHAPTERS, I have had occasion more than once to speak of the dominant contemporary conception—traceable to the so-called Enlightenment—that religion is a purely private affair, about which we should studiously avoid making waves in the public square. Religion is like a hat or a coat you take off and hang at the entrance before going into the offices of government or business.

The Christian's vocation cannot be confined or clipped off in that manner. This is not because it is political first and foremost, but rather because it is a total vision of life in all its dimensions, natural and supernatural, and therefore has implications for the whole of the world in which man lives.

When the gospel entrusted to the Church first entered the world, there was no program or plan for "taking over the state." Because Christ had died for the salvation of sinners, and baptism into His death was the only way to receive the blessing of eternal life, Christians sought not only to follow Christ zealously but also to persuade as many of their fellow citizens to follow "the Way"[1] as they possibly could. It was love (Greek, *agapē*; Latin, *caritas*) that compelled the Christians to Christianize the world around them—soul by soul, family by family, city by city, people by people. The Middle Ages were not a "Five-Century Plan"

---

[1] Acts 9:2; 19:9, 23; 22:4; 24:14, 22.

that someone implemented; it was the organic result
of many generations of clergy, religious, and laity who
lived their faith with gusto. Christian citizens trans-
formed the world by the energetic exercise of moral
and theological virtues. Pope Leo XIII memorably
described this Christian phase of the West:

> There was once a time when states were gov-
> erned by the philosophy of the gospel. Then
> it was that the power and divine virtue of
> Christian wisdom had diffused itself through-
> out the laws, institutions, and morals of the
> people, permeating all ranks and relations of
> civil society. Then, too, the religion instituted
> by Jesus Christ, established firmly in befitting
> dignity, flourished everywhere, by the favor of
> princes and the legitimate protection of mag-
> istrates; and Church and state were happily
> united in concord and friendly interchange
> of good offices.
>
> The state, constituted in this wise, bore
> fruits important beyond all expectation, whose
> remembrance is still, and always will be, in
> renown, witnessed to as they are by countless
> proofs which can never be blotted out or ever
> obscured by any craft of any enemies. Chris-
> tian Europe has subdued barbarous nations,
> and changed them from a savage to a civilized
> condition, from superstition to true worship.
> It victoriously rolled back the tide of Moham-
> medan conquest; retained the headship of civ-
> ilization; stood forth in the front rank as the
> leader and teacher of all, in every branch of
> national culture; bestowed on the world the
> gift of true and many-sided liberty; and most
> wisely founded very numerous institutions for
> the solace of human suffering.
>
> And if we inquire how it was able to bring
> about so altered a condition of things, the
> answer is, beyond all question, in large measure

through religion, under whose auspices so many great undertakings were set on foot, through whose aid they were brought to completion.[2]

Leo XIII goes on to say that this state of affairs could have peacefully continued if the two powers, the civil and the ecclesiastical, "kingdom and priesthood," had continued to cooperate towards the common good, both natural and supernatural. Yet rebellion is always possible in beings with free will, whom God does not compel to stand in the blessings they have, but who, like Lucifer and Adam, may throw away their glory out of disordered self-love:

> But that harmful and deplorable passion for innovation which was aroused in the sixteenth century threw first of all into confusion the Christian religion, and next, by natural sequence, invaded the precincts of philosophy, whence it spread amongst all classes of society. From this source, as from a fountainhead, burst forth all those later tenets of unbridled license which, in the midst of the terrible upheavals of the last century [viz., the eighteenth], were wildly conceived and boldly proclaimed as the principles and foundation of that new conception of law which was not merely previously unknown, but was at variance on many points with not only the Christian, but even the natural law.[3]

For the past several centuries, Western man has been constructing bit by bit an anthropocentric society, in opposition to the theocentric society of the Middle Ages, when the mystery of the Incarnation permeated the intellectual, cultural, and social fabric as fully as it is ever likely to do short of the Parousia. The ecclesial order, the political order, the moral order, the very

---

[2] Leo XIII, *Immortale Dei* 21.
[3] *Immortale Dei* 23.

order of reason, would each be compromised and corrupted as the West, in its "flight from God" (to use
a phrase of Max Picard's), drifted ever further from
its foundational principles. Indeed, the unraveling of
the West may be compared to a descent into madness.
Is my description exaggerated? Let's see: if a human
being is not a human person just because of its age
and location (unborn, in the womb); if everyone has
the right to make up reality according to his whims;
if a man may marry a man or a woman a woman; if a
man may decide he is a woman or vice versa; then I
think that my description is perfectly accurate.[4]

The avowed goal of the Christian is to work out one's
salvation in fear and trembling,[5] and, along the way, to
win over souls for Christ; the goal of the Catholic is
to make the world Catholic. Impelled by the Spirit of
truth and of love, believers must be restless and pained
as long as the world around them is *not* Christian in
its attitudes and appearance, its desires and deeds — and
all the more pained to the degree that it is *opposed*
to the mind which is in Christ Jesus.[6] So obviously
is it the duty of believers to "re-establish all things
in Christ, things in heaven and things on earth"—the
motto and program of Pope St. Pius X, *Instaurare omnia
in Christo*[7]—that even the Second Vatican Council could
not avoid reiterating it several times, in language that
bears the stamp of Leo XIII. I say this because, while

---

[4] I refer, in part, to three major decisions of the US Supreme
Court: *Roe v. Wade, Planned Parenthood v. Casey, Obergefell v. Hodges.*
In the second of these, Justice Kennedy wrote the most metaphysically absurd sentence ever penned: "At the heart of liberty
is the right to define one's own concept of existence, of meaning,
of the universe, and of the mystery of human life." And, although
Roe fell with *Dobbs*, many states immediately passed savagely pro-
abortion laws in order that the carnage might continue unabated,
slaking the Moloch of materialism.
[5] See Phil 2:12.
[6] Cf. Phil 2:5.
[7] Eph 1:10; see Pius X, *E Supremi* 8.

I share misgivings about that Council, *even there*, in the very midst of a progressive *coup*, strong echoes of the traditional doctrine still resounded, showing that it can never be repudiated without rejecting the essence of Christianity itself.[8]

"*INSTAURARE OMNIA IN CHRISTO*"

Progress does not consist in separating still further the state from the Church—"equivalent to the separation of human legislation from Christian and divine legislation," as Leo XIII succinctly put it.[9] True progress, for Catholics, occurs when the laity infuse the spirit of the gospel into temporal realities. The Pastoral Constitution on the Church in the Modern World, *Gaudium et Spes*, exhorts the laity to "impress the divine law on the affairs of the earthly city."[10] That does not sound like a secularist or liberal viewpoint; instead of privatizing religion, it insists that the truth about God and man, as revealed by God Himself, should be, as the text literally says, "written into" (*inscribatur*) the civil society here below. Neither Aquinas nor Leo would have said it differently.

The Decree on the Apostolate of the Laity, *Apostolicam Actuositatem*, recognizing the "intrinsic value" of temporal realities (7), notes how easily they can be perverted to the grave harm of mankind, and issues a call to Christians, especially the laity, to *transform* the temporal order according to the gospel—without,

---

[8] Thomists and Molinists, who fought bitterly for centuries about grace and predestination, were of one mind about the impossibility of a separation of Church and state. That goes to show how self-evident a conclusion this is, if we move from the data of the Deposit of Faith.

[9] Leo XIII, *Au Milieu des Sollicitudes* 28; see also *Immortale Dei*.

[10] The original text in no. 43, speaking of the laity: "*Ad ipsorum conscientiam iam apte formatam spectat, ut lex divina in civitatis terrenae vita inscribatur.*" For commentary, see "The Laity's Role in the World—and in the Church," in Kwasniewski, *Ministers of Christ*, 65–80, as well as Storck, *Foundations*.

needless to say, attempting a mistaken fusion of temporal and spiritual societies, as has occurred historically in a number of ways: the Caesaropapism of Byzantium, the Erastianism of some Western nation-states, the Gallicanism and Josephinism of the Enlightenment. Modern Christians have tended towards the opposite extreme, the divorcing of personal conviction from public life, which is a perilous attitude ceaselessly opposed by CST.[11]

The conclusion in *Apostolicam Actuositatem* 7 is unequivocal:

> The whole Church must work vigorously in order that men may become capable of rectifying the distortion of the temporal order and directing it to God through Christ. Pastors must clearly state the principles concerning the purpose of creation and the use of temporal things and must offer the moral and spiritual aids by which the temporal order may be renewed in Christ.

The "distortion of the temporal order" occurs precisely when it is not "direct[ed] to God through Christ." Pastors, too, have the responsibility to provide support to the laity in their efforts to Christianize society and government. The same document defines the "apostolate in the social milieu" as "the effort to infuse a Christian spirit into the mentality, customs, *laws*, and *structures* of the community in which one lives."[12] Catholics are urged to take an active interest in the reconstruction and perfection of civil society according to unchanging principles, so that citizens may be prepared for receiving the gospel (14).

Such passages from Vatican II necessarily prompt the question: Why did the Council's implementation

---

[11] See the Congregation for the Doctrine of the Faith's *Doctrinal Note on Some Questions Regarding the Participation of Catholics in Political Life*, November 24, 2002.
[12] Vatican II, *Apostolicam Actuositatem* 13, emphasis added.

so rapidly abandon the traditional doctrine that its own texts echoed? The answer is not far to seek: the Council had *simultaneously* accepted the Liberal separation of Church and state in *Dignitatis Humanae*. Ironically, in light of the much-ballyhooed breakthrough attributed to Henri de Lubac's *Surnaturel*, the abandonment in *Dignitatis Humanae* of the truth of the intrinsic ordering of the natural to the supernatural—of the earthly city to the City of God on behalf of which the Catholic Church teaches and sanctifies—made it impossible to work seriously and effectively toward the fulfillment of the principles espoused in *Apostolicam Actuositatem*. The relaxed and worldly Liberal policy of the Declaration on Religious Freedom won out over the repetition of traditional teaching elsewhere. As the Council gently endorsed integralist theses in one place, it boldly adopted a two-tier anthropology in others. And like the statue beheld in the vision of Daniel, the fusion of incompatible pieces allowed for its ready shattering into fragments.

PROPER RELATIONSHIP BETWEEN CHURCH AND STATE

Although the Church rejects the *separation* of Church and state, she upholds the *distinction* between the two: they are not the same power, nor are they in the same hands (except in rare cases). Yet they cannot act separately because they operate on the same unitary subject, namely, the individual man who is both a citizen and a Christian, a child of his people and a son of God. In no way has the Church called for theocracy as the ideal form of government; on the contrary, throughout history the spiritual power, represented by the clergy, has continually had to extricate itself from distracting and burdensome business that was not properly its own, while extracting the hand of civil rulers from ecclesiastical affairs that were not theirs to determine.

What, after all, is civil government *for*? Of course it must secure a safe public space in which citizens may travel, talk, and trade, keep garbage off the streets, and respond to emergencies that affect large numbers of people at once. But its most serious purpose is to aid citizens in acquiring the panoply of natural virtues on which such great goods as friendship, the family, and the common good of the entire people depend, and to render as easy as possible the attainment of happiness, which consists in the knowledge and love of God. This is not my idea, but Pope Leo XIII's:

> Civil society, established for the common welfare, should not only safeguard the well-being of the community, but have also at heart the interests of its individual members, in such a manner as not in any way to hinder, but in every manner to render as easy as may be, the possession of that highest and unchangeable good for which all should seek.[13]

In practical terms, the question of the proper relationship between Church and state comes down to this: Are the laws and customs of the state, are the cultural practices of the people, supposed to reflect and embody Catholic truth, or not? The answer is yes — contrary to the modern insistence that the state should always be religiously neutral and separated from all supernatural concerns. The reason why is explained by the same pope in the letter *Au Milieu des Sollicitudes* sent to the clergy and faithful of France in 1892. Having stated that "the principle of the separation of the state and Church . . . is equivalent to the separation of human legislation from Christian and divine legislation," he continues:

> As soon as the state refuses to give to God what belongs to God, by a necessary consequence it refuses to give to citizens that to

---

[13] Leo XIII, *Immortale Dei* 6.

which, as men, they have a right; as, whether agreeable or not to accept, it cannot be denied that man's rights spring from his duty toward God. Whence it follows that the state, by missing in this connection the principal object of its institution, finally becomes false to itself by denying that which is the reason of its own existence. These superior truths are so clearly proclaimed by the voice of even natural reason, that they force themselves upon all who are not blinded by the violence of passion; therefore Catholics cannot be too careful in defending themselves against such a separation.[14]

In the aftermath of the anticlerical "Law of Separation" in France in 1906, Leo XIII's successor, St. Pius X, spells out the traditional teaching most forcefully:

That the state must be separated from the Church is a thesis absolutely false, a most pernicious error. Based, as it is, on the principle that the state must not recognize any religious

---

[14] Leo XIII, *Au Milieu des Sollicitudes* 28. This is why the same pontiff is careful to explain to the bishops of the United States of America in *Longinqua Oceani* 6: "Thanks [for the flourishing of the Catholic Church in the USA] are due to the equity of the laws which obtain in America and to the customs of the well-ordered Republic. For the Church amongst you, unopposed by the Constitution and government of your nation, fettered by no hostile legislation, protected against violence by the common laws and the impartiality of the tribunals, is free to live and act without hindrance. Yet, though all this is true, it would be very erroneous to draw the conclusion that in America is to be sought the type of the most desirable status of the Church, or that it would be universally lawful or expedient for State and Church to be, as in America, dissevered and divorced. The fact that Catholicity with you is in good condition, nay, is even enjoying a prosperous growth, is by all means to be attributed to the fecundity with which God has endowed His Church, in virtue of which, unless men or circumstances interfere, she spontaneously expands and propagates herself; but she would bring forth more abundant fruits if, in addition to liberty, she enjoyed the favor of the laws and the patronage of the public authority."

cult, it is in the first place guilty of a great injustice to God; for the Creator of man is also the Founder of human societies, and preserves their existence as He preserves our own. We owe Him, therefore, not only a private cult, but a public and social worship to honor Him. Besides, this thesis is an obvious negation of the supernatural order. It limits the action of the state to the pursuit of public prosperity during this life only, which is but the proximate object of political societies; and it occupies itself in no fashion (on the plea that this is foreign to it) with their ultimate object which is man's eternal happiness after this short life shall have run its course. But as the present order of things is temporary and subordinated to the conquest of man's supreme and absolute welfare, it follows that the civil power must not only place no obstacle in the way of this conquest, but must aid us in effecting it.[15]

Both popes were addressing a nation that had long been Catholic and was still largely Catholic, and which therefore had solemn public obligations to the true religion. But what about secular and pluralistic societies—should their citizens and statesmen, too, aspire to an explicitly Christian and Catholic government?

Let us think this through. Wherever the faith is vibrantly and courageously lived—and even if this is no longer the case at the moment in most of our nations, it has been in the past, and it could be again in the future—it is not only possible but likely that large numbers of citizens will become imbued with the Faith, and over time, statesmen will arise from this citizenry. Being thus imbued with Catholic truth will affect for the better their way of life and practical judgments. A practicing Catholic politician will never "leave his faith behind" in his decisions; he will view temporal

---

[15] Pius X, *Vehementer Nos* 3.

realities from the eternal and divine perspective of revealed truth.

If we accept St. Thomas's definition of natural law as a participation in the eternal law—that is, in eternal wisdom, the mind of the Creator Himself[16]—then even reason's act of judging "according to natural law" is a way of applying the divine measure to human realities. (As many magisterial texts declare, the Church is the guardian and interpreter of natural law in its purity; without giving ear to her teaching, it would be impossible for a state to follow the natural law consistently and stably.[17]) Failure to do this is not just an incidental failure, it is the total failure of prudence—above all, of political prudence. A ruler cannot be a ruler at all, let alone a good one, if he is not seeking to judge and regulate the affairs of temporal life according to unchanging principles of the divine law.

The Catholic view is simply that such principles *may* and *should* include supernatural principles as well as natural ones. Catholics reject any understanding of politics that would remove or relativize fixed natural principles by making the will of a majority, or the will of a dictator, the source of right. Fascist Germany, Soviet Russia, contemporary France, Communist China, Canada and the United States in their liberal drift, are no different from each other in one fundamental way: each has pretended that what is right and wrong can be determined by the autonomous will of man, whether by electorates or by politicians acting (truly or supposedly) in their name. We have seen where this ends up: the Gulag, the concentration camp, the abortion mill, the anti-culture of "whatever." If we want to end up in a better place, and ultimately in heaven, we need to rethink, from the ground up, what government is *for*,

---

[16] See *Summa theologiae* I-II, QQ. 93–94.
[17] See, *inter alia*, Pius XI, *Quadragesimo Anno* 41; Paul VI, *Humanae Vitae* 4; *CCC* 2035–36.

what transcendent norms it ought to follow, and how it must justify itself before the eyes of God and men.

Far from being "pre-Vatican II," this position is exactly what one finds in John Paul II's encyclical letters *Veritatis Splendor* and *Evangelium Vitae,*[18] although unfortunately the Polish pope passed up no opportunity to mix in his liberal views on religious freedom. This much we should admit: John Paul II was not a secularist pure and simple, for no secularist could demand that states and societies make due efforts to preserve and promote man's *integral good*, which transcends the order of material creation and life in this world, as the Polish pope ceaselessly proclaimed against the Siamese twins of dialectical Marxism and materialistic capitalism. He seemed nevertheless unable or unwilling to draw the Leonine conclusion that, since religion—taken in the Thomistic sense of the virtue by which we offer due and right public worship to God—is the first and highest moral virtue,[19] the state has a solemn obligation to promote precisely *this* virtue and its exercise. He was likely caught in the modern confusion between *confessionalism* (politically-recognized subordination of state to Church) and *theocracy* (exact overlap of Church and state), and since he rejected the latter, as did Leo XIII, so he rejected the former.

Moreover, on a pragmatic level, John Paul II, like Pius XII, was anxious about the incompetence of the modern state to legislate well in regard to the highest conditions of human flourishing, that is, anything concerning the spiritual domain. Who could blame him for being skeptical? In a period of decadence and disintegration, there is a lot to be said for the rough-and-ready attitude met with every day in the American

---

[18] So much so that the encyclicals immediately generated a predictable reaction from liberals: "John Paul II is turning back the clock to preconciliar days!"

[19] See *Summa theologiae* II-II, Q. 81, and Staudt, *The Primacy of God.*

West: "Let me have my gun, livestock, and truck, and leave me and my wife in peace to bring up our children in the fear of the Lord."

A CATHOLIC VISION FOR SOCIAL LIFE

Nevertheless, the Church has always advocated something more than this minimalism as an ideal to be pursued. Catholicism should be *a socially privileged reality*. What would this look like in practice?

Businesses would be closed on Sundays and holy days.[20] Hospitals would be forbidden to perform unethical practices. Doctors and pharmacists could not prescribe or distribute contraceptives. Parliament or congress would open and close with prayer, perhaps led by a chaplain. Proposed legislation could be evaluated by a council of bishops or moral theologians they appointed.[21] Movies would require pre-screening and some kind of *"nihil obstat"* before they could be distributed. The construction of mosques or Mormon temples would be prohibited. Some of these examples are more appropriate to nations with a majority Catholic population, while others are pertinent to all.

The state's *minimum* obligation would be to protect "natural religion," in such a way that atheism and all its expressions (e.g., pseudo-scientific literature arguing for a purely materialistic process of evolution) as well as metaphysical absurdities (e.g., Mormonism or New Age superstitions; polytheistic pagan religions) could be prohibited *tout court*, with no allowance of public activity or propaganda. For in such errors the intellect is denying first principles and thus cannot be said to be pursuing truth; it is only corrupting itself.

---

[20] As expressly called for by John Paul II in his Apostolic Letter *Dies Domini* of May 31, 1998.

[21] Admittedly, we might hesitate about this provision at the present moment, but we should take the long view of things and hope to see someday better bishops than we now have.

That John Paul II himself would be logically forced to this position is clear from what he taught repeatedly about culture, as in this famous remark: "A faith that does not become culture is not fully accepted, not entirely thought out, not faithfully lived."[22] A succinct and illuminating definition of culture is provided by Tate Hilgefort: "Culture is made up of three elements: what we think (mentality), what we do (habits), and what we're surrounded by (environment). These elements directly relate to the transcendentals of truth, goodness, and beauty."[23] Is not the way people organize and govern themselves politically an immensely important element of their culture—one that is particularly influential over all other aspects of culture?[24] Is this not, then, prime missionary territory to be evangelized and converted? And if this domain is converted, will it not mature into something like Christendom, in the model depicted by St. Thomas Aquinas?[25]

Similarly, in the Apostolic Exhortation *Ecclesia in Oceania*, John Paul II wrote: "It is vital that the Church

---

[22] John Paul II, Address to the Italian National Congress of the Ecclesial Movement for Cultural Commitment, January 16, 1982. Regis Martin, in a series of articles, eloquently argues that the Christianization of culture is an imperative that necessarily arises from the Incarnation and from our baptism into the God-Man: "Cultivating the Soil"; "Configuring All Things to Christ"; "Rediscovering Our Roots"; "Living an Integrated Life."

[23] Hilgefort, "Parish Priests Are the Cure to the Crisis."

[24] It is obvious that people can organize themselves politically in *evil* ways, in anti-Christian ways, as noted by John Paul II in his Address to Members of the Pontifical Council for Culture, January 12, 1990 (see no. 1), and as demonstrated by the news every day. Does it not follow that Christians may and must organize themselves in *good* ways—in ways expressly Christian?

[25] I have in mind Aquinas's opusculum *On Kingship*, where he argues in favor of a hierarchical society ruled by a Christian prince, himself subject to the pope and the priests of the Roman Church. Over against this "consecrational Christendom" Jacques Maritain and Charles Journet attempted to articulate what a "secular Christendom" might look like, but I am not convinced they did not create a chimera, a contradiction in terms.

insert herself fully into culture and from within bring about the process of purification and transformation" (16). Again: "It is the fundamental call of lay people to *renew the temporal order in all its many elements.* In this way, the Church becomes the yeast that leavens *the entire loaf of the temporal order*" (43).[26] He rightly complains that "the Christian concept of marriage and the family is being opposed by a new secular, pragmatic, and individualistic outlook which has gained standing in the area of legislation" (45). This statement implies that once upon a time, it was the natural and even the Christian concept of marriage that had authoritative standing in the area of legislation — and that it ought to regain it. This is something John Paul II consistently demanded, confident that he was asking the state to undertake a task essentially within its competence — confident, indeed, that he was stipulating a basic requirement for the survival and prosperity of the people.[27]

LONGING FOR CHRISTENDOM

If the popes, bishops, clergy, and faithful of the Dark Ages had decided at one point to give up their quest for a Christian society (you can imagine them sighing and saying to one another: "It's awfully depressing, all these

---

[26] Emphases added.

[27] "More than ever, man is seriously threatened by an *anti-culture* which reveals itself, among other ways, in growing violence, murderous confrontations, exploitation of instincts and selfish interests" (John Paul II, Address to Members of the Pontifical Council for Culture, January 16, 1984, no. 8). "The challenge of the twenty-first century is to humanize society and its institutions through the gospel; to restore to the family, to cities, and to villages a soul worthy of the human person, created in the image and likeness of God.... The Christian leaven will enrich living cultures and their values and bring them to full flower. In this way, hearts will be penetrated and cultures renewed by Christ, the Way, the Truth, and the Life (cf. Jn 14:6) who 'has brought complete newness by bringing Himself,' as Irenaeus of Lyons wrote (*Adv. Haer.*, IV, 34, 1)" (John Paul II, Address to Members of the Pontifical Council for Culture, January 10, 1992, no. 9).

plagues and barbaric tribes and crumbling buildings and corrupt kings. Why don't we just forget all about justice and peace in this world, which is a rotten place anyhow, and flee to the forests with the hermits?"), the Middle Ages, the Age of Faith and Chivalry, of Cathedrals and *Summae*, would never have been born.

Tempted by discouragement in the face of so many and such great evils as our times are burdened and burgeoning with, we must learn the same lesson: If we truly love Christ, then we will love and long for Christendom, which is the flowering of His grace in this vale of tears. This means we will do everything we can, *as individuals*, to make this world more welcoming to Christ, to His Church, to His saving gospel and to its sanctifying power. This will be the only long-term solution to our short-term problem: the want of authentically Catholic statesmen. It is a want that faith, hope, and charity, working against all odds and human calculations, have inherent power to supply, but not before many grains of wheat have first fallen into the ground and died.[28] "I planted, Apollos watered, but God gave the growth.... For we are God's fellow workers."[29]

---

[28] Cf. Jn 12:24.
[29] 1 Cor 3:6, 9.

THE CATHOLIC STATE:
ANACHRONISM, ARCHENEMY,
OR ARCHETYPE?

I T IS ASSUMED BY MANY THAT THE
age-old problem of Church-state relations, a problem that grew ever more intense from the Reformation era through the so-called Enlightenment, has
been uneasily resolved, *de facto* and *de iure*, in favor
of democratic pluralism and a benign liberal ideology
to which even the Church has found it possible to
reconcile herself, in exchange for common recognition
of basic human rights. From this perspective, Vatican
II's *Dignitatis Humanae* is taken as a watershed in CST,
which had traditionally emphasized the Catholic confessional state as the ideal, and the non-Catholic or
pluralistic state as an evil that prudence could tolerate
but never approve.

Careful students of the Church's magisterium have
found this view a troubling simplification. If the Church
has, in fact, changed so consistent, long-standing, and
significant a teaching, what does this mean for doctrinal
continuity with the past? To paraphrase Pope Benedict
XVI, can a Church be trusted who changes her mind
on matters of such weight, lauding as modern progress
that which she condemned as godless apostasy only a
few decades earlier? Moreover, is reconciliation with
the aggressive secularism of the Enlightenment really
as easy as blessing democracy while adding a few stern
reminders about the need for religious underpinnings?
Finally, if the Fathers of Vatican II had truly wanted a
sea-change in Catholic political doctrine, how can one

explain the persistent footnotes—in conciliar documents, in the encyclicals of John Paul II, in the new *Catechism*, in doctrinal interventions of the CDF—that refer the reader to the unambiguous formulations of Pius IX, Leo XIII, Pius XI, Pius XII, and John XXIII?

One begins to suspect that we are dealing not with any substantive doctrinal change, but rather with a rhetorically palatable, diplomatic reclothing that downplays the doctrine's controversial elements. Yet if this is true, the choice prompts a serious objection. Would not such a reclothing amount to a form of dishonesty, if not a craven relinquishment of mission?

To help sort through these matters, I will define the concept of "the Catholic state." Then I will turn to Vatican II and, drawing chiefly upon *Gaudium et Spes* and *Apostolicam Actuositatem*, establish that the essence of the doctrine is restated by the Council, albeit in terms believed to be more adapted to the present historical situation.[1] I will show that it is impossible to repudiate the ideal of the Catholic state without implicitly repudiating the claims of Jesus Christ and His Church over mankind as a whole and over each individual. A society and government imbued with reverence for the divine law is the full, natural embodiment of the Faith in the midst of the world Christ redeemed and wishes to save.[2]

WHAT IS A CATHOLIC STATE AND HOW DOES IT ARISE?

Materially, a Catholic state is a sovereign political entity made up of a people predominantly Catholic in

---

[1] I do not take up here the question of whether this attempt at a new formulation has been successful either in transmitting true doctrine to Catholics or in opening those outside the Church to her beneficent influence; I think not, but to elaborate on that skepticism would take us too far afield. See "Vatican II: *Requiescat in Pace*" in Kwasniewski, ed., *Sixty Years After*, 93–122.

[2] Cf. Jn 3:17.

profession. Formally, it is defined as a nation with a regime or government whose constitution commits it to the support of the one true Faith, whose laws are in harmony with the teaching of the magisterium on faith and morals, and whose policies implement CST to the widest extent possible.[3]

The Catholic state is the natural, organic outcome of the Faith when it is fully *lived* by a people. As we saw in the last chapter, the most recent Ecumenical Council invites the laity to make it a matter of conscience "that the divine law be impressed on the affairs of the earthly city" (*ut lex divina in civitatis terrenae vita inscribatur*).[4] When this is done consistently, on a broad scale, over some length of time, the natural and proper result is a Catholic society, culture, and state. The Church and her faith will be, for the majority of citizens, the point of reference for understanding themselves and the world, the framework of their daily lives, customs, arts, letters, festivities, rituals. She will be the dominant presence in the life of the individual as in the life of the community. This has never ceased to be the ideal towards which the Church strives. In an address to the Tenth International Congress of Historical Sciences in Rome in 1955, Pope Pius XII stated:

> While the Church and state have known hours and years of conflict, there were also from the time of Constantine the Great until the contemporary era and even recently, tranquil periods, often quite long ones, during which they collaborated with full understanding in the education of the same people. The Church does not hide the fact that she considers such collaboration normal, and that she regards the

---

[3] For a schematic overview of the nine possible relationships between Church and State, with concrete examples, see Crean, "The Nine Choirs of Politics."

[4] Vatican II, *Gaudium et Spes* 43.

unity of the people in the true religion and
the unanimity of action between herself and
the state as ideal.[5]

Permit me to quote once more the last Council's teaching on the apostolate proper to the laity, which differs
in no way from the traditional doctrine:

> The whole Church must work vigorously in
> order that men may become capable of recti-
> fying the distortion of the temporal order and
> directing it to God through Christ. Pastors
> must clearly state the principles concerning the
> purpose of creation and the use of temporal
> things and must offer the moral and spiritual
> aids by which the temporal order may be
> renewed in Christ.[6]

Tellingly, the Council defines the lay apostolate as "the
effort to infuse a Christian spirit into the mentality,
customs, laws, and structures of the community in
which one lives" (13). Note that *laws* and *structures* are
expressly specified; it is not merely attitudes, social
graces, and public demonstrations of piety that must
take their determinate bearings from Christ and His
Church, but also the concrete content and manner of
political life. In giving this advice, the Council was doing

---

[5] See Msgr. Joseph Clifford Fenton's illuminating commentary in
Michael Davies, *The Second Vatican Council and Religious Liberty*,
179–81. The statement of Lefebvre that Davies quotes on p. 181 is
surely exaggerated, since it fails to recognize the equally constant
teaching of the popes that the *least* right to which the Church lays
claim is the freedom to perform her mission without interference,
e.g., freedom to appoint bishops, freedom of communication
between the bishops and the pope, freedom of promulgation and
publication of documents, and freedom to influence laws, customs,
and constitutions. As we know, the Church in modern times
has rarely been given even this *minimal* freedom by supposedly
Catholic states; one need only think of France or Austria. Hence
Dignitatis Humanae's demand for rigorous respect for "the freedom
of the Church" is anything but an empty phrase. See Hittinger,
"How to Read *Dignitatis Humanae* on Establishment of Religion."
[6] Vatican II, *Apostolicam Actuositatem* 7.

no more than echoing Pope Leo XIII, who frequently made such exhortations — as when he encourages the faithful "to use their best endeavors ... to infuse, as it were, into all the veins of the state the healthy sap and blood of Christian wisdom and virtue."[7]

WHY IS A CATHOLIC STATE DESIRABLE?

Since the Catholic faith is revealed by God as the one true religion from which derives not only spiritual perfection (which is the decisive thing for our eternal destiny) but also the highest moral, intellectual, and cultural perfection achievable by man, it is desirable that this faith become the sovereign, pervasive principle of the public life of a people, just as it should be the principle of the personal life of its adherents. In this way, more men will be perfected with the full complement of virtues and more souls will attain the heavenly reward promised by Christ to those who believe in Him. Put negatively, to the degree that a society, culture, and state are non-Catholic (or worse, anti-Catholic), to that degree perfection in virtue is less likely among citizens, and the number of souls in danger of damnation greater. For a non-Catholic society, culture, or state to be a good thing in itself, the Catholic faith would have to be false. Because the Faith is true, however, the only "end game" scenario as far as Christians are concerned is a converted nation of explicitly Christian institutions, deliberately working hand-in-hand with the hierarchy of the Church.

The common good of any political community is twofold: the extrinsic common good, God; the intrinsic common good, namely, true peace, the "tranquility of order," which is achieved by the study of truth, the impartial administration of justice, and a fitting provision and distribution of earthly goods — all of which contribute to what may be called social happiness. Now,

---

[7] Leo XIII, *Immortale Dei* 45.

in a Catholic society, the extrinsic common good is all the more easily and widely attained due to adherence to the true religion, which furnishes the sovereign and infallible means for attaining it. Moreover, the study of truth will consist of the promotion of naturally knowable as well as revealed truth, together with the repression of natural and supernatural errors. The administration of justice will conform to Catholic moral teaching, including the wise use of capital punishment. Marriage and family law will be regulated according to the principles of natural and divine law, and parents, *not* the state, will be regarded as the primary educators of their children. Material goods will be traded, bought, sold, provided, in the context of a strong juridical order inspired by the principles of CST. All of these elements pertain to the true common good of a Catholic society. It is therefore the duty of government officials to ensure that this common good is zealously guarded from harm, without, at the same time, attempting to interfere with the private religious acts of non-Catholics[8] or altogether excluding a limited public exercise of that right where public order and the common welfare of the people do not demand its restraint.[9]

Notwithstanding the obvious benefits of a thoroughly Catholic society and regime, we need to consider a corresponding danger that tends to arise and grow almost imperceptibly, as the history of Europe proves in a dramatic fashion. After centuries have passed from the time of a nation's initial conversion, it is possible that the Faith will come to be taken for granted; that

---

[8] This private exercise is equivalent to acts of intellect and will that can be externalized in the family forum. As soon as they are brought into the political or public forum, they become subject to the governance of the state for the same reason that any human act does. This I take to be the only possible orthodox interpretation of *Dignitatis Humanae*.

[9] For further clarifications, see Storck, *Foundations*, 27–49 and 171–85.

many citizens will be poorly educated, being Catholics more by custom (often trustingly accepted and sincerely practiced) than by instruction and zealous conviction. There is thus great danger of a slow drift into an increasingly worldly mentality, as well as the danger of perversion and corruption of citizens by errors in faith or morals spread by persuasive representatives of sects that manage to gain entrance into that society. A Catholic government that really holds the common good of its people at heart is therefore obliged to limit severely the public activities of such sectarians and the public expressions of their beliefs (e.g., to prohibit entry of such people or the publication of their pamphlets), while at the same time continuing to promote, in every way possible, the institutions that keep the Faith alive and well in the hearts of the people: families, parishes, monasteries, schools, guilds, hospitals, clubs, and the like.

FURTHER DEFINITIONS AND A COROLLARY

A non-Catholic state may be defined as one that is, or claims to be, officially neutral vis-à-vis the Church, recognizing civilly its special laws as binding on its own members, and allowing it full freedom of ministry. There are, of course, varying degrees of neutrality, ranging from "warm" to "cold." The general philosophical framework of such a state is liberalism: *de facto* recognition of pluralism and the toleration of all views compatible with basic public order (as construed by current officeholders). An anti-Catholic state may be defined as one that denies the Catholic Church those rights that are due to her as a perfect society with a divine mandate, or, in a worst-case scenario, actively persecutes and penalizes her members.[10]

---

[10] The United States of America is an anti-Catholic state to the extent that it allows Catholics to get divorced (and, *a fortiori*, to be civilly remarried) or to have abortions when such acts ought to be illegal unless the Catholics in question formally apostatize

A corollary: to the extent that modern democracies place limits on all *formal* intersection between the Catholic faith and the ordering of political society and temporal affairs, to this extent they are both anti-Catholic and tyrannical. The goal of the Enlightenment social contract theorists was to design a society from which the Catholic Church was effectively excluded, a society therefore "free" to reject with impunity all rules of faith and morals. Hence, we find a consistent exclusion of practicing Catholics from social contract experiments — one need only read Hobbes's *Leviathan*, Locke's *Letter Concerning Toleration*, Samuel Adams's *The Rights of Colonists*, and countless other examples from the eighteenth century.[11] It follows that when Catholics *are* permitted to live within such societies or under such regimes, it is virtually at the cost of renouncing the social dynamism and authoritative structure of the Faith itself. No less a churchman than Archbishop Charles Chaput has recognized this dark logic in John F. Kennedy's Address to the Greater Houston Ministerial Association in 1960, and in the continual stream of U.S. "Catholic" politicians who, abusing the noble title of conscience, throw their support behind sexual immorality and the slaughter of the

---

and depart from the society of the Church, even as in some European countries Catholics and Protestants are legally obliged to pay church taxes until and unless they renounce their church membership. A state that permits Catholics routinely to break their solemn oaths and promises is a state that, in its official capacity, considers anything religious or spiritual to be mumbo-jumbo with no discernible public, objective meaning or value.

[11] From Adams, *The Rights of the Colonists*: "Mr. Locke has asserted and proved, beyond the possibility of contradiction on any solid ground, that such toleration ought to be extended to all whose doctrines are not subversive of society. The only sects which he thinks ought to be, and which by all wise laws are excluded from such toleration, are those who teach doctrines subversive of the civil government under which they live. The Roman Catholics or Papists are [thereby] excluded..."

unborn.[12] At its root, the social contract demands a common creed of relativism and public indifference to the highest things.

What, then, of *Dignitatis Humanae*—what kind of state, or what range of states, is this declaration addressing? Both its textual genesis and its internal preoccupations show us that *Dignitatis Humanae* is addressed to the two situations that had become dominant in the contemporary world: non-Catholic liberal pluralistic states (e.g., the United States) and anti-Catholic ideological states (e.g., Soviet Union, China). As Russell Hittinger convincingly argues in his book *The First Grace*, the declaration never takes up in a systematic way the question of a "normative" Catholic state, being content to mention it in passing:

> If, in view of peculiar circumstances obtaining among peoples, special civil recognition is given to one religious community in the constitutional order of society, it is at the same time imperative that the right of all citizens and religious communities to religious freedom should be recognized and made effective in practice.

Yet surely the declaration's unqualified reaffirmation that "it [the teaching on religious freedom] leaves untouched traditional Catholic doctrine on the moral duty of men and societies toward the true religion and toward the one Church of Christ" can only be construed as support for the possibility, desirability, and ideality of such a state, regardless of what some authors or promoters of the document may have wished it might have said or may have personally believed.[13]

---

[12] See Chaput, "The Vocation of Christians in American Public Life."

[13] See Harrison, "Is John Courtney Murray a Reliable Interpreter of *Dignitatis Humanae*?" Murray's life raises many questions about the soundness of his views: see Green, "The Crisis in the Church Is an LSD Trip."

The final document neither excludes the Catholic confessional state nor omits to mention essential limitations on, or norms for, the public expression of religious belief—limitations and norms that at least imply the traditional teaching.[14]

WHAT IS AT STAKE

In an age of confusion, it is very important that we correctly conceptualize the political question—that is, the one central question on which everything else hinges. The political question *par excellence* is this: What is the status or place of the Catholic Church within a civil society and its regime?[15] The "thesis," i.e., the norm, the ideal, is nothing less than a fully Catholic culture, in which all the arts, economic life, and government are thoroughly "baptized." The pragmatic situation of pluralism (also called the "hypothesis") is any partially or scarcely Catholic culture, whose arts, economy, and government follow principles that vary from being merely compatible with, to being violently opposed to, the Catholic faith. A civil society animated by a non-Catholic or anti-Catholic worldview will be imperfect according to both natural and supernatural criteria, and its existence can only be tolerated, never approved in itself or as a model.

---

[14] Here we refer to the role in *Dignitatis Humanae* that "norming concepts" such as "due (or just) public order," "common good," and "the objective moral law" play in respect to the exercise of any and every civil liberty—even those rooted in human nature and pertaining directly to human dignity. Admittedly, this Declaration remains a most vexing trial of interpretation (see note 6 on page 20). We should also be prepared to admit that many things done in its name were not, in fact, required by its actual prima facie teaching but were rather the consequence of the progressive faction insisting on a certain "spirit" of the Council that went beyond the text. Thus, nothing in *Dignitatis Humanae* demanded that the special standing of the Church in Spain or Italy be canceled.

[15] See Manent's penetrating remarks along these lines in *An Intellectual History of Liberalism*.

What are the implications of abandoning the "thesis"? The three fundamental forces motivating the Christian in the world are the theological virtues of faith, hope, and charity. Whenever the goal of a thoroughly converted (that is, Catholic) culture and state is no longer aspired to — even if only remotely, by sighs and prayers, when its realization seems humanly impossible — then sadly, it must be the case that faith, hope, and charity are no longer the operative principles of life. They are replaced by worldly prudence, a heavenless horizon, an all-too-human love that contradicts the missionary impulse of charity. To let go of the gospel as the norm for *everything human* is to consign oneself and society to the mediocre exercise of mediocre virtues, at best; and given human sinfulness, it may also mean throwing open the house to the expert exercise of inhuman vices, as modern political history has shown all too vividly.

We are living in an era characterized by profound unrest: the increasing rationalism of science fueling technological barbarism, the increasing irrationalism of non-Christian religions feeding horrific violence, the increasing secularization of Western societies driving them to the brink of insanity as every perversion and aberration is not only permitted but celebrated. We must not underestimate the extent to which false ideas in philosophy, religion, and politics have brought about this world situation, nor the extent of Catholics' complicity in it by their willingness to listen to the siren song of the Enlightenment, luring us with empty promises of a universally respectful and benevolent, value-neutral, open-ended social order where religion would be the special preserve of the sovereign individual conscience — and never would the Catholic Faith be the public principle of social cohesion, moral orientation, intellectual light, and spiritual vitality. As the wake-up call becomes increasingly shrill, it is high time for us to rise from the drugged sleep of modernity and embrace a fully *Catholic*, fully *traditional* vision of the political order and the common good. It may not be ours to see such an order rise up from the ashes of the corrupt West, but it is our duty and privilege to embrace it in spirit and to advance its dawning in any great or small way the Lord empowers us to do.

PURIFYING PATRIOTISM
OF AMERICANISM

CATHOLIC PATRIOTISM OR AMERICANIST INCULTURATION?

IN THE PRE-1955 ROMAN CALENDAR, July 4 would have been a day within the octave of the Holy Apostles Peter and Paul, with the Mass "Mihi autem." Current Ordos usually say "feria." After the canonization of Pier Giorgio Frassati on September 7, 2025, July 4 (his *dies natalis*) has been appointed his feastday.[1] Secularly speaking, the fourth of July is, in most parts of the world, a day like any other. In the United States of America it is quite noisily otherwise, as millions set off fireworks in celebration of the chief national holiday.

"Independence Day" is a secular holiday if ever there was one, celebrating rebellion against political authority, a victory of Deism and Freemasonry over European tradition, and a culture of secularizing Protestantism. It may be fun to shoot off fireworks, enjoy barbecues with family and friends, and be proud of what our nation has accomplished (while not thinking too closely about how we have treated native Americans and countless other "inferiors" over the centuries), but one thing's absolutely certain: it's not a religious feast. This holiday is no holyday.

When I first learned of the existence of a Mass for the Fourth of July, I could not restrain my curiosity to

---

[1] Indeed, according to the norms of the Decree *Cum Sanctissima* of February 22, 2020, St. Pier Giorgio Frassati could be honored in the Traditional Latin Mass by using the Common of Confessors.

see what it was like. As one who had been nourished on the sober words of Leo XIII in *Testem Benevolentiae* and *Longinqua Oceani*—where that great pope warns the American hierarchy not to over-celebrate aspects of the United States that are merely tolerable, not ideal, from a Catholic point of view, such as the "wall of separation" between Church and state, or the appetite for ecumenical ventures, or the tendency to exalt active and pragmatic approaches over contemplative and principled ones[2]—I was eager to see how the prayers devised by the U.S. bishops would deftly embody the great social doctrine of Leo XIII, so that July 4th, for those who attended Mass, might become a moment of "formation," as everyone likes to say nowadays: a time when our parochial patriotism could be expanded to embrace the social Kingship of Jesus Christ,[3] the primacy of religion and the things of the spirit, and the unique vocation of American Catholics to convert and make disciples of their fellow citizens.

The reality was far different. Not wishing to miss any opportunity for postconciliar "inculturation," the U.S. bishops devised a perfectly ridiculous "Mass for Independence Day" that reeks of Masonic "Manifest Destiny" patriotism—a Mass of pan-Christian, flag-waving, self-glorifying sentimentalism. Let's have a look at a few of its texts.

> COLLECT. Father of all nations and ages, we recall the day when our country claimed its place among the family of nations; for what has been achieved we give you thanks, for the work that still remains we ask your help, and as you have called us from many peoples to be one nation, grant that, under your providence, our country may share your blessings with all

---

[2] On all these points, see Kwasniewski, *Resurgent in the Midst of Crisis*, 57–70; also above, note 14 on page 155.
[3] See Br. André Marie, "For Christ the King."

the peoples of the earth. Through our Lord
Jesus Christ...

Manifest Destiny, anyone? Shades of Mormonism, and
support for the Pentagon, which knows how to share
the blessings of democracy and freedom—whether their
recipients like it or not!

> PRAYER OVER THE OFFERINGS. Father, who
> have molded into one our nation, drawn from
> the peoples of many lands, grant, that as the
> grains of wheat become one bread and the
> many grapes one cup of wine, so we may
> before all others be instruments of your peace.
> Through Christ our Lord.

Should the unification of former British colonies under
a Protestant-Deist constitutional regime be compared
to the manufacturing of the bread and wine for the
Eucharistic sacrifice? The phrase "before all others" is
especially unfortunate, since it has a double meaning:
"in the sight of others," and "holding the primacy above
others"—a view known as American exceptionalism.
In this prayer, America is presented as the Eucharistic
city on the hill offered to God to bring about peace
in the world.

> PREFACE. It is truly right and just, our duty
> and our salvation, always and everywhere to
> give you thanks, Lord, holy Father, almighty
> and eternal God, through Christ our Lord. He
> spoke to us a message of peace and taught us
> to live as brothers and sisters. His message took
> form in the vision of our founding fathers as
> they fashioned a nation where we might live
> as one. His message lives on in our midst as
> our task for today and a promise for tomorrow.
> And so, with hearts full of love, we join the
> angels today and every day of our lives, to sing
> your glory as we acclaim: Holy, Holy, Holy
> Lord God of hosts...

"His [Christ's] message took form in the vision of our founding fathers as they fashioned a nation where we might live as one." Are we so certain of that? Pope Leo XIII had his doubts, which he expressed on numerous occasions, about Enlightenment social contract regimes and their understanding of liberty and secularity. The mystical language applied to old Israel and to the Church, new Israel, is now being applied to the Nation. "His message lives on in our midst as our task for today and a promise for tomorrow." This sounds like the rhetoric of a ghostwritten State of the Union address.

> PRAYER AFTER COMMUNION. By showing us in this Eucharist, O Lord, a glimpse of the unity and joy of your people in heaven, deepen our unity and intensify our joy, that all who believe in you may work together to build the city of lasting peace. Through Christ our Lord.

What "city" is this referring to? If the heavenly Jerusalem, the prayer should be clearer. It is ambiguous, allowing "social justice warriors" to confuse the earthly city with the heavenly one, in the way familiar to the utopian and Marxist thought in vogue today in so many putatively Catholic quarters.

None of this is defensible liturgical language. It has in fact nothing to do with the Sacrifice of the Mass and the worship of God. It is fluff and bilge.

The Mass for Independence Day even prescribes a Gloria—the great hymn of the angels and saints that the new missal of Paul VI excluded from nearly every feastday. But we must not neglect to sing it (or more probably, recite it) on so momentous a secular holiday!

This is not how Catholics in the United States of America should celebrate their nationhood or patriotism. We can do this far better by using traditional votive Masses: a votive Mass in honor of the Immaculate Conception, the country's patroness; a Mass of thanksgiving for favors received; a Mass of reparation for sins committed; a Mass to beg for peace; a Mass for the conversion of the enemies of the Church. All of these are provided for in the traditional *Missale Romanum* and some still exist, albeit hobbled, in the Pauline missal. The Church always gives us appropriate ways to mark national holidays, without the need for recourse to a fabricated feastday with problematic propers.

FOUNDERING FATHERS

How did we arrive at this nadir, where not even the sanctuary of the temple is free from Americanist propaganda?

At this time in its history, the United States of America is — or at least is in continual danger of — devolving into violence and anarchy. Some would blame this on very recent social movements and educational failure; others would see it as rooted in longstanding philosophical errors and habits of life the consequences of which take time to unfold.

As a student of political history I find fascinating the genre of dreamy praise directed to the U.S. government and its founding documents as practically the best the world has ever seen, and this, not on the lips of secularists or Protestants, from whom one might expect the message, but on the lips of important Catholic figures.

Let's begin with Cardinal Gibbons, who stated in a speech at the Catholic University of America on January 19, 1897:

> If I had the privilege of modifying the Constitution of the United States, I would not expunge or alter a single paragraph, a single line, or a single word of that important instrument. The Constitution is admirably adapted to the growth and expansion of the Catholic religion, and the Catholic religion is admirably adapted to the genius of the Constitution. They fit together like two links in the same chain.

The same prelate returned to this theme twelve years later in the *North American Review* of March 1909: "American Catholics rejoice in our separation of Church and state, and I can conceive no combination of circumstances likely to arise which would make a union desirable for either Church or state."

It seems to me exceedingly unlikely that the Leo XIII whose gigantic and impressive statue sits in the grand foyer of CUA's McMahon Hall would be able to approve of these sentiments. Indeed, he expressly taught the contrary in his encyclical *Longinqua Oceani* and in his letter *Testem Benevolentiae* directed, meaningfully, to this very cardinal, not to mention a host of social encyclicals like *Immortale Dei* and *Libertas Praestantissimum*.[4]

Another Americanist of distinction was Isaac Hecker (1819–1888), founder of the Paulist Fathers, who is quoted as saying:

> The form of government of the United States is preferable to Catholics above other forms. It is more favorable than others to the practice of those virtues which are the necessary conditions of the development of the religious life of man. This government leaves men a larger margin of liberty of action, and hence for cooperation with the guidance of the Holy Spirit, than any other government under the sun. With these popular institutions men enjoy greater liberty in working out their true destiny. The Catholic Church will therefore flourish all the more in this republican country in proportion as her representatives keep, in their civil life, to the lines of their republicanism.[5]

---

[4] Tradition-loving Catholics are not all agreed, however, on how best to interpret the founding philosophy of the American Republic, nor do they equally bemoan the Americanism identified by Pope Leo XIII. See Jay, "Americanism—A Phantom Heresy?"; Vree and Storck, eds., *Catholics and the American Polity*.

[5] Elliott, *The Life of Father Hecker*, 293.

And yet, even one so wedded to Vatican-II-style religious liberty and the separation of Church and state as John Courtney Murray had the perspicacity to see, and the honest to state, the real situation "on the ground" (this, in a lecture at Loyola University in Baltimore in 1940):

> American culture, as it exists, is actually the quintessence of all that is decadent in the culture of the Western Christian world. It would seem to be erected on the triple denial that has corrupted Christian culture at its roots, the denial of metaphysical reality, the primacy of the spiritual over the material, of the social over the individual.... Its most striking characteristic is its profound materialism.... It has given citizens everything to live for and nothing to die for. And its achievement may be summed up thus: It has gained a continent and lost its own soul.[6]

Such a blistering assessment brings to mind G. K. Chesterton's quip in the *New York Times* of February 1, 1931: "There is nothing the matter with Americans except their ideals. The real American is all right; it is the ideal American who is all wrong."

Traditionalist historian Henry Sire — a man of dual origin, Spanish and English — offers critical remarks about the role America played in the dechristianization of the world and the decatholicizing of the Church:

> Across the Atlantic, there was a new Protestant power, adding its strength to those of Europe, and here, too, the work of sapping Catholic societies was prominent. It had already been seen in the French Revolution, in which the American example was influential, and the process continued in the nineteenth century. The United States, like Britain, supported the

---

[6] Murray, "The Construction of a Christian Culture."

revolt of Spanish America, and in 1867 they
were directly responsible for the victory of an
anti-clerical regime in Mexico.

A less commonly noticed achievement was
that of decatholicising the lands—the seaboards
of the Gulf of Mexico and the Pacific—which
the United States acquired by purchase or conquest between 1803 and 1848. For a contrast,
we may look to the case of Quebec after its
annexation by Britain; a policy of respecting
the native institutions allowed Quebec to sur-
vive essentially as a traditional Catholic society.
A different fate was that of the Spanish and
French colonies that fell to republican expansion, as their institutions were overruled in
favour of the self-evident truths of Thomas
Jefferson. Yet it would be petty to find fault
with the American Republic merely for what
it did to Catholic societies. It also followed
the career of territorial expansion led by its
Protestant precursors, Holland and Britain.
The empire that those powers built up in far-
off lands was available to the Americans on
their doorstep.

It is not generally remarked that the United
States is the only country in the modern world
which in the recent past—specifically the years
from 1811 to 1898—has acquired its national territory by dispossessing the existing inhabitants
and by launching wars of aggression against its
neighbours; but that record has not hampered
the United States from presenting itself as the
world's moral pastor in international affairs, so
successfully has democracy been identified
with virtue and innocence.

Internally, the years after the Civil War
became known for their corruption and political manipulation, and for the rise of the rob-
ber barons of large-scale capitalism, showing
that the country's domestic morality matched

that in foreign relations. By that period, the United States was taking the place of Britain as the example of modernity. American society became the leader in advances against the older Christian ethos, a trend that became stronger in the twentieth century. The undermining of sexual morality included, amongst other signs, a growing fashion for divorce, encouraged by the strength of the feminist movement. A Protestant tradition that busied itself in imposing teetotalism and biblical literalism was engaged in looking the wrong way while these vices stole upon it.[7]

After that sobering passage, it does not seem quite right to say among ourselves in the USA, "Happy Independence Day!," much less (in keeping with the *faux* new rite optional memorial) "*Blessed* Independence Day!" Rather, we might say, as indeed all Catholic citizens of any Western country at this time must say: *Miserere nostri, Domine, quia peccavimus tibi.*

All Catholics should be patriots, meaning, lovers of their land, people, upright customs, and homegrown arts — and, moreover, should desire and work for the conversion of their nation to the one true Faith so that Church and state may rule harmoniously together. For these reasons, American Catholics cannot be too careful to purify their patriotism of the defects of Americanism.

---

[7] Sire, *Phoenix from the Ashes*, 133–34.

14

....

CONSERVATISM IS PART OF
THE PROBLEM, NOT PART
OF THE SOLUTION

IN THESE DARK TIMES OF OURS,
both in the state and in the Church, one cannot
help musing on some of the essential differences
between Christian conservatives and traditional Catholics. I am writing with the American situation in
mind, but elements of this reflection admit of application to other Western countries.

For the conservative (whether Catholic or evangelical), the solution or restoration begins with the Declaration and the Constitution, with the reclaiming of the
public sphere. We are Americans, and our government
system gives us the tools to solve our problems. The
fundamental thing is *action*. The enemy is taking the
ground because we are not fighting, not voting, not
pressing our cause through thick and thin.

The central organizing concept for the conservative
is *American citizenship*. It is around this axis that all
other aspects of life and action revolve.

Discipleship is understood as *engagement with the
world*. All other things are judged according to how they
fit or seem to fit with this goal.

Evangelization is understood as going out into the
street and bringing a certain message to people. It means
ecumenical and interreligious outreach to make common
cause, looking for strength in numbers—often, in consequence, grouped around a lowest common denominator.
("You're heterosexual and believe that marriage has something to do with children? Fantastic! Let's join forces.")

For a conservative, the liturgy is a means — one means among many. It is a useful tool. One does not concern oneself much with it, or the manner of its offering, whether or not it has suffered damage at the hands of clumsy repairmen, how it is expressive and formative, and if it could be more or less pleasing to God or even displeasing to Him. It is part of a toolkit we have been given by the authorities, and we make use of it to support the cause. Ours is not to reason why; if it's good enough for the authorities, it's good enough for me.

For the traditional Catholic, the solution or restoration begins with and remains centered on the Holy Sacrifice of the Mass. It must begin with the recovery of the sacred liturgy, font and apex of the Church's life and mission,[1] and with it, the contemplative orientation of life as a whole. The fundamental thing is *prayer*, public and personal. The enemy is winning because we have been lazy, contemptuous, irreverent, and worldly, when we should have been seeking first the kingdom of God and His righteousness.[2] "We have here no abiding city, but we seek one that is to come."[3]

The central organizing concept is *our citizenship in heaven.*[4] We know that our spiritual identity as members of the Body of Christ makes continual demands of us in this world — we are, after all, pilgrims working out our salvation here and now, as we travel and travail. At the same time, however, our heavenly rebirth and destiny decisively subordinate and relativize everything worldly, because our own salvation and that of the whole human race depends on God's grace and our spiritual bond with Him. This, therefore, is what has to come *first* and receive our best focus and energy, or else everything else will fall apart and even turn against us. We will be in danger of manicuring the lawn and painting the shutters while family relationships deteriorate indoors.

---

[1] Cf. Vatican II, *Sacrosanctum Concilium* 10 and *Lumen Gentium* 11.
[2] Mt 6:33   [3] Heb 13:14.   [4] See Phil 3:20.

Discipleship means, above all, entering into the prayer of Christ and the Church through the sacred liturgy, integrally received, reverently celebrated, fully lived. Evangelization is understood as building a city on a hill, putting the light on top of the bushel basket, and letting the beauty of Christian life exercise an attractive force of its own. It means prioritizing the affairs of our *own* house, adhering to the fullness of the Faith and settling for no internal compromises, and accepting—in a time of growing infidelity and persecution—a process of social marginalization that also brings about purification.

Can conservatives and traditionalists work together? In one sense, it's obvious that they have to try. There is, after all, *some* wisdom in making a common cause against the enemy, in spite of a lack of total agreement. But it won't be easy, because there is a lack of clear agreement about the very nature of the crisis we are facing and, consequently, the response called for.

Indeed, there is alarming evidence that many conservatives, who tend to think on the procedural plane of politics and economics, do not even recognize the deeper spiritual, liturgical, and metaphysical crisis, and get impatient with those who point in that direction.[5] One is reminded of members of the hierarchy who say that issues like immigration, unemployment, climate change, or loneliness among senior citizens are the great challenges of our age. One wonders whether the sense of the supernatural survives at all.

It is so easy for our priorities to get shuffled and out of order, from the best of motives as well as the worst. We can start to feel as if we will lose everything if we lose our government, our place in society, our semi-Christian culture, our Western civilization—or, for that matter, our clean air and clean water. We have put all our eggs in a worldly basket, and the basket's being

---

[5] See Morello, *Mysticism, Magic, and Monasteries* and *Unto the Ages of Ages.*

taken away. The "free world" is in a state of freefall, as rulers and citizens welcome with open arms the demons of the seven capital sins. The public square, which was already full of mendacity, rancor, avarice, and incredible obtuseness, is gearing up for full-scale persecution of Catholics, Christians, believers, sane men. Why is all of this being permitted to happen before our very eyes?

Why did the Lord permit the Jews to be carried off in captivity to Babylon, their temple in Jerusalem destroyed, their lives ruined and wrecked, their future utterly bleak, as if He had abandoned them? He was always going to save them—but not before they had been thoroughly purged of their vices and converted from the depths of their souls. They had to get over being their own king and awaken to a longing for the Messiah. Salvation history "rhymes" and we are at one of those rhyming moments. The same captivity is being allowed to befall us, for much the same reason, and with much the same purpose.

The Lord is telling us something that we have been ignoring in our distracted rushing around as well as in our satisfied indolence.

> *Be still, and know that I am God. I am your Creator and Ruler. I am your merciful Savior—and I demand your entire mind and heart because I am merciful and you need Me. I am a consuming fire. I am the Judge of the living and the dead. I have put you on this earth for a short time, to know, love, and serve Me.*

"You have looked for more, and behold it became less, and you brought it home, and I blowed it away: why, saith the Lord of hosts? Because my house is desolate, and you make haste every man to his own house."[6]

> *Put first things first, and I will give you everything else that you need. Put second things first,*

---

[6] Hag 1:9.

and I will take away from you both the second things and the first, because you deserve neither of them. My servant Augustine said: The sinner is not worthy of the bread he eats. Do you grasp this difficult truth?

Another of my servants, Benedict, said: Put nothing before the work of God, that is, the worship of My Holy Name. Get your temple in order—offer Me due sacrifice, the praise of pure hearts and holy lips—and I will visit you again with My fruitfulness, and you will flourish once more in the lands and in the cities.

* * *

The reaction to Archbishop Viganò's revelations in the summer of 2018—at least in the United States—should give us heart: there are still bishops of orthodox faith who respect human rights and divine justice.[7] Moreover, in spite of the almost daily bad news from Rome, we find dioceses in which vocations are on the rise and traditional religious communities that are flourishing. After decades of amnesia, sacred music is returning to cathedrals and parishes. Recognizably Catholic churches are being raised once more to the glory of God. Good news is not lacking if one looks for it.

Nevertheless, we can also still see a longstanding problem that slows down the pace of overdue reform and genuine renewal in the Church: the predominance of the basic stance of *conservatism* among bishops, priests, and faithful.

A conservative is one who wishes to *conserve* the good at hand, which means maintaining the status quo while correcting notorious deviations. But the conservative has no principled motivation to return to and recover what has been lost, for he has no compelling

---

[7] In recent years, Viganò has wandered along questionable paths, but as my concern is not with him personally, I will leave aside further discussion of him at present.

reason to see it as *more* precious, *more* valuable, than a constellation of goods that happens to exist right now. ("Are there religious sisters who wear a kind of uniform and a crucifix? Great! Let's keep that going, for we don't want to lose it. After all, something's better than nothing.") The lover of tradition, on the other hand, has the mind of the fifth-century father of the Church, St. Vincent of Lérins. For Vincent, as for a host of fathers, doctors, and popes, tradition *as such* is superior to novelty; novelty is to be distrusted, resisted with all one's might. ("If nuns are not wearing full habits with veils, time to give them two alternatives: embrace the traditional attire, or return to the world.")

Consequently, wherever traditional things have been lost, the traditionalist strives to restore them as fully as possible, whereas the conservative contents himself with preserving what is at hand—even if it may be mediocre in itself or was a novelty only a few years back. This helps explain the bizarre fact that, after so much bitter experience and so many irrefutable critiques, one still finds Catholic conservatives defending the Novus Ordo and popular church music. "These things are a few *decades* old, you know, and they're what we've got right now, so we might as well conserve them!"

Thus, conservatism, in the end, turns out to be a slower, less self-conscious version of liberalism. Liberalism takes as a principle that change is inherently good and, thus, that faster change is even better—as long as the change is in any direction *away* from tradition. Conservatism takes as its supposedly contrary principle that it is better to hold on to what one has than to give it up without a fight, but it fails to recognize the problem that, due to the prevailing liberalism, more and more good things are ignored, undermined, and surrendered with each passing year, leaving less and less to conserve.

For these reasons, *conservatism is liberalism in slow motion.* What conservatives preserve, they preserve by force of custom and free choice, not by the firmness of a non-negotiable principle. As the truth fades away and people grow accustomed to its loss, the conservative has no ground to stand on; he wrings his hands while he watches beautiful things getting dismantled and sent away. Sometimes it's worse than that: the conservative will drive himself insane, zealously defending the same horrible novelties he would have decried only a few years before. We've seen this rubbery allegiance time and again. For example, it's wrong to wash women's feet at Mass on Holy Thursday—until the pope says it's okay. Suddenly, out come the specious arguments to back it up, as if it had been true all along! "A conservatism of the wrong, the false, and the hideous means only degradation."[8]

In contrast, adherence to tradition goes beyond conservation of whatever minimal good (let alone whatever tolerated but customary evil) is at hand, for such adherence demands the love and honorable defense of an inheritance that is received and must not be squandered. And if part of this inheritance *has* been lost, the traditionalist endeavors to restore it. Accordingly, traditionalists are and must be, by the nature of their allegiance to tradition, reformers, in the same way that figures like St. John of the Cross and St. Teresa of Avila were reformers. Wherever a traditionalist sees a serious deviation from tradition, he strives to reinstate what is venerable. "So what if we've had fifty-five years of vernacular Novus Ordo Masses, facing the people, with bad music? That's nothing in comparison with well over 1,500 years of tradition. We must return to what is most richly and most perfectly Catholic."

The problem comes down to this. If you do not understand Tradition, both as a formal principle and as material content, you cannot possibly see what is wrong with the status quo—you have no means of comparison, no proportionality. If you hold on to something not

---

[8] Birzer, *Beyond Tenebrae*, 5.

because of principle, but only out of sentimentality or habit, it will sooner or later be taken away from you. The inverse is also true: if you hold on to something because it is true and good and beautiful, it can never be taken away from your mind and heart, even if it may be suppressed in the world and you may suffer persecution. In due time, the Lord will raise it from the dead and give it a new life, contrary to all the predictions of the "experts."

Because many of the "best" bishops today are merely conservatives and not lovers of tradition, they have little desire to recover, to restore, to hand down the inheritance in full. It seems to me that there are three reasons for this flaw: (1) they are not intimately acquainted with tradition, nor with how it has been lost; (2) they do not *desire* to know its worth, or even to inquire what kind of tragedy its loss might be; (3) they are content with the status quo, provided it be kept free from what they see as obvious excesses or distortions.

On this third point, major subjectivism enters in, because what is seen as a deviation will vary a great deal from one conservative to another. For instance, one conservative will see lay extraordinary ministers of Holy Communion and female altar servers as they truly are — an offensive break with unanimous Eastern and Western tradition going back to the earliest liturgical and canonical records available to us — while another may see such practices as mere administrative or bureaucratic decisions, with no serious repercussions. In this way, conservatives end up losing their influence because their lack of principled adherence to tradition leaves them splintered, tentative, and unwilling to draw any line in the sand. They wait ... and watch ... and lose Catholicism, bit by bit, year by year.

It is the argument of cowardice, or at the very least, a sad lack of imagination, to say: "It's just not possible in this day and age to implement this or that reform" or

"It's been too long—we can't recover that old belief or practice," or "don't let the best be enemy of the good." Yes, but the bad or the worst is also the enemy of the good; old things are continually being revived, such as the Hebrew language in Israel; and why are we putting limitations on ourselves and especially on God as to what is possible and what is impossible? *Do we know what is possible until we try it or pray for God to grant it?*

Every serious reform movement in the history of the Church has risen up against impossible odds and won by God's grace. Every serious reform movement has based itself on past tradition that had been lost, obscured, or diluted. The victories we enjoy in the midst of this vale of tears will always be temporary, but they are not unreal for not being eternal, and they were purchased not without unbending faith, hope against hope, and the gritty charity that seeks the best and thrusts away evil.

If we do not fight for tradition, we will end up fighting for yesterday's status quo, which gets worse and worse with the passing of each godless decade of the post-Christian secular world. That is why we have all experienced or known about parishes where things never seem to get much better, regardless of how well-intentioned the new pastor may be. Out there in the mainstream world inhabited and fought over by liberals and conservatives, the "bar," the standard of Catholicism, is always sinking, sometimes faster, sometimes slower. There is no upward force of tradition to prevent it from sinking into Gehenna.

Why is Divine Providence permitting catastrophic or cowardly pontificates, with all the evils they spawn or bring to light? I truly believe (to the extent that any of us can discern the mysterious ways of God) that He is issuing a stern wake-up call to serious Latin-rite Catholics everywhere: abandon the sinking ship of Vatican II Catholicism; abandon the fabricated liturgy of Paul VI;

abandon a confused theology that wants to speak out of both sides of the mouth; abandon compromise with worldliness in morals; and return to the safe, spacious, and sustaining haven of Tradition—traditional doctrine as found in Sacred Scripture, dogmatic councils, and countless old catechisms; traditional morals as exemplified in the lives and exhortations of the saints; traditional theology as practiced by the Church Fathers and Doctors; and most importantly, *traditional liturgy*, stretching from before the time of St. Gregory the Great (d. 604) through St. Pius V (*Quo Primum*, 1570) and beyond, handed down and received as a precious inheritance, without any massive break or reconstruction according to the Zeitgeist.

If our ecclesiastical crisis is telling us anything, it is telling us this: stop pretending the Church can accommodate modernity and its panoply of errors, just as long as she window-dresses everything with pious language and vague appeals to a hermeneutic of continuity. Stop reassuring yourself that *aggiornamento*, contrary to the frequent admissions of its advocates and the plenteous ruination caused by their ideas, meant just an updating of incidentals and didn't touch the essence of the Faith. Stop thinking you can serve two masters: "What concord hath Christ with Belial? Or what part hath the faithful with the unbeliever?"[9]

In short: *Give up the conservatism.* Replace low-fat liberalism with the raw milk of tradition. Begin the longed-for renewal of the Church by nourishing your soul on the feast God has been preparing for you for 2,000 years, "a feast of fat things, a feast of wine, of fat things full of marrow, of wine purified from the lees."[10] As for recent novelties, it seems best—indeed, it seems unavoidable—to let the dead bury the dead.

---

[9] 2 Cor 6:15.
[10] Is 25:6.

15

IMPLACABLE ENEMIES

A S WE HAVE ARGUED, THE CONVER-
sion of societies is the natural consequence of
the conversion of souls. Those who receive
Christ in their hearts receive Him also into the world
they live in, and progressively change it for the better.
There will never be "heaven on earth" for fallen man,
but the Christian life can be heaven's antechamber, with
blessings from above descending on families, friendships,
and cultural pursuits here below.

The Father of Lies and the Enemy of Human Nature
despises the love, joy, stability, and sanctity that Jesus
Christ brings into the world of sinners. The devil and
his minions labor to deceive the children of light with
promises of a new and better light—one that will liberate them from law, faith, and self-denial. Nor does
he show himself manifestly; rather, he works through
"fronts" in the form of movements and organizations
that advance his will without exposing his hand.

When it comes to the nature and aims of the international, quasi-religious society known as Freemasonry,
disagreement has been the rule, not the exception.
For every book that emphasizes the law-abidingness,
philanthropy, and tolerant universalism of masonic
organizations, another book condemns them for their
hidden role in political upheavals or the *Kulturkampf*
against the Catholic Church, while still others extol, or
mock, their esoteric doctrine and elaborate ritualism.
Research is complicated by the fact that Freemasonry
is not a single entity, but a conceptual whole made up
of regional networks of lodges and sister organizations,
each with rituals, doctrines, and enterprises more or

less similar to those of others—rather as we speak of "Protestantism" when there are hundreds of independent sects with more or less overlapping beliefs and practices.[1]

Freemasonry may be defined as "a system of morality veiled in allegory and illustrated by symbols,"[2] or, as a German handbook from 1822 puts it,

> the activity of closely united men who, employing symbolical forms borrowed principally from the mason's trade and from architecture, work for the welfare of mankind, striving morally to ennoble themselves and others and thereby to bring about a universal league of mankind, which they aspire to exhibit even now on a small scale.[3]

"The origin of Freemasonry is one of the most debated, and debatable, subjects in the whole realm of historical inquiry," declares Frances Yates. One must carefully separate what can be established by serious historical investigation from the legendary and fanciful accounts found in traditional texts, both masonic and anti-masonic. Modern Freemasonry emerged not in eighteenth-century England, as is often asserted, but in early seventeenth-century Scotland, when the "medieval contribution of craft organisation and legend" was combined with "aspects of Renaissance thought . . . along with an institutional structure based on lodges and the rituals and the secret procedures for recognition know as the Mason Word."[4]

Originally, lodges concerned themselves with the working lives of stonemasons (in this respect, as also in the use of religious symbolism and paraliturgical ritual, continuing the precedent of medieval trade guilds), but by the middle of the seventeenth century a significant number of members had no real connection with this craft, and were assembling for social and ritual purposes. By the start of the eighteenth century, the

---

[1] Whalen, *Christianity and American Freemasonry*, 169–86 *et passim*.
[2] Whalen, 15.   [3] Gruber, "Freemasonry."
[4] Stevenson, *Origins of Freemasonry*, 6.

English lodges, composed mainly of gentlemen and not of working stonemasons, assumed a certain preeminence, and began shifting the theoretical platform toward the cutting edge of Enlightenment thought. By the middle of the same century, this English brand of Freemasonry had spread to every corner of Europe and the New World, changing rapidly into an agent of revolutionary ideology and praxis.[5]

It was this Enlightenment Freemasonry that the popes so vehemently opposed, once they had seen the danger it represented for integrity of faith and tranquility of order.[6] Radicals among eighteenth-century Freemasons openly supported secularizing policies such as the dissolution of religious orders, the expropriation and redistribution of church property, civil marriage and divorce legislation, political toleration for non-Catholic religions, and compulsory state-run schooling for children, all of which became hallmarks of nineteenth-century continental European liberalism.

The Church's reaction began in earnest during the pontificate of Clement XII (1730–1740), who with his constitution *In Eminenti* of 1738 became the first pope to condemn Freemasonry. (For context, the Grand Lodge of London, a foremost symbol of the organization, was founded in 1717, and the first Provincial Grand Master in North America was appointed in 1730.) Condemnations were repeated, often with mounting severity and appeals to civil authorities to take action, by Benedict XIV in 1751, Pius VII in 1821, Leo XII in 1825, Pius VIII in 1829, Gregory XVI in 1832, and Bd. Pius IX in a number of documents ranging from *Qui Pluribus* of 1846 to *Etsi Multa* in 1873.

The papal objections against Freemasonry may be reduced to four heads: its commitment to a philo-

---

[5] For a good overview of the different kinds of Freemasons and for discussion of how they nearly destroyed the country of Mexico, see Ravasi, *The Cristero Counterrevolution*, 165–81.

[6] See Whalen, *Christianity and American Freemasonry*, 136–49.

sophical naturalism that inevitably results in religious indifferentism; its character of secrecy, which cloaks evil designs; its demand for oaths of total fidelity when such oaths cannot be morally justified; the danger presented to the security and tranquility of the civil order by the existence of secret societies.

Of the papal encyclicals dedicated to the subject, the greatest and most influential has been *Humanum Genus*, promulgated by Leo XIII in 1884. After reminding his readers of the Church's unchanging verdict, Leo XIII offers a summary and critique of Freemasonry's philosophico-religious principles and revolutionary activities. "Their ultimate purpose," he writes, is

> the utter overthrow of that whole religious and political order of the world which the Christian teaching has produced, and the substitution of a new state of things in accordance with their ideas, of which the foundations and laws shall be drawn from mere naturalism. (10)

Since the "fundamental doctrine" of this system is "that human nature and human reason ought in all things to be mistress and guide" (12), "they endeavor to bring [it] about . . . that the teaching office and authority of the Church may become of no account in the civil state" and "imagine that states ought to be constituted without any regard for the laws and precepts of the Church" (13). They hold, too, that "power [to rule] is held by the command or permission of the people" and so "the source of all rights and civil duties is either in the multitude or in its governing authority when this is constituted according to the latest [Enlightenment] doctrines" (22).

Leo XIII identifies a number of characteristic tenets or tendencies of masonic thought: a humanism aspiring to universal brotherhood apart from obedience to Christ and the Church; a moral Pelagianism that denies original sin and locates the spring of virtue and happiness primarily in the self-governed human will; a

deism that accepts the existence of a God conceived of
as architect of nature while rejecting special revelation,
miracles, and the divinity of Christ; an indifferentism
whereby all religions are held to be equal in value when
reduced to analogous symbolic languages for hinting
at divine things. These views are unequivocally condemned by the pope as contrary to the Catholic faith
and, not seldom, as contradicting reason itself (24).[7]

Though issued almost a century and a half ago, *Humanum Genus* has lost none of its relevance; one may note,
for instance, its searching analysis of the consequences
of masonic principles. What the pope predicts will
happen has now happened throughout the Western
world, and for exactly the reasons he gives. The critique
is accompanied by a counter-proposal to find in the
Christian gospel the liberating power for human society
vainly sought for in ideologies. Indeed, the slogan of the
French Revolution, a veritable motto of Freemasonry, is
invested by the pope with a Christian meaning:

> The *liberty*, We mean, of sons of God, through
> which we may be free from slavery to Satan or
> to our passions...; the *fraternity* whose origin
> is in God, the common Creator and Father
> of all; the *equality* which, founded on justice
> and charity, does not take away all distinctions
> among men, but, out of the varieties of life,
> of duties, and of pursuits, forms that union
> and that harmony which naturally tend to the
> benefit and dignity of society. (34)

Though it was the most important, *Humanum Genus*
was not the sole word of Leo XIII on Freemasonry;
he also censured it in documents from the years 1882,
1890, 1894, and 1902.

In the twentieth century, pronouncements specifically targeting Freemasonry are scarce, not because

---

[7] See "Freemasonry and Allied Societies" in Cahill, *Framework
of a Christian State*, 221–41.

the Church renounced or modified her stance, but because that stance needed no further clarification in the wake of Leo XIII. From Clement XII down to Leo XIII, a single, most severe penalty was appointed for any Catholic who joined the Lodge: *latae sententiae* excommunication. The *Code of Canon Law* issued by Benedict XV in 1917 expressly repeated this warning.

In the wake of Vatican II, some suggested that the time for rapprochement between Catholics and Freemasons was at hand. This idea was taken seriously by the German bishops who entered into dialogue with representatives of the German lodges between 1974 and 1980. The ensuing inquiry led to an unsurprising judgment: "Simultaneous membership of the Catholic Church and of Freemasonry is impossible."[8] When the new *Code of Canon Law* was issued in 1983, certain people interpreted its lack of any explicit mention of Freemasonry as a quiet softening of the Church's prohibition. To quell this false interpretation, in the same year the Congregation for the Doctrine of the Faith, with the approval of John Paul II, published a Declaration stating that

> the Church's negative position on Masonic associations ... remains unaltered, since their principles have always been regarded as irreconcilable with the Church's doctrine. Hence joining them remains prohibited by the Church. Catholics enrolled in Masonic associations are involved in serious sin and may not approach Holy Communion.[9]

Bishop Athanasius Schneider has done the Church a signal service by once again highlighting the issue. His talk "The True Face of Freemasonry," given in 2017

---

[8] *Amtsblatt der Erbistums Köln,* June 1980, cited in Whalen, *Christianity and American Freemasonry,* 144. Whalen's is the best book in English that I know of concerning the opposition in principles between modern Freemasonry and the Catholic religion.

[9] The Declaration may be found in Whalen, 195–96.

on the three-hundredth anniversary of the founding of modern Freemasonry in London, is well worth reading.[10]

One should not be misled into thinking that the Catholic Church stands alone in her suspicion of the Lodge. Leaving aside the condemnations of Freemasonry by Protestant and Eastern Orthodox Christians,[11] monarchs and statesmen of the last two hundred years took an active interest in so-called secret societies, which were assumed, and very often proved, to be entertaining views or promoting schemes subversive of the established order, often functioning as nerve-centers of intrigue on a global scale.

Far from being idle guesswork, the involvement of Freemasons in anti-authoritarian (particularly anticlerical) ventures from the Enlightenment period well into the twentieth century can be taken as a basic fact of modern history, though evidently it cannot be assumed that the lodges of each country were equally occupied with political machinations (the lodges of the Grand Orient in continental Europe and Latin America, considered "heretical" by the mainstream English-speaking Freemasons, contain the highest concentration of anticlericals and revolutionaries), nor that lower-ranking members knew what their superiors were doing or why; arguably the majority of Freemasons have only a superficial interest in the religious and political doctrine of the Lodge. Given the discipline of secrecy that has reigned among them for centuries, many historical lines of causality remain at best obscure, at worst unknowable.

Nevertheless, that the Freemasons are witting or unwitting collaborators of the deceiver, the father of lies, the accuser, the "light-bearer," is, given what we do know, beyond all reasonable doubt. A future pope in the image of Leo XIII will once more become their implacable antagonist, and future states, recast on Christian lines, will once again rightly seek their suppression.

---

[10] Schneider, "The True Face of Freemasonry."
[11] See Whalen, *Christianity and American Freemasonry*, 150–68.

16

....

THE GLORY OF THE
CHRISTIAN RAINBOW

T HERE IS SOMETHING NOT ONLY
publicly offensive but positively demonic about
the way in which both the rainbow and the
month traditionally dedicated to the Sacred Heart of
Jesus have been violently appropriated by one of the
most socially and morally destructive forces in the
world, the LGBTQ+ movement. Thus, when Fr. James
Martin, SJ, says that churches ought to observe June
as "Pride Month"[1] and that in so doing, they would be
embodying the message of the Sacred Heart devotion,
he could not be more mistaken.

It hardly needs to be stated among Christians that
the rainbow is, first and foremost, *God's* sign, and any
legitimate use of it must be tied back to the significa-
tion *He* gave it:

> I will set my bow in the clouds, and it shall
> be the sign of a covenant between me, and
> between the earth. And when I shall cover the
> sky with clouds, my bow shall appear in the
> clouds: And I will remember my covenant with
> you, and with every living soul that beareth
> flesh: and there shall no more be waters of a
> flood to destroy all flesh. And the bow shall
> be in the clouds, and I shall see it, and shall
> remember the everlasting covenant, that was
> made between God and every living soul of all
> flesh which is upon the earth. And God said
> to Noe: This shall be the sign of the covenant

---

[1] Haynes, "Fr. James Martin urges Catholics to celebrate LGBT
'Pride Month.'"

which I have established between me and all
flesh upon the earth.[2]

Noah's Ark is a scriptural image of the vessel of God's
salvation. Being in the Ark is being in Christ, in His
Body, the Church. The raging flood of sin and vice
drowns and destroys those who are caught up in it,
but those who pass through the waters of baptism—
through the mystery of the death and resurrection
of Christ—have their sins washed away and receive
the grace of divine adoption. As the human race was
preserved for temporal life in Noah and his family, so
is it saved for eternal life in the Church.

The rainbow, one of the most uplifting glimpses of
beauty in the natural world (and also, like the wind of
the Holy Spirit that "blows where it will," one of the
most elusive and surprising), was given as a divine sign
and symbol of the promise following upon salvation
from the flood-waters of destruction. God would not
destroy the earth again . . . by *water*. Next time, at the
end of time, the earth will be destroyed by *fire*. The
ambivalence of the water imagery (drowning or giving
life) is paralleled by the ambivalence of the fire imagery
(burning up with lust or enkindling with love).[3]

REAL (NOT PRETEND) DIVERSITY

In addition, the rainbow reminds us of the *genuine*
diversity to be found in the Church of Christ, which
brings together Jews and Gentiles, slaves and free, men
and women, all nations, cultures, races, peoples, into
a single family of God. The saints, perfected by their
union with Christ, are at the same time the most vivid
personalities in human history, with the most distinctive faces. Theologian Sergius Bulgakov calls the host
of saints "God's rainbow":

---

[2] Gen 9:13–17.
[3] See Kwasniewski, "God as Fire."

I pray to the saints of God, I look upon their faces in their icons and call them each by name, I converse with them, I pray to them for my needs and together with them I pray to the Lord of glory. The saints in their icons surround my home altar and serve with me, praying along with me. Wondrous is God in His saints [Ps. 67:36 Douay-Rheims], and blessed is the man who is with God's saints. *This is God's rainbow*, this is the angelic-human choir that, together with us sinners and together with me, a wretch, prays to God. They do not abhor my wretchedness, and I do not grow ashamed, but instead I call upon them. Our love for the saints becomes ever warmer, more palpable, more vital, the more we pray to them, and their love for us in return becomes even more ardent—if this "more" is even possible for them. And yet the saints of God are people, and for them there exists an eternal more, and they grow richer in God by love for us through our prayers to them. This is the circle of human interconnectedness, linking heaven with earth, sinful humans and the saints of God; this is the palpability of the church visible and invisible, *this is the rainbow*, the bridge of our ascension from earth to heaven. And all the saints respond to our prayers, each saint to every prayer, regarding whatever we ask of them, and they speak in their own tongue to their own people: St. Nicholas to his, St. Sergius to his, St. Seraphim to his, the Greatmartyr Panteleimon to his, Mary Magdalene, the Greatmartyr Barbara...Wondrous is God in His saints, the God of Israel![4]

In the wonderful painting of the Last Judgment by Marx Reichlich (South German, active ca. 1485–1520), Our Lord is depicted as seated on a rainbow that joins

---

[4] Bulgakov, *Spiritual Diary*, 122–23, emphasis added.

Our Lady and the Forerunner to Him. He is the Lord
of creation and the King of the saints, the unity from
which all diversity flows, and to which all must return
in order to be natural, right, good, and blessed. This
too is what the month of June, traditionally dedicated
to the Sacred Heart—since the year 1673, I have seen
it said—is meant to remind us of: He loved us first,
and by His love, by what He did for us and gives to us,
we learn whom to love and how to love. Apart from
Him there is only demonic unnaturalness, perversity,
malice, and misery.

INVERTING THE SYMBOL

> The worst month of the year begins. June—the
> month of the Sacred Heart—has been taken
> over by perversion. The love that dares not
> speak its name screams all month long in our
> faces. You cannot get away. Rainbows every-
> where. You are tempted to stay inside, lower
> the shades, like the three days of darkness,
> praying for the demons to pass by.[5]

It is a very ancient understanding of the spirit of Antichrist that it mimics and mocks Christ. It takes what is
His, and inverts it. A moral or doctrinal inversion of a
Christian symbol perforce becomes a demonic symbol.
For example, an upside-down cross—if it is not in the
specific context of a depiction of the Apostle Peter,
who was martyred upside-down—is an anti-cross or
a rejection of the cross of Christ. That the rainbow,
sign of God's covenant with restored creation, was
affixed to a flag representing grave depravity and even
the misanthropic destruction of humanity (since "God
created them *male and female*"), is already a clear sign
of the spirit of Antichrist. But we are given one more
indication of this, hiding in plain sight. The demonic

---

[5] Ruse, "Lighting a Candle to Rainbow Zeus."

symbol represents the rainbow with *six* colors—six being the number of *man*, according to ancient numerology—and not *seven*, the number of the divine, as in a natural rainbow.

Any place this flag is hoisted or displayed will be a target of demonic activity and possibly infestation. Wherever it is flown, the banner of Satan is unfurled, in a public contest with the *Vexilla Regis*, the standard of the King.

The connection between, on the one hand, disordered sexuality culminating in one of the "sins that cry out to heaven for vengeance"—sodomy or unnatural sexual relations—and, on the other hand, apostasy, atheism, hatred of God, violent rejection of all sacredness, and idolatry or worship of demons, is a connection illustrated in many pages of Sacred Scripture, particularly in the Old Testament. Into the cauldron may now be stirred the ingredient of transgenderism, which adds to sexual perversion crimes of self-mutilation. The devil, the father of lies, is the ape of God: he cannot create, he can only mock and mar. He will not come up with a new symbol; he will always take an old one and desecrate it, and with transhumanism the ultimate symbol can now be corrupted: the human body.[6]

SOCIAL RESPONSIBILITY: CHRISTIANS, WHERE ARE YOU?

The connection between LGBTQ+ and Satanism isn't even hiding itself any more: Target brought out a "Satan respects pronouns" T-shirt[7] that was quickly scuttled off the floor due to the volume of protests.[8] It is good, of course, that there *were* protests (as with Bud Light's Dylan Mulvaney stunt, which backfired so badly that it

---

[6] See Kwasniewski, *Ministers of Christ*, 3–12.
[7] Sadler, "Designer for Target's pro-LGBT 'pride' collection promotes satanism."
[8] Lamb, "Target removes some LGBT merchandise."

cost the company an astronomical $5 billion),[9] but the forces of darkness are numerous, powerful in worldly resources, and stubborn as hell, and will continue to push the envelope day by day, month by month, year by year, wearing down opposition and winning over the non-committal. We should not give up doing what we can, but we should also recognize that the primary reason to refuse to buy from certain companies is that it would be wrong for us to support them, regardless of whether or not our refusal purchase will make any difference. On Facebook, I saw the following timeline:

> In 1999, Democrat President Bill Clinton declared June "Gay and Lesbian Pride Month." Every year since, the first week in June, Disney uses its facilities to kick off homosexuals' month-long victory celebrations over Christianity. Then 13th thru the 15th of June Disney hosts gay "pride nite" parties in its parks. In 2010 Disney supported Democrat President Barrack Obama's transformation of our military into a sanctuary for homosexuals to openly defy God. Disney vigorously backed the legalization of same-sex marriages. Between 2010 and 2015 Disney and a cooperative America coerced Christian Boy and Girl Scouts clubs into accepting active homosexuals as members, mentors, and Scoutmasters.
>
> Disney movies and cartoons shown in theaters and other venues are riddled with homosexual characters, some blatant, others subtle, subliminal, and suggestive, while others are full-blown homosexual movies. Most of Disney's children's literature is subliminally laced with suggestive homosexualism. Disney is a strong advocate of homosexualizing school children.
>
> Romans 1:26–28 along with 25 other gospels [Bible passages?] emphatically states God

---

[9] Sadler, "Bud Light sales crash 26%."

condemns homosexual conduct: including behaving contrary to one's birth gender. This homosexual depravity condemned by God is Disney-promoted, government-sanctioned, approved by hordes of corporations & companies, embraced by likeminded Americans, and accommodated and tolerated by the majority of Christians. Amazing. How are we Christians handling this? Or are we?

Focused boycotts on Bud Light and Target have had a real effect and have sent signals that capitalists are likely to take seriously, since the only language they speak is money. This is something we all should be much more conscientious about—not that we can avoid every single company or store that promotes the woke agenda, but at least we can avoid the worst of the worst, like Disney. Why give them a single cent or any free rent in our souls? We should have the same attitude toward woke companies that we have toward dioceses where the bishop is running roughshod over the rights of the faithful or promoting an evil agenda: *give them not so much as a penny.*

Our brethren in Africa are setting an example to the whole world by keeping the Faith and choosing truth over the idolatry of Western money, working to pass salutary and sane legislation against the LGBTQ+ agenda—"for our children," as they say.[10] Should we be surprised that Uganda is leading the world in reasonable, correct, proportionate, and sufficient laws on behalf of the family and against moral perversion, when the Ugandan Martyrs died rather than commit the abomination of sodomy with their king?[11] Or that the African

---

[10] Sadler, "Uganda's tough anti-sodomy bill"; Wailzer, "Burkina Faso votes to ban homosexual acts." Currently, homosexual acts are illegal in 60% of African nations.

[11] See Brankin, "Homosexual Immorality Pointed Out by Martyr Charles Lwanga and Companions."

bishops on the whole rejected *Fiducia Supplicans* in a stunning blow to papal power abused?

Wherever they live worldwide, all parents must act now in accord with the law of God and follow their parental instincts, even if the whole world rises up against them, or the progressivist brigade at the Vatican betrays them. Our children are worth every sacrifice to protect them from this Satanic filth.

THE DIFFICULTY OF DIALOGUE

Well-meaning people tell us that we must learn to dialogue with the LGBTQ+ community. I have no doubt that we should try to find effective ways to reach them. But dialogue is often impossible, for the reason that it always goes something like this (as I once saw someone spell it out):

Person: I want to do "X."

Catholic Church: You are free to do it.

Person: But you think "X" is wrong.

Catholic Church: Yes.

Person: Because you want to control me?

Catholic Church: No. You are free to do what you want.

Person: But you think "X" is wrong.

Catholic Church: Yes. But only because I want your ultimate good.

Person: But I want to do "X."

Catholic Church: You are free to do it.

Person: But I want you to say that "X" is good.

Catholic Church: I cannot say that.

Person: Why do you hate me?

Now, more than ever, it will be the *example*, out in the open, of normal, relatively happy, peaceable, compassionate, and clear-thinking Christians that may win over those who find themselves eventually exhausted and disgusted by a life lived contrary to nature and to nature's God, contrary to Christ and His Church, which means, contrary to the basic requirements of human sanity and joy. When someone begins to question what he/she (or any other preferred pronoun) is doing with himself/herself—begins to have doubts, regrets, questions—let us be there to listen and to answer.

But most of all, let us be witnesses to the gospel of life by faithful marriages and children generously welcomed, loved, educated. With God's help, let us fill the world with lovers of God and lovers of each other, in all our wondrous God-willed diversity. This is how we will vindicate the true meaning of the rainbow symbol, which for now lies captive in the hands of our enemies at this stage of the "cosmic edition" of Capture the Flag that we are playing for eternal stakes.[12]

---

[12] One small thing we can do is fly a Sacred Heart flag during June. See Flanders, "It's Time to Purchase Your Sacred Heart Flag for June."

THE KINGSHIP OF JESUS CHRIST

FONT AND APEX OF
THE SOCIAL ORDER

RETRACING OUR STEPS

L ET US RECALL SOME OF THE MAJOR
truths defended thus far.
In Part I, I established that it is legitimate for
the Church to teach on matters of social ethics in the
political, economic, and cultural domains, because moral
theology embraces all the free actions of men—actions
that will be virtuous or vicious, leading individuals
closer to or further away from their single ultimate
end, the Beatific Vision, and leading societies closer
to or further away from the supporting role they are
supposed to play in this attainment of human perfection in Christ. We know, in any case, that the Church
is permitted to teach on social ethics because she *has*,
in fact, over many centuries exercised her magisterium
in precisely this way, and as Catholics we learn from
the magisterium, rather than telling it *a priori* what
subjects it is or is not allowed to engage.[1]

In Part II, I showed that any society, whether it
be the family, the state, or the Church, is necessarily
hierarchical, and that the Christian understanding of
equality, which did more to rid the world of slavery
than anything else has ever done or could do, is at
the same time incompatible with the egalitarianism

---

[1] At the same time, we should be careful not to inflate or exaggerate the status of non-definitive teaching. John Joy is a well-
informed Thomistic guide to this minefield-studded terrain: see
his works *On the Ordinary and Extraordinary Magisterium* and
Disputed Questions on Papal Infallibility.

characteristic of modernity. The division into classes is an inevitable and in fact beneficial aspect of civil society; these classes are capable of working together for the common good.

Since the trio "liberty, fraternity, and equality" is the illusory mantra of modern political revolutions, I turned in chapter 7 to the question of how true liberty, the freedom of the sons of God to pursue excellence and happiness, differs from the licentiousness that leads to misery and nihilism. The relationship between law and liberty is not what moderns have been brainwashed into thinking it is. Good law protects and nurtures the faculty of free will, guiding it along the path of proper growth to maturity, where one desires the good and freely embraces it. Free will, in man's fallen condition, always brings evils in its wake; hence arises the problem of toleration. We saw that the Church has a wise understanding of the balance between tolerating evils that cannot be readily eradicated and succumbing to a relativist mentality that refuses to condemn evils and to work prudently towards their removal.

After these more political topics, the chapters of Part III delved into controversial economic questions that, after all, have profound political implications: the nature of private property in its relationship to the good of the family and the common good of the larger society, and the Church's repeated call for a more equitable distribution of the goods of creation, so that no one may suffer wretched want while another fattens himself off of excess — a situation too easily taken advantage of by socialism and communism, which offer cures worse than the disease. In particular, I tried to show how distributism translates magisterial teaching into practical policies for gradually increasing private ownership without violent upheaval or the need to increase government ownership. It is true that dyed-in-the-wool capitalists will never be convinced,

but the effort to explain how there *are* real alternatives to plutocratic oligarchy is not in vain. Sooner
or later, our decadent civilization will collapse and
another must take its place. Perhaps some version of
distributism will, at that time, find its place in the
rebuilding of a Christian world.

Part IV turned to a category broader than either
politics or economics, namely, the cultural milieu out of
which political regimes and economic practices emerge.
Human beings are political animals who express their
inner world in their outer actions, products, structures,
and systems. Religious people, if they are true to their
religion, will necessarily generate societies that are
religious; this includes governments and markets in
their day-to-day operation. In other words, a Christian
regime and a market that favors truly human goods over
inhuman or anti-human "goods" is a natural outgrowth
of the Faith truly believed and lived.

The Catholic cultural synthesis that was European
Christendom is the great evidence and exemplar of
this process, but it can be seen throughout Western
history at various times and in various places, even if
on a more modest scale. We would risk falling into the
sin of despair if we yielded to discouragement in the
face of the increasing hostility not only towards the
Catholic Church but also towards the natural law and
human reason, for we should see, with supernatural
faith, that the more the truth is rejected, the more its
enemies will suffer deformation and dissolution; and
the more we ourselves live it and defend it, the more
our sweat, and, if God wills it, our blood, will be the
seed of a future Catholic culture out of which a confessional state may in due course arise. "Behold, the
hand of the Lord is not shortened that it cannot save,
neither is His ear heavy that it cannot hear."[2]

---

[2] Is 59:1.

MOUNTING THE SUMMIT

In this fifth and final part, we can step back and take the loftiest as well as the most comprehensive perspective on Catholic Social Teaching by turning to its starting point and goal, the Kingship of Christ. One of the truest, most-quoted, but, alas, least followed teachings of the Second Vatican Council is that the Holy Eucharist is "the source and summit of the Christian life"—or, as other translations read, "font and apex."[3]

By means of an exact analogy, we may say that the Kingship of Christ is the font and apex of the family and of civil society, as well—of any and every human society. Jesus Christ is the God-man from Whom all reality comes and to Whom all rational beings must return for judgment, resulting in either glorification or condemnation. He, as the eternal Word of God and Image of the Father, is the one "through Whom *all things* were made"[4]—including man's social nature and all of its natural and supernatural consequences. As the popes teach, the family as well as the civil order proceeds from God and stands beholden to Him no less than isolated individuals.[5] The preeminent magisterial source on the Kingship of Christ is Pope Pius XI's encyclical *Quas Primas*, which not only expounded the truth out of Scripture and Tradition but also introduced a feast in its honor, beloved to traditional Catholics for a century now.

The month of November begins with the great Solemnity of All Saints. But in the traditional Roman calendar, All Saints is preceded shortly before by an even greater feast—that of the heavenly King who creates and sanctifies the citizens, ambassadors, and soldiers of His Kingdom. When Pius XI instituted the feast of Christ the King in 1925, he was, one might say, supplying in

---

[3] Vatican II, *Lumen Gentium* 11.
[4] Niceno-Constantinopolitan Creed.
[5] See, e.g., Leo XIII, *Immortale Dei* 3 and 6; Pius X, *Vehementer Nos* 3.

the Church's calendar the missing invisible cause of All Saints, as well as making clear just what the mission of the saints in history is: to be living members of the Mystical Body under Christ its Head, and to extend this body across the whole earth. Our Lord Jesus Christ is the King of all men, all peoples, all nations, and His saints are those who, taking up their cross and following Him, have conquered their own souls and won over the souls of many others for this Kingdom.

Pius XI knew that in modern political circumstances, it was absolutely necessary to make this truth explicit:

> All men, whether collectively or individually, are under the dominion of Christ. In Him is the salvation of the individual; in Him is the salvation of society.... He is the author of happiness and true prosperity for every man and for every nation. If, therefore, the rulers of nations wish to preserve their authority, to promote and increase the prosperity of their countries, they will not neglect *the public duty of reverence and obedience to the rule of Christ....* (18)

> When once men recognize, both in private *and in public life*, that Christ is King, society will at last receive the great blessings of real liberty, well-ordered discipline, peace, and harmony.... (19)

> That these blessings may be abundant and lasting in Christian society, it is necessary that the kingship of our Savior should be as widely as possible recognized and understood, and to the end nothing would serve better than the institution of a special feast in honor of the Kingship of Christ. (21)

A little further on (in no. 29), Pius XI makes his intention clear: to emphasize the glory of Christ as the terminus of His *earthly* mission—a glory and mission *visible and perpetuated in history* by the saints. Hence, the feast's placement on the last Sunday of October, shortly before that of All Saints, underlines that the work of salvation inaugurated by Christ in His own person before ascending in glory is then carried further in societies, cultures, and nations by His holy ones. In short, the feast celebrates Christ's ongoing kingship over all reality, *including this present world*, where the Church must fight for the recognition of His rights, the actual extension of His dominion to *all* domains, individual *and social.*[6]

Pius XI unambiguously declared that the feastday he was instituting had *social* dimensions and demands attached to it. "If We ordain that the whole Catholic world shall revere Christ as King," he writes, "We shall minister to the need of the present day, and at the same time *provide an excellent remedy for the plague which now infects society.* We refer to the plague of anticlericalism, its errors and impious activities" (24).[7] With the term "anticlericalism," Pius XI sums up the multifaceted war waged against Catholicism by modern revolutions, characterized by a ferocious and indeed demonic hatred of the clergy, celibacy, religious life, the Holy Sacrifice of the Mass, crucifixes, church buildings, parochial schools, and anything that belonged to or bore the mark of the Church. "Anticlericalism" is a fitting term for all this, because the symbol *par excellence* of Catholicism is the priest vested for Mass, standing at the high altar, facing East towards the Sun of Justice.[8]

---

[6] See Kwasniewski, "Should the Feast of Christ the King Be Celebrated in October or November?"

[7] Here and in other quotations from *Quas Primas*, italics are editorial additions.

[8] It is all the more disturbing that many at the Vatican, including Pope Francis during his twelve-year reign, have aligned themselves with yesterday's and today's anticlericals on so many subjects— attacking clerical attire, traditional rites and devotions, adherence to doctrine, and the effort to keep Europe Christian, while winning praise from Freemasons, environmentalists, global investors, and imams eager to see the continent flooded with Muslims.

When Pius XI established the feast of the Kingship of Our Lord Jesus Christ, the world was in a precarious condition (as it often seems to be). The evils of the first World War were still fresh in everyone's minds, and the European political and economic situation in the mid-twenties was bleak. A pervasive worldliness had arisen, including open demands for contraception and abortion, that portended the abandonment of natural law morality we have seen rapidly accelerating since the 1960s. In short, it was an age that had already turned its back on God's law, His truth, His wisdom, His love, and His actual rulership over human hearts *and societies*. The pope summarizes the roots and consequences of this rebellion:

> This evil spirit, as you are well aware, Venerable Brethren, has not come into being in one day; it has long lurked beneath the surface. *The empire of Christ over all nations was rejected.* The right which the Church has from Christ himself, to teach mankind, to make laws, to govern peoples in all that pertains to their eternal salvation—that right was denied [in the Enlightenment era]. Then gradually the religion of Christ came to be likened to false religions and to be placed ignominiously on the same level with them. It was then put under the power of the state and tolerated more or less at the whim of princes and rulers. Some men went even further, and wished to set up in the place of God's religion a natural religion consisting in some instinctive affection of the heart. There were even some nations who thought they could dispense with God, and that their religion should consist in impiety and the neglect of God. (24)

For Pius XI, true to the teaching of his predecessors, the Church, by God's decree, is Christ's empire over all nations. The nations must therefore respect her unique nature and prerogatives. Catholicism cannot without injustice be placed on the same level with other religions, or be treated like a member of a "world parliament of religions," even for seemingly noble purposes like seeking peace or human fraternity or the common good.[9]

> The rebellion of individuals *and states* against the authority of Christ has produced deplorable consequences. We lamented these in the encyclical *Ubi Arcano*; we lament them today: the seeds of discord sown far and wide; those bitter enmities and rivalries between nations, which still hinder so much the cause of peace; that insatiable greed which is so often hidden under a pretense of public spirit and patriotism, and gives rise to so many private quarrels; a blind and immoderate selfishness, making men seek nothing but their own comfort and advantage, and measure everything by these; no peace in the home, because men have forgotten or neglect their duty; the unity and stability of the family undermined; society, in a word, shaken to its foundations and on the way to ruin. (24)

There is no question that Pius XI, already in 1925, is describing a secularized world, stripped of ultimate meaning and transcendent purpose. What would he say today?

One thing we must never forget: God is the King of all creation, *whether we want Him to be or not*; we do

---

[9] The interreligious gatherings in Assisi over which John Paul II and Benedict XVI presided, and the declaration that Francis signed with the Grand Imam in Abu Dhabi, are thus ruled out in *Quas Primas* as offenses against the rights of God. Moreover, the policy of an official stance of neutrality towards religion, with a total separation of Church and state, is likewise condemned. This is not the only encyclical one could point to on these points — there are many others from Leo XIII, Pius IX, Pius X, Pius XI, and even Pius XII.

not get to decide by means of a Brexit-type referendum whether or not He will be King, but only whether we will submit humbly to His just and merciful reign, or rebel against it to our own detriment. Civil societies will reflect this orientation on the part of their leaders and the preponderance of their citizens: the society itself, including its government, can bow before God willingly and, even here on earth, begin to experience a certain foretaste of salvation and happiness; or it can chafe at the yoke, sin mightily, and call down upon itself the punishment of bitterness, aridity, and compounding cruelty. In other words, heaven and hell begin *here and now*, on earth, among us, depending on the choices we make, individually *and* socially.

Maintaining his focus on the *social* kingship of Christ, Pius XI gently reproaches Catholics for their weak efforts, perhaps stemming from a misplaced sense of meekness or politeness on their part, or a fear of encountering opposition or suffering persecution:

> We firmly hope that the feast of the King-ship of Christ, which in future will be yearly observed, may hasten *the return of society* to our loving Savior. It would be the duty of Catholics to do all they can to bring about this happy result. Many of these, however, have neither the station in society nor the author-ity which should belong to those who bear the torch of truth. This state of things may perhaps be attributed to a certain slowness and timidity in good people, who are reluc-tant to engage in conflict or offer but a weak resistance [to evil]; thus the enemies of the Church become bolder in their attacks. But if the faithful were generally to understand that it behooves them ever to fight courageously under the banner of Christ their King, then, fired with apostolic zeal, they would strive to win over to their Lord those hearts that are

bitter and estranged from Him, and would
valiantly defend His rights.[10]

At this point, a century after Pius XI was writing, we
can see rather clearly why Catholics do not enjoy high
stations or much authority in civil society. Regardless of
our sins of omission or commission in the past, Western
democratic systems today are dominated by morally
corrupt or compromised liberals (both classical liberals
and "progressives"), a rogue's gallery of the ambitious,
avaricious, and salacious, who either hate Catholics
passionately (as witness the Democrat contenders for
the U.S. presidential nomination) or are willing to use
them when convenient.

In a system so ideologically inhospitable and colos-
sally rigged, there is no chance of a wholesale Catholic
or Christian "takeover" such as Pius XI might have
thought still possible when he first established this
great feast. Indeed, when Paul VI in 1969 changed the
feast in both concept and calendrical placement (as I
will discuss in the next chapter), he effectively replaced
Pius XI's Thomistic incarnational integralism with a
cosmic and eschatological mysticism more amenable to
the Age of Aquarius. It is not merely the government
that doesn't want Christ as King; it seems to be the
postconciliar Church as well.

It would be no exaggeration to say that if we reject
the Kingship of Our Lord in regard to any detail of
our personal and social lives—if we hold back any small
piece and say "this domain is ours and ours alone; we'll
have no king over it!"—we are already theoretically
rejecting God; and this rejection, at first subtle and
abstract, will soon enough lead to rejecting Him in the
practical order as well.[11] God is one, and reality is one;

---

[10] *Quas Primas* 24.
[11] For examples of liturgical acceptance and rejection of Christ's
kingship, see "Why We Follow Inherited Rituals and Strict
Rubrics" in Kwasniewski, *Turned Around*, 79-108.

there is no way to bifurcate life into what belongs to Him and what belongs to us.

> The very first expression of the Kingship of Christ over man is found in the natural moral law that comes from God Himself; the highest expression of His Kingship is the sacred liturgy, where material elements and man's own heart are offered to God in union with the divine Sacrifice that redeems creation. Today, we are witnessing the auto-demolition of the Church on earth, certainly in the Western nations, as both the faithful and their shepherds run away and hide from the reality of the Kingship of Christ, which places such great demands on our fallen nature and yet promises such immense blessings in time and eternity. The relentless questioning of basic moral doctrine (especially in the area of marriage and family), the continual watering down of theology and asceticism, the devastation of the liturgy itself—all these are so many rejections of the authority of God and of His Christ.[12]

The faithful who still revere Christ as King and understand that He deserves to reign in every heart and home, in every tribe and tongue and people and nation, know what can and must be done right now. We work to improve local conditions and to build Catholic "cells" within society so that, at least for a while, we might fly under the radar screen of Big Brother and bring up another generation or two in the fear and love of the Lord, preparing them either for martyrdom or for a new Christendom. We know neither the day nor the hour of Christ's coming; to those who live a hundred or a thousand years hence, we have no obligation but to ensure, as much as lies in our power, that

---

[12] Kwasniewski, "Should the Feast of Christ the King Be Celebrated in October or November?"

the Catholic Faith remains in the world for them, and reaches them intact.

We pray and we work; we work and we suffer; we hand on the Faith, and we beg the Lord to save us, to save His Church, from the unprecedented double attack of external *and* internal anticlericalism.

CHRIST MUST ONCE AGAIN BE HAILED AS KING

There is urgent need for the Church on earth to hail Christ once again as her King, and as the ruler of all men—with the mightiest, including all rulers of the earth, and the pope himself, being the most subject to Him. For let us make no mistake about it: even if *Dignitatis Humanae* was intended to be a teaching about the modern secular state, it quickly became, by a kind of reflex effect, a teaching about the modernized and secularized Church. It was the Church, now, that could no longer confess Christ unambiguously as the one and only Savior of mankind; it was the Church that was not permitted to go forth to convert Jews, Muslims, Protestants, or pagans; it was the Church that needed to bend the knee, not before the King of kings, but before presidents and parliaments, before international organizations and environmentalist summits. The Covid debacle cleared away any lingering doubts that the effect, whether intended or not, of the social dethronement of Christ was His spiritual dethronement in the Church.

> Do Catholics *understand* how we got to a situation where millions of unborn children are murdered in the womb each year, and people think that men can marry men, or women women? This did not happen overnight, the result of an avalanche of money and political pressure. It is the culmination of a long historical process, the accelerating application of a process of revolt against first

principles of nature and grace, beginning with the Protestant Revolt against ecclesiastical authority and sacred tradition, achieving its paradigm in the French Revolution's rejection of temporal authority and human tradition, and sliding downhill to the Sexual Revolution's rejection of social co-responsibility and self-restraint....

If the kingship of Christ is not understood to have profound, immediate, and uncompromisable political and economic ramifications for all mankind, *including Americans* (no "Enlightenment exceptionalism" allowed!), then it is not understood *at all*. Or rather, it has been domesticated, defanged, and declawed by the self-worshiping modern state — a Catholicism rendered harmless as a vague spirituality to which none can object as long as it has no worldly consequences. This purely subjective feel-good "religion" is *not* the incarnational confession of the Son of God by the Church of God, stretching from the first Adam to the last man before the trumpet sounds, and we would do well to spew it forth as the poison it is, knowing there can be no harmony between Christ and Belial (see 2 Cor 6:14–17). The only antidote is the traditional, authentic, full-bodied, sacramental, incarnational social doctrine of the Church, given its fullest and most classic expression in the magisterium of Leo XIII.[13]

Again and again, we circle back to Leo XIII, the "pope of the social question," who, in reality, was much more than that: he was the pope who successfully brought the Church into dialogue with modernity — unlike the Second Vatican Council, which placed the Church into dhimmitude. Leo XIII's engagement was,

---

[13] Kwasniewski, *Treasuring the Goods of Marriage*, 113–14.

however, not in the style of Pope Francis but rather in that of *Saint* Francis, who marched straight into the enemy (Islamic) camp and began to preach the gospel of conversion for the salvation of souls. And although he did not succeed, he made it clear where he stood, and won grudging respect for his courage. The wordy and worldly encyclical *Fratelli Tutti* of Francis falls into shadow compared with the pure and luminous doctrine of Leo XIII's *Humanum Genus*.

We know where to find the uncorrupted springs of CST; it is now for us to drink deeply, and gain strength. The only basis on which we can proceed today is the clarity of the truth, spoken out of love for souls. The conversion, the Christianization, of our societies will not come easily; they have been inoculated, as it were, against Christ. Our task, at any rate, is simple enough: to exemplify the good fruits of embracing Him as the Truth, to help our neighbors in every way we can to draw nearer to Him, and to be prepared to suffer, *usque ad sanguinem*, if the New World Order tells us to trample on the image of the Crucified and Glorified King.

BETWEEN CHRIST THE KING AND "WE HAVE NO KING BUT CAESAR"

I N THE LAST CHAPTER, WE SAT AT the feet of Pope Pius XI, absorbing his sound teaching on the kingship of Christ as transmitted in the encyclical *Quas Primas.*

That was 1925.

In Advent of 1969, a tidal wave of changes in Catholic worship came rolling through the Church. Among these changes was the relocation of the feast of Christ the King from the last Sunday of October to the last Sunday of the liturgical year, at the end of November. Yet as Michael Foley shows, the feast was not merely moved; it was transmogrified. It was given a new name and new content that deemphasized the social reign of Christ and put in its place a "cosmic and eschatological Christ" (in the words of liturgical reformer Pierre Jounel). Foley:

> According to no less an authority than Pope Paul VI, the Feast of Christ the King was not merely changed or moved; it was *replaced.* In *Calendarium Romanum*, the document announcing and explaining the new calendar, the Pope writes: "The Solemnity of Our Lord Jesus Christ King of the Universe occurs on the last Sunday of the liturgical year *in place of* the feast instituted by Pope Pius XI in 1925 and assigned to the last Sunday of October...." The key word is *loco*, which means "in place of" or "instead of." The Pope could have simply stated that the Feast occurs on a different date (as he did with the Feast of the Holy Family) or that it is being moved (*transfertur*) as he

did with Corpus Christi, but he did not. The
Novus Ordo's Solemnity of Christ the King,
he writes, is the *replacement* of Pius XI's feast.[1]

Paul VI abolished Pius XI's feast and replaced it with a new
feast of the Consilium's devising. There is some common
material, of course, but the observance is by no means
intended to be the same feast on a different Sunday.[2]

DETHRONING THE KING

Archbishop Marcel Lefebvre, Michael Davies, Michael
Foley, myself, and many other traditionalist authors have
noted how radically Paul VI modified Pius XI's feast,
in many ways neutralizing its significance.

The removal to the last Sunday of the liturgical year
gives it an "end of the world" twist, as if to say: the
Kingdom of Our Lord does not enter into and per-
meate history as a leaven, but is postponed to the end
of time like a *Deus ex machina*. The working model is
not King St. Louis IX or King St. Stephen of Hungary,[3]
but Teilhard de Chardin's Omega Point.

Paul VI stripped away anything from the Mass or
Divine Office of the day that had reference to the conversion of nations and their subjection to the Church.
Again, as I discussed in chapters 5 and 11, we are not
speaking of theocracy but of a correct ordering of
Church and state whereby, as Leo XIII teaches, the
former stands to the latter as the soul to the body, and,
as Pius XII adds, the former illuminates the meaning
of the natural law so that the latter may translate it
more successfully into civil law. The 1925 version of

[1] Foley, "A Reflection on the Fate of the Feast of Christ the King," emphasis added.
[2] For examples of the kinds of changes made—some glaring and others subtle—see Foley, "A Reflection on the Fate" and "Orations of the Feast of Christ the King"; Schrader, "The Revision of the Feast of Christ the King."
[3] See Kwasniewski, "Fiddling with the Collects of Ss Henry II and Louis IX."

the Collect of the day (still prayed by traditionalists) conveys the traditional doctrine:

> Almighty everlasting God, who in Thy beloved Son, King of all men, hast willed to restore all things; mercifully grant that all the families of nations, rent asunder by the wound of sin, may be placed under His most pleasant rule. Who liveth and reigneth...[4]

The 1969 text substituted for it sharply departs from this integralist vision:

> Almighty ever-living God, whose will is to restore all things in your beloved Son, the King of the universe, grant, we pray, that the whole creation, set free from slavery, may render your majesty service and ceaselessly proclaim your praise. Through our Lord Jesus Christ, your Son, who lives and reigns...

Or consider these verses of the hymn *Te Saeculorum Principem*, written for the original feastday's Office by the Jesuit V. Genovesi in 1925:

Te nationum praesides	Let the rulers of nations
Honore tollant publico,	extol Thee with public honor;
Colant magistri, judices,	let governors and judges
Leges et artes exprimant.	worship Thee, the laws and arts make Thee known.
Submissa regum fulgeant	Let kings find renown
Tibi dicata insignia	in their submission and dedication to Thee;
Mitique sceptro patriam	bring under Thy gentle rule
Domosque subde civium.	the fatherland and our homes.

In verse 2, *Scelesta turba clamitat / Regnare Christum nolumus* (the wicked crowd cries out / "We don't want Christ

---

[4] Translation by Foley, "Orations of the Feast of Christ the King." As Foley details, the contrasts between the other orations — Secret/Prayer over the Offerings and Postcommunion/Prayer after Communion — are no less striking.

as king") connects the rejection of Christ's Kingship with the rejection, played out dramatically before Pontius Pilate, of His mission of salvation that culminates in the Cross and Resurrection; in verse 8, the second line *Qui sceptra mundi temperas* (Who govern the scepters of the world) reminds us that Christ is, right now, actually the Governor of the governors of the world, whether they acknowledge Him now or will be compelled to acknowledge Him in the life to come. These verses reflect the older theological paradigm of Gregory XVI, Pius IX, Leo XIII, St. Pius X, Pius XI, and plenty of other popes to boot. When Paul VI's *Liturgia Horarum* was published a few years after Vatican II, verses 6 and 7 were omitted altogether, and the other verses cited were replaced with more "politically correct" material. It is a thoroughly disgraceful episode, among many others like it which can be found in the liturgical "reform."[5]

Why did this happen? The simplest explanation, indeed the only one that fits the evidence, is that the apparent "integralism" of Pope Pius XI had become an embarrassment to such as Montini, Bugnini, and other progressives of the 1960s and 1970s. They had bought into the philosophy of secularism and wanted to make sure the liturgy did not celebrate either the authority of Christ over the socio-political order or the regnant position of His Church within it. The modernized feast has to be about "spiritual" or "cosmic" or "eschatological" things, with a seasoning of "social justice." As Foley writes: "The new feast guts the original of its intended meaning.... The liturgical innovators kicked the can of Christ's reign down the road to the end of time so that it will no longer interfere with an easygoing accommodation to secularism."[6] Not for them was the potent teaching of St. Pius X, quoted earlier in chapter 11:

---

[5] See Kwasniewski, ed., *Illusions of Reform.*
[6] Foley, "A Reflection on the Fate."

That the state must be separated from the Church is a thesis absolutely false, a most pernicious error. Based, as it is, on the principle that the state must not recognize any religious cult, it is in the first place guilty of a great injustice to God; for the Creator of man is also the Founder of human societies, and preserves their existence as He preserves our own. We owe Him, therefore, not only a private cult, but a public and social worship to honor Him. Besides, this thesis is an obvious negation of the supernatural order. It limits the action of the state to the pursuit of public prosperity during this life only, which is but the proximate object of political societies; and it occupies itself in no fashion (on the plea that this is foreign to it) with their ultimate object which is man's eternal happiness after this short life shall have run its course. But as the present order of things is temporary and subordinated to the conquest of man's supreme and absolute welfare, it follows that the civil power must not only place no obstacle in the way of this conquest, but must aid us in effecting it.... Hence the Roman Pontiffs have never ceased, as circumstances required, to refute and condemn the doctrine of the separation of Church and state.[7]

What, then, are we to make of the countless saints over the centuries who completely *upheld* this traditional doctrine, lived by it and for it, defended and promoted it, advanced it to victory against every heathen and heretic? What of the saints who owed the birth and growth of their vocations—we could even say, in a way, the human conditions of their very sanctity—to the full-bodied, full-blooded Catholic society and culture in which they lived? And what, above all,

---

[7] Pius X, *Vehementer Nos* 3.

do we make of that host of royal saints and blesseds whose holiness took the form of supporting the true Faith in their exercise of politics; people who saw the state as subordinate to the Church, this earthly life as subordinate to the life of the world to come, and believed that, in St. Pius X's words, they "must not only place no obstacle in the way of this conquest [of heaven], but must aid us in effecting it"? Surely these saints have a special place in the Kingdom of God, where they rejoice in the just and pacific reign of Christ the King. They, above all, grasp the inner rationale of the close proximity of November 1 to the last Sunday of October.

When I taught CST to college students, I never ceased to be surprised at how many of them displayed the knee-jerk reaction of automatically assuming that monarchy is "mostly evil" and that democracy is "obviously good." This seems to be a secular dogma imposed by our age and drilled in from tender years, especially in public schools. I like to shake people up by handing out the mighty catalog of saintly royals and nobles—the kings, queens, princes, princesses, dukes, duchesses, and other ruling aristocrats who are officially venerated by Catholics, Orthodox, or Anglicans. The lists are eclectic and ecumenical, to be sure, but offer plenty of food for thought, since all of these individuals in obvious ways promoted and defended Christianity (and often Christendom, its full flowering) using their God-given political authority or leveraging their social position.[8]

---

[8] These lists are taken from Wikipedia's "List of royal saints and martyrs," which more than suffices for our purpose here. Incidentally, it is obvious from the magisterium of the Church that even non-Catholic rulers have their authority from God and received it precisely to promote natural law morality and the Christian religion: see, *inter alia*, Leo XIII's Encyclical *Diuturnum Illud*.

CHRISTIAN SOVEREIGNS

Abgar V of Edessa
Ælfwald I of Northumbria
Æthelberht II of East Anglia
Æthelberht of Kent
Alexander Nevsky
Alfred the Great
Amadeus IX, Duke of Savoy
Andrey Bogolyubsky
Archil of Kakheti
Ashot I of Iberia
Baudouin of Belgium
Boris I of Bulgaria
Brian Boru
Brychan Brycheiniog
Canute IV of Denmark
Causantín mac Cináeda
Ceolwulf of Northumbria
Charlemagne[9]
Charles I of England
  and Scotland
Charles the Good
Clovis I
Constantin Brâncoveanu
Constantine I
Constantine IV
Constantine of Cornwall
Constantine of Strathclyde
Constantine XI Palaiologos
Cormac mac Cuilennáin
Cynehelm
Dagobert II
David I of Scotland
David IV of Georgia
David of Trebizond
Demetrius I of Georgia
Demetrius II of Georgia
Eberhard of Friuli

Edgar the Peaceful
Edmund the Martyr
Edward the Confessor
Edward the Martyr
Edwin of Northumbria
Eric IX of Sweden
Ezana of Axum
Fedelmid mac Crimthainn
Ferdinand III of Castile
Francis II of the Two Sicilies
Guntram
Henry II the Pious
Henry II, Holy Roman
  Emperor
Henry VI of England
Hermenegild of the Visigoths
Hoel, King of Cornouaille
Humbert III of Savoy
Isabella I of Castile
Jadwiga of Poland
James I of Aragon
James VII of Scotland
John III Doukas Vatatzes
John IV Laskaris
Judicael of Brittany
Justinian I
Justinian II
Kaleb of Axum
Karl I of Austria
Ladislaus I of Hungary
Lazar Hrebeljanović
Leo I the Thracian
Leopold III
Louis IX of France
Luarsab II of Kartli
Lucius of Britain
Ludwig IV of Thuringia

---

[9] The cultus of Charlemagne is permitted in the diocese of Aachen.

Magnus of Orkney
Malcolm III of Scotland
Malcolm IV of Scotland
Manuel II
Marcian
Mikhail of Tver
Milutin Nemanjic
Mirian III of Iberia
Neagoe Basarab
Nicholas II of Russia
Nikephoros II
Olaf II of Norway
Oswald of Northumbria
Oswine of Deira
Pabo Post Prydain
Peter I of Bulgaria
Peter of Murom
Pompeia of Langoat
Salomon
Sigebert III
Sigismund of Burgundy
Solomon II of Imereti
Stefan Dragutin

Stefan Lazarević
Stefan Nemanja
Stefan Nemanjić
Stefan Uroš III
Stefan Uroš V
Stephen I of Hungary
Stephen the Great,
    King of Moldavia
Tamar of Georgia
Theodosius I, Roman
    Emperor
Theodosius II, Roman
    Emperor
Tiridates III of Armenia
Vakhtang I of Iberia
Vakhtang III of Georgia
Vladimir I of Kiev
Vladislav
Wenceslaus I, Duke
    of Bohemia
Wigstan of Mercia
William of Gellone
Yaroslav the Wise

OTHER CHRISTIAN ROYALTY AND NOBILITY[10]

Adela of France
Adela of Normandy
Adelaide of Italy
Adelaide of Metz
Æbbe of Coldingham
Ælfflæd of Whitby
Ælfthryth of Crowland
Æthelberht, Prince of Kent
Æthelburh of Barking
Æthelburh of Faremoutiers
Æthelburh of Kent
Æthelburh of Wilton
Æthelnoth of Canterbury

Æthelred, Prince of Kent
Æthelthryth
Æthelwine of Athelney
Afrelia, Princess of Powys
Agnes of Bohemia
Alexandra Feodorovna
Alexei Nikolaevich
Anastasia Nikolaevna
Andrew Bertie
Anna of Kashin
Arnulf of Metz
Ashkhen, Queen of Armenia
Avitus of Vienne

[10] Non-sovereign royalty would include consorts of rulers.

Balthild
Begga
Bertha of Kent
Blanche of Castile
Bojan Enravota
Boris, Prince of Kiev
Budoc
Cadfrawd [Adelphius]
Cainnech of Aghaboe
Canute Lavard
Casimir Jagiello
Clotilde
Clotilde of France
Columba
Constance of Sicily
Constantine Constantinovich
Cunigunde of Luxemburg
Darerca of Ireland
Dimitry (Dmitry) of Moscow
Dinar of Hereti
Dubricius
Edburga of Bicester
Edburga of Minster-in-Thanet
Edburga of Winchester
Edith of Wilton
Edmund of Scotland
Egwin of Evesham
Elena of Montenegro
Eleonora d'Este
Elgiva of Wessex
Élisabeth of France
Elisabeth of Hungary
Elizabeth Fyodorovna
Elizabeth of Portugal
Emeric of Hungary
Emma of Hawaii
Ermenilda of Ely
Fevronia of Murom
Gleb, Prince of Kiev
Gummarus

Hedwig of Andechs
Helena of Constantinople
Himelin
Ignatius Spencer
Igor Konstantinovich
Illtud
Ingegerd of Sweden
Ioann Konstantinovich
Irene of Hungary
Isabel de Bragança Bourbon
Isabelle of France
Jeanne de Valois
Joana of Portugal
Jolenta of Poland
Juthwara
Kea
Kentigern
Ketevan the Martyr
Khosrovidukht
Kinga of Poland
Kyneburga
Kyneswide
Leonorus
Louise of France
Ludmila
Mafalda of Portugal
Margaret of Hungary
Margaret of Savoy
Margaret of Scotland
Maria Clotilde of Savoy
Maria Cristina of Savoy
Maria Nikolaevna
Matilda of Ringelheim
Matilda of Scotland
Matilda of Tuscany
Mildburh
Mildrith
Mlada
Nana of Iberia
Odilia of Cologne

Olga Nikolaevna	Tatiana Nikolaevna
Olga of Kiev	Teneu
Padarn	Teresa of Portugal
Paul Aurelian	Theodora, consort
Philomena	of Justinian
Pulcheria	Theodora, consort
Ragnhild of Tälje	of Theophilos
Richeza of Lotharingia	Tibba
Rumbold of Mechelen	Tudwal
Rumwold of Buckingham	Umbrafel
Sæthryth	Ursula
Saizana	Vladimir Paley
Samson of Dol	Walstan
Sancha of León	Werburgh
Sancha of Portugal	Wigstan
Scaeva	Wihtburh
Seaxburh of Ely	Wilgyth
Senara	Wulfthryth of Wilton
Shushanik	Wulvela
Sidonius Apollinaris	Wynthryth
Sidwell	Zita of Bourbon-Parma

Does democracy have a track record of sanctity like that? Where are the dozens of holy presidents, prime ministers, cabinet members, congressmen, mayors? You may object: Monarchy had many centuries of time during which saints could arise. Democracy as we know it is still relatively young. Give it a chance! To which I respond: modern democracy has been around now for over two centuries, and its track record is abysmal. One could count on both hands the men and women involved in democratic governments who have a reputation for sanctity, let alone an acknowledged cultus.[11] Besides, look around you: do you think the prospects

---

[11] An example would be Robert Schuman, one of the founding fathers of the European Union—the contemporary debased form of which he would scorn. Other examples might be António de Oliveira Salazar in Portugal, Engelbert Dollfuss in Austria, and Gabriel García Moreno of Ecuador.

for great holiness emerging within democratic regimes are *increasing* as time goes on? In this case, it is no exaggeration to say that the myth of Progress looks more mythical than ever.

In a fallen world where all of our efforts are dogged by evil and doomed (eventually) to failure, Christian monarchy is, nevertheless, the best political system that has ever been devised or could ever be devised.[12] As we can infer from its much greater antiquity and universality, it is the system most natural to human beings as political animals; it best reflects the Fatherhood of God and the domestic patriarchy derived therefrom; it is the system most akin to the supernatural government of the Church; it is the system that lends itself most readily to collaboration and cooperation with the Church in the salvation of men's souls. Yes, it goes without saying that there have been plenty of tensions all along between Church and state—but will those *ever* be absent, in any political arrangement whatsoever? Are they absent in democracy—or have we obtained what seems like peace at the steep cost of relinquishing any real influence in society? Has not the Church simply been demoted to the status of a private bowling league that can be permitted or suppressed at whim? The usual defense of religious liberty today is only as strong as the Enlightenment concepts it depends upon, and these concepts were already branded as falsehoods by a string of popes from the time of the French Revolution down to Pius XI.

The two wisest men of pagan antiquity, Plato and Aristotle, maintained that democracy, far from being a stable form of government, is always teetering on the edge of anarchy or tyranny. In spite of his predilection for democracy, Pope John Paul II could not fail to acknowledge the same danger in three separate encyclicals:

---

[12] See Coulombe, *The Compleat Monarchist.*

Nowadays there is a tendency to claim that agnosticism and skeptical relativism are the philosophy and the basic attitude which correspond to democratic forms of political life. Those who are convinced that they know the truth and firmly adhere to it are considered unreliable from a democratic point of view, since they do not accept that truth is determined by the majority, or that it is subject to variation according to different political trends. It must be observed in this regard that if there is no ultimate truth to guide and direct political activity, then ideas and convictions can easily be manipulated for reasons of power. As history demonstrates, a democracy without values easily turns into open or thinly disguised totalitarianism.[13]

Today, when many countries have seen the fall of ideologies which bound politics to a totalitarian conception of the world — Marxism being the foremost of these — there is no less grave a danger that the fundamental rights of the human person will be denied and that the religious yearnings which arise in the heart of every human being will be absorbed once again into politics. This is *the risk of an alliance between democracy and ethical relativism,* which would remove any sure moral reference point from political and social life, and on a deeper level make the acknowledgement of truth impossible.[14]

If the promotion of the self is understood in terms of absolute autonomy, people inevitably reach the point of rejecting one another. Everyone else is considered an enemy from whom one has to defend oneself. Thus society becomes a mass of individuals placed side

---

[13] John Paul II, *Centesimus Annus* 46.
[14] John Paul II, *Veritatis Splendor* 101.

by side, but without any mutual bonds. Each
one wishes to assert himself independently
of the other and in fact intends to make his
own interests prevail.... This is the sinister
result of relativism which reigns unopposed:
the "right" ceases to be such, because it is no
longer firmly founded on the inviolable dignity
of the person, but is made subject to the will
of the stronger part. In this way democracy,
contradicting its own principles, effectively
moves towards a form of totalitarianism....
Even in participatory systems of government,
the regulation of interests often occurs to the
advantage of the most powerful, since they are
the ones most capable not only of maneuvering
the levers of power but also of shaping the
formation of consensus. In such a situation,
democracy easily becomes an empty word.[15]

We may have deluded ourselves into thinking that we
have stability, peace, and justice — "Where's the anarchy?
Where's the tyranny?"—but, as Hans Urs von Balthasar
once wrote, the entire contemporary Western social
order is founded on the blood of millions of butchered
unborn children, whose murder is permitted and protected by the state. And this is only *one* of the many
pervasive sins of our democratic era that cry out to
God for vengeance. This hardly sounds like a system of
which Catholics ought to be proud. Rather, they should
rue it, repent of it, and beg the Lord for deliverance.

Right now, the prospects for Catholic monarchy
seem dim, to say the least. But we ought to have the
courage to admit that what we are doing is *not working*, that we are digging ourselves collectively into the
deepest and darkest pit the human race has ever seen.
Compared to this, I would prefer to take my chances
on monarchy. In spite of its checkered history, it still

---

[15] John Paul II, *Evangelium Vitae* 20; 70.

has a proven track record of sanctity and defense of the Faith. Nothing else does.

This leads me back to Pope Paul VI's suppression of one feast of Christ the King and his creation of another. What is really going on here? It seems to me that the original feast of Christ the King represents the Catholic vision of society as a hierarchy in which lower is subordinated to higher, with the private sphere and the public sphere united in their acknowledgment of the rights of God and of His Church. This vision was put aside in 1969 to make way for a vision in which Christ is a king of my heart and a king of the cosmos — of the most micro level and the most macro level — but *not* king of anything in between: *not* king of culture, of society, of industry and trade, of education, of civil government.

In other words, for such middling spheres, "we have no king but Caesar."[16] The impious cry of the ancient Jews has become our foundational creed. We have bought into the Enlightenment myth of the separation of Church and state, which, as Leo XIII says, "is equivalent to the separation of human legislation from Christian and divine legislation."[17] The result cannot but be catastrophic, as we unmoor ourselves from the very aids God has provided for our human weakness.

If we see a world crashing around us into unimaginable deviancy and we seek the cause, let us not be afraid to pursue it back to the rebellion of the modern revolutions — from the Protestant Revolt down to the French Revolution and the Russian Revolution — against the social order of Christendom, which blossomed in the sacral kingship of Christian monarchs.

I am certainly not saying that we can snap our fingers and find ourselves in a renewed Christendom. The original version took *centuries* to build up. It would

---

[16] Jn 19:15.
[17] Leo XIII, *Au Milieu des Sollicitudes* 28.

take several centuries to build up a new Christendom.
But the only way we are going to get there is by seeing
the ideal for what it is, yearning for it, and praying for
the reign of Christ the King to descend into our midst
with all the realism of the Incarnation, that He may
sanctify anew the world He came to save. In this time
of struggle before the end of time—that day when all
politics and all visible rites will give way to the blazing
glory of His advent—we are not allowed to throw up our
hands, yielding everything to the juggernaut of "Progress," which is another word for decadence and depravity.
It belongs to soldiers of Christ to acknowledge their
King and to fight for His acknowledgment. Come what
may, this is how each one of us shall win through to an
imperishable crown in the eternal kingdom of heaven.

ADDENDUM

A reader who had seen my defense of the superiority
of Catholic monarchy over other forms of government
posed a question:

> I was wondering, given the absence of true
> Catholic Monarchy today, our duty to submit
> to legitimate authorities, and "a world crashing
> around us into unimaginable deviancy," what
> you thought our best options were. My feeling
> is that *any* form of theistic integralism—Calvin-
> ist, Lutheran, Mohammedan, or Jewish—would
> be preferable to the twin visions of Hell shown
> us by the Renegade Mainland Provinces and
> the Rebel North American Colonies. What
> do you think?

I replied that one might be torn on the question of
whether a non-Catholic but religious regime is better
than a secular one. It was surely not good for English
Catholics when they suffered under Queen Elizabeth I,
and it's not good for today's Catholics to be in Saudi
Arabia or Pakistan. On the other hand, there's the saying

about how the lukewarm will be vomited forth. People go more easily from false zeal to true zeal than they do from total indifference to religious faith. In that sense, a religious society is better off than an irreligious or non-religious society, and the same would seem to be true of governments.

When I wrote this, I had no idea that my interlocutor actually lived in Saudia Arabia! In response, he told me what it's been like to live for two years in that Islamic kingdom. He admitted that he's in a privileged position as a white-collar worker in a part of the country where crossing the causeway to Bahrain to attend Mass is possible, but he feels less under siege as a Catholic in Saudi Arabia than he did in a quiet university town in Australia, for the following reasons.

The rules in Saudi Arabia are settled and stable, and being based on an authority that is seen as divine, bind the king as much as the least of his subjects. While the details may change over time, the extent of possible change has been pretty well-established by historical experiment, so the map of possible permutations is not hard to predict. It is not like the West today, where politicians are making rules up as they go along, and where each year brings fresh hell for Christians and conservatives.

The things he's not allowed to say are relatively few, and are not things he feels tempted to say anyway. Practically every day at his Australian university, on the other hand, he had to choke back something he wanted desperately to say that he knew would get him in trouble.

Moreover, "locals think better of the Christians than we deserve, and assume all Westerners are Christians." Even Saudi co-workers who earned graduate degrees in Chicago or Manchester cannot really process that atheists exist in the world. So one would have to go out of one's way to *deny* Christ in Saudi Arabia. In Australia, on the other hand, the default assumption of most people he met socially was that he would surely be a progressive atheist (since that's seen as the only intelligent view), and he was often faced with the temptation to keep quiet to avoid an uncomfortable argument. In other words: in the Moslem country, faith is assumed; in a modern Western country, faithlessness is assumed.

Most movingly, he wrote: "It is a tremendous joy for me to wake up every morning in a place where the unborn are not being legally slaughtered. It is a lesser joy, but still a great one, to wake up every morning and know that the public square will not be pushing perversion at me all day long, in whatever 'woke' form it happens to take in the current calendar year."

He said he appreciated the fact that there are things the state forbids him to do *for the good of his soul*—limits on his liberty that are less onerous than the ones Westerners put up with all over the world solely for the good of their bodies. Even if many of the Saudi restrictions may not actually be good for one's soul, there is at least an acknowledgement that the soul is real and primary. In other parts of the so-called "free world," the government is either studiously indifferent to the eternal welfare of its citizens, or actively (though, one would hope, unwittingly) working to ensure their damnation.

His concluding thought was powerful: "So, although I considered myself fairly integralist before moving to Saudi Arabia, I am now much more integralist, having seen the 'form' of integralism in action, without its true 'matter.' In short: I would love to live in a Catholic version of this country, for that would unite the correct formality of government with the content of the truth."

The perhaps surprising reflections of this Australian Catholic residing in Saudi Arabia help us to step outside the bubble of our comfortable liberalism. The lack of secularism and the insistence that there is a

divine order and that the political order must correspond to it makes an environment more true to
reality and more human, even when religious error
predominates. It shows the naturalness and rightness
of integralism as a logical, coherent, and supportive
mode of living. Liberalism is the illusion that it is
possible to separate politics from its divine origin and
finality and to understand citizenship in abstraction
from the personal religious commitment of citizens.
Liberalism seduces us into creating what we think is
a neutral "God-free" space, which turns out to be a
shrine in which the ego is erected as an idol. Where
God is dethroned, the world, the flesh, and the devil
rush in to fill the void.

19

CHRISTIAN MILITANCY IN
THE PRAYER OF THE CHURCH

A T THE REPUBLICAN NATIONAL
Convention in 2020, a religious sister named
Deirdre Byrne gave a rousing pro-life speech
that concluded with a promise of prayers for then-Pres-
ident Trump: "You'll find us here with our weapon of
choice, the Rosary." The liberal Franciscan theologian
Fr. Daniel P. Horan reacted with what a well-known
blogger calls a spittle-flecked nutty: "Weapons are, by
definition, instruments of violence. Prayer is NOT a
weapon, sacramentals for prayer like rosaries are not
weapons. Christ preached and lived a message of non-
violence, and prayer is always about love—God's love!
Weaponizing faith is disgusting and idolatrous." Here
Dede and Daniel offer us a perfect contrast: you might
even call them "Sr. Rambo and Br. Bambi." Which one
has the right perspective on Christianity?

It would seem that Fr. Daniel hasn't cracked open the
letters of St. Paul in a good long while, for he might
have stumbled across verses in 2 Corinthians that could
have put ideas into Sr. Deirde's head: "As servants of
God we commend ourselves in every way: through great
endurance, in afflictions, hardships, calamities...with
the weapons of righteousness for the right hand and for
the left" (that's from chapter 6); and again, "the weapons
of our warfare are not worldly but have divine power
to destroy strongholds" (that's from chapter 10).[1] One
is reminded of how the late pope once said that "faith

---

[1] 2 Cor 6:4, 7b; 2 Cor 10:4. On Sr. Deirdre and Fr. Daniel, see
MacDonald, "A Tale of Two Religious."

is not a suit of armor," seeming to forget that St. Paul
in Ephesians tells Christians to "take up the full amor
of God" and to use the "shield of faith."[2] One would
think scriptural literacy is a job requirement for the
papacy, but I guess there are exceptions to every rule.

"The life of man upon earth is a warfare."[3] These
words from the Book of Job express a fundamental truth
of the Christian life. We are born into enemy territory:
the world is in the grip of the Evil One, to whom our
first parents gave the keys to the city. Scripture really
leaves no doubt about it. The Apostle John writes:
"We know that whosoever is born of God does not
sin, but the generation of God preserves him and the
wicked one does not touch him. We know that we are
of God and the whole world lies in the power of the
evil one [*mundus totus in maligno positus est*]."[4] Within
this world Christ has established a fortress, a beachhead,
a kingdom that is at the same time *not* of this world
but of the enduring world of heaven, where the Evil
One has already decisively lost. The fury with which
he campaigns on earth is an expression of his despair
at having been driven forth from heaven into hell.
Either from malice or from ignorance and foolishness,
many men end up enlisting in Satan's army, and we are
engaged with them in a struggle not only to repel their
attacks but to capture them, if possible, and bring them
over to our side. The life of man is a battle in another
and more distressing way: we have enemies *within* us,
too, that we can never fully escape from—disordered
concupiscence, bad habits, the memories of our past
sins—although we can bring them into subjection. That,
indeed, is what the season of Lent is supposed to help
us to do. To paraphrase St. Benedict, our whole life
should be salted with a Lenten spirit, but the Church

---

[2] Francis, Homily for the Feast of the Epiphany, January 6, 2022.
[3] Job 7:1.
[4] 1 Jn 5:18-19.

wisely asks us to set apart a segment of time each year when we can hit the spiritual "restart" button.

We are not alone in the fight: we have many allies, many powerful friends. The most powerful weapons in our arsenal are the Holy Sacrifice of the Mass and the other sacraments, the Divine Office, and the sacramentals (especially the Rosary), which Christ and the Church provide for our sanctification, the strengthening of the inner man, the conquest of enemy territory within and without. These things are not just individual actions we perform; they are acts of the Mystical Body that carry the full weight of its indestructible essence. Taymans d'Eypernon writes:

> This, then, is the reason why God in His love has stooped so low to us. It is in a material universe that our destiny is shaped and shattered and remade. The material world is a vast plain of battle, scarred with the marks of our defeat, or resplendent with the trophies of victory. Matter is man's strength and his weakness, for it is by his life amid material things and by his use of them that man rises above himself; and on the other hand, it is the material part of our nature that bleeds and is broken in the press of life. It was divinely fitting that God should come and apply His saving Omnipotence to this essential part of His creation, the most vulnerable of all. He does this by the sacraments. They not only are signs of His coming, they actually contain the divine healing power and apply it to our souls. In them, matter is elevated to the rank of a bond between God and man, and a symbol of the infinite mystery of God's love. Raised to sacramental dignity, matter is not only the channel by which the thought and prayer of the creature rise to the Uncreated, but the channel by which God Himself really comes

to His creatures to dwell in them forever. *Et mansionem apud eum faciemus*: And we will make our abode with him (Jn 14:23).[5]

Without this help from God throughout our lives, above all in the Most Holy Eucharist, the vast plain of battle *will* be scarred with the marks of our defeat, rather than resplendent with the trophies of victory. By God's grace, given to us under material forms (even as the Son of God was "given to us" in the man Jesus of Nazareth), we can find healing, rise above ourselves, and join Christ our victorious King.

Fr. Christopher Smith has these rousing words for us:

> As Christians we know that peace comes from the social reign of Christ as King over all peoples, and to establish that peace we engage first of all in a spiritual battle within ourselves. We absolutely must not be afraid to declare total war on the world, the flesh, and the Devil, which seek to carry our souls away from peace, away from the Prince of Peace. But that spiritual battle also means that we must learn how to defend our Faith and engage others for our freedom to practice what we know is the true religion. Now of course every age has its own particular fight for right. The spiritual battle takes on a different quality in different times and places but there is a very particular quality to what that looks like today.

Part of this "very particular quality" is surely fighting for the Church's traditional rites of divine worship, which candidly acknowledge the spiritual battle we are facing and boldly assist us in the fray. In this concluding chapter I will show some of the many ways in which the traditional Roman liturgy recognizes the true state of affairs, with realism and supernatural hope. Roberto de Mattei notes that "the Church is the Mystical Body

---

[5] d'Eypernon, *The Blessed Trinity and the Sacraments*, 15.

of Christ: a reality that transcends history, but *in history* lives and battles and hence is called the Church Militant."[6] "The Church here on earth is not simply 'on the pilgrim's way,' but it is rather a militant Church (*ecclesia militans*). Her ranks are called to battle."[7]

Tragically, nearly all of the things I will be writing about were either greatly reduced or abolished altogether in the liturgical reform of the 1960s — a process of pacification that had the predictable and now undeniable result of blunting our blades, snapping our shields, hobbling our horses, and subverting our strategy. In order to avoid monotony, I will not always explicitly say "this thing I'm describing was chucked out by the liturgical reformers," but you can assume that that is the case.

BATTLES FOR CHRISTENDOM

First, let's look at the traditional liturgical calendar. Every year, Holy Mother Church reminds us again and again of battles fought by Christians to preserve the true Faith on earth. For the Kingdom of God is not far removed from us, in a heaven that cannot be reached, but is a reality present also on earth, albeit in the form of sacramental signs administered and received by imperfect men, and in the form of a hierarchical social body that coexists with the cities and nations of men. Wherever Christ is present, His kingdom is present; we are living at the fringes of His realm, with access to the King Himself. We do not pray "Thy Kingdom stay away," but "Thy kingdom *come*." We do not pray: "Thy will be done only in heaven, and as for earth, forget about it, it's a hopeless disaster." We pray: "Thy will be done *on earth*, as it is in heaven." In Our Lord's parable of the mustard seed, we should not overlook the fact that a seed must be planted in the earth, where it germinates and puts down its roots in order to grow into the heavens.

---

[6] De Mattei, *Love for the Papacy*, 180.
[7] Fiedrowicz, *The Traditional Mass*, 244.

Christians are called first and foremost to beg the
Lord for deliverance, but we are also called to make
a good use of the natural gifts and abilities He has
given us for living with dignity here below. That is the
reason why, when the blossoming of the human-divine
civilization known as Christendom was attacked by its
enemies, Christians reasonably and rightfully took up
arms to defend themselves, their families and peoples,
their holy religion. In fact, historian Phillip Campbell
describes ancient liturgies intended to be offered at the
army camp or the proposed field of battle for success
in warfare. A supplication from one such Mass, in the
time of the emperor Justinian, prays: "Look upon the
Romans at last, look, O Highest God...[and] with Your
power, I beseech You, smash the proud pagans. Let
the peoples recognize you alone as Lord and powerful,
while You crush the enemy and save Your own kind by
battle."[8] We may find *ourselves* in the future needing
our weapons to defend the most fundamental human
and Christian rights against totalitarian progressivism
in the state and Modernism in the Church. None of
us can know exactly what this will look like, but it is
important to see that we are not wrong to be thinking
along these lines.

The traditional Roman Martyrology, which is read as
part of the office of Prime, puts us in mind of this fact
over and over again.[9] Some examples: on September 12,
we read about "The Feast of the Most Holy Name of
the Blessed Virgin Mary, which Pope Innocent XI com-
manded should be celebrated by reason of the famous
victory obtained over the Turks at Vienna in Austria
by the help of the Blessed Virgin," and on the 16th
of the same month, "At Monte Cassino, blessed Pope
Victor III, who...shed a fresh lustre on the Apostolic

---

[8] Campbell, *Power from on High*, 65.
[9] See Kwasniewski, "The Great Cloud of Witnesses in the Roman
Martyrology."

See, and with God's help gained a famous victory over the Saracens." On May 1, we hear of St. Pius V that "he battled against the enemies of the Christian name." On October 7, we hear of "the Feast of the Blessed Virgin Mary of the Rosary and the commemoration of St. Mary of Victory, which Pope St. Pius V instituted to be kept yearly in memory of the glorious victory obtained on this same day in a naval battle by the Christians against the Turks [at Lepanto in 1571], by the help of the same Mother of God." (And, in fact, it was a *second* victory over the Turks in Hungary in 1716 that prompted Pope Clement XI to extend the feast to the entire Catholic world.[10] Can you imagine what these popes would think about Abu Dhabi and *Fratelli Tutti*?) In his 1937 encyclical on the Rosary, Pope Pius XI expressly recalled Lepanto:

> When the impious Mohammedan power, trusting in its powerful fleet and war-hardened armies, threatened the peoples of Europe with ruin and slavery, then—upon the suggestion of the Sovereign Pontiff—the protection of the heavenly Mother was fervently implored and the enemy was defeated and his ships sunk. Thus the faithful of every age, both in public misfortune and in private need, turn in supplication to Mary, the benignant, so that she may come to their aid and grant help and remedy against sorrows of body and soul. And never was her most powerful aid hoped for in vain by those who besought it with pious and trustful prayer.[11]

We are reminded by this simple historical fact that Christianity, although supernatural in origin and oriented to the life to come, is nevertheless realistic in its willingness to confront and defeat evils in this world

---

[10] *St. Andrew's Daily Missal* (1945), 1491.
[11] Pius XI, *Ingravescentibus Malis* 3.

that would threaten the good of souls delivered by Our Lord's precious Blood. The Rosary is indeed a weapon by which spiritual and *temporal* victories are won.

On October 23, we read about "the birthday of St. John of Capistrano, Priest of the Order of Friars Minor, Confessor, a man illustrious for holiness of life and zeal for the spreading of the Catholic faith. He by his prayers and miracles delivered from siege the town of Tornau, which was wasted by a powerful Turkish army."[12] In the entry for "St. Stephen, King of Hungary, Confessor, who was adorned with divine virtues," we learn that "his feast is especially kept, by decision of Pope Innocent XI, on September 2, on which day the strong fortress of Buda, by the aid of the holy king, was valiantly recovered by the Christian army."

One might also recall the entry in the Martyrology for August 18, which speaks of "that most religious Emperor Constantine the Great, who was the first to show to other princes an example of the manner in which the Church should be protected and enriched." For it was the appearance of the Chi-Rho in the heavens with the words *En touto nika*, "in this sign conquer," that brought the persecution of Christians to an end and laid the first foundations of Christendom.

The traditional Martyrology mentions over 360 martyrs to Islam on over thirty separate dates in the year, with no month skipped. The Church does not want us to forget the memory of these heroes of the Faith who surrendered their lives for the love of Christ and the love of His truth. They were not combatants, but neither were they milquetoast Christians who apologized for offending people with the gospel or who preached human fraternity and boundless tolerance of error. One of my favorite entries in the Martyrology appears on February 21: "At Damascus, St. Peter Mavimenus, who said to certain Arabs who came to

---

[12] His actual feast is celebrated on March 28.

him in his sickness: 'Every man who does not embrace the Catholic Christian faith is damned as Mohammed, your false prophet, was,' and was slain by them." Not a surprising conclusion to *that* "interreligious dialogue."

SOLDIERS FOR CHRIST

Then there are the soldiers: the ancient Roman calendar is full of soldier-saints. In antiquity, the Church wrestled with the issue of whether believers ought to enlist (or remain in) the imperial army. The liturgy answered the question with a paradox: yes, there were many just men who fought for the emperor, but their righteousness was displayed above all when they refused to worship the emperor's idols and, throwing down their arms, embraced martyrdom for the heavenly King, which is the ultimate act of fortitude or courage.[13] In this way we see that being a soldier is not, in itself, incompatible with professing the Christian Faith—but also that our ultimate allegiance cannot be to any earthly ruler or his campaigns. As I said, the old calendar is full of these soldier-saints. Just to limit ourselves to the sanctoral cycle in the traditional Roman Missal: St. Sebastian (January 20), the Forty Holy Martyrs of the garrison of Sebaste (March 10), St. George (April 23), Sts. Nereus and Achilleus (May 12), Sts. Basilides, Cyrinus, Nabor, and Nazarius (June 12), Sts. John and Paul (June 26), Sts. Processus and Martinian (July 2), St. Romanus (August 9), St. Hippolytus (August 13), St. Gorgonius (September 9), St. Eustace and Companions (September 20), St. Maurice and Companions (September 22), St. Theodore (November 9), St. Martin of Tours (November 11), and St. Mennas (also November 11). That's over sixty soldiers commemorated at Mass each year! While it is true that these soldiers are celebrated by us at Mass because they are martyrs for the Faith, not because they fought for the Roman

---

[13] See *Summa theologiae* II-II, Q. 124.

Empire, they are not *condemned* for having been in the
imperial army, even when it was a pagan army—and
subsequent devotion to them has emphasized their
military attire, virtues, and patronage, seeing in them
models of Christian warfare on battlefields both literal
and metaphorical.

The reason I make a point of mentioning Christian
soldiers is that, in our own times, the Church on earth
has been corrupted by the error of pacifism in various
forms. We are not sure anymore if we are allowed to
fight anyone about anything. Isn't it mean and nasty to
speak against someone's lifestyle choices, their opinions
and views, their "orientation," or whatever? Isn't it lacking in meekness to resist attacks against our persons
or our property? Shouldn't we always "turn the other
cheek" and let God alone defend us? This mentality was already influential during the Second Vatican
Council, when memories of the horrors of World War
II, together with a secular humanistic optimism about
the potential of democratic government and the peace-
keeping role of the United Nations, led all too many
churchmen into believing that humanity had somehow "come of age" and could now deal with evils not
by warring against them, or even condemning them,
but rather by the gentle touch of negotiation and the
warmth of universal benevolence. This attitude, alas, is
reflected in certain texts drawn up for the Novus Ordo,
which are notable for their naïveté and chumminess.
And nearly all the soldier saints were removed from
Paul VI's calendar.

Catholics have never thought or acted this way until
quite recently. According to St. Thomas Aquinas, some
souls are called to a meekness that is supererogatory
(that is, above-and-beyond-the-call-of-duty), even as
some souls are called to the evangelical counsels of
poverty, chastity, and obedience. It would not be edi-
fying to see a Dominican friar wielding an AK-47. Yet

Aquinas also notes that the structure of justice inherent to God's creation is not suppressed or contradicted by divine revelation, but rather reinforced by it. This is why at least we the *laity* are allowed to defend ourselves, our families, our communities, our nation, our Church—with violence if necessary. One can put it this way: just as the advent of the more perfect way of the religious life does not cancel out the natural and supernatural goodness of marriage and family, so too the choice of some to allow themselves to be tortured and killed does not cancel out the natural and supernatural goodness of proportionate resistance to evil. While normally our fight against evil will take place in the spiritual domain and in the political arena, there is no reason to exclude the possibility that it may sometimes rightly take place on the physical level too.

Roberto de Mattei has spoken frequently of the danger of what he calls "catacombism." Here is how he explains it:

> Catacombism is the attitude of those who retreat from the battlefield and hide themselves in the illusion of being able to survive without fighting. Catacombism is the denial of the militant conception of Christianity. The catacombist does not wish to fight, because he is convinced of having already lost the battle; he accepts the situation of the inferiority of Catholics in the culture as a given, without going back to the causes that have determined it. But if Catholics today are in the minority, it is because they have lost a series of battles; they have lost these battles because they have not fought them; they have not fought them because they have removed the very idea of the "enemy," turning their backs on the Augustinian concept of the two cities fighting each other in history, the only concept that can offer us an explanation of what is happening,

and what has happened. If one rejects this militant concept, one accepts the principle of the irreversibility of the historic process, and from catacombism one inevitably passes to progressivism and modernism....

Wishing to portray that valorous Church [of ancient times], always ready to live on the forefront, as a community of draft dodgers, hiding themselves for embarrassment or cowardice, would be an insult to their virtues. They were fully aware of their duty of conquering the world for Christ, to transform private and public life according to the doctrine and law of the Divine Savior, out of which a new civilization could be born—another Rome, springing forth from the tombs of the two Princes of the Apostles. And they reached their goal. Rome and the Roman Empire became Christian.

In times past it was said that the Sacrament of Confirmation made us "soldiers of Christ," and Pius XII, addressing the bishops of the United States, said: "The Christian, if he does honor to the name he bears, is always an apostle; it is not permitted to the Soldier of Christ that he quit the battlefield, because only death puts an end to his military service." We need to recover this militant conception of the Christian life.[14]

A favorite hymn, "For All the Saints," delivers this message loud and clear in one of its verses: "O may Thy soldiers, faithful, true, and bold, / Fight as the saints who nobly fought of old, / And win with them the victor's crown of gold. / Alleluia, alleluia!"

THE PRAYERS OF THE MISSAL

More telling than the mere presence of saints in the calendar are the prayers we use at Mass for their

---

[14] De Mattei, *Love for the Papacy*, 149–50.

feasts and commemorations. Among the most important public prayers of the Church are those we call "orations"—namely, the Collects, Secrets, and Postcommunions of the Mass. The Collect itself is of special importance because it recurs throughout the Divine Office as well. If we want to understand how the Catholic Church prays—and therefore, what we should believe and how we should live—we must look carefully at these orations.

Now, "the prayers [of the old missal] identify those enemies and adversaries that the Church militant must continually encounter in the temporal as well as the spiritual life."[15] Comparing these old prayers with their newer (post-1969) substitutes is eye-opening, to say the least. In the Novus Ordo, the Collect for the *optional* memorial of St. John of Capistrano, who spurred the Christian army to victory in 1456 at Belgrade, goes like this:

> O God, who raised up Saint John of Capistrano
> to comfort your faithful people in tribulation,
> place us, we pray, under your safe protection
> and keep your Church in everlasting peace.

By contrast, here's the prayer found in the traditional missal for the *obligatory* feast of the same saint:

> O God, Who through blessed John didst enable Thy faithful people to triumph over the enemies of the Cross by the power of the Most Holy Name of Jesus: grant, we beseech Thee, that by his intercession we may overcome the snares of our spiritual enemies and be found worthy to receive from Thee the crown of justice.

The traditional Collect for St. Patrick notes that he brought the gospel not only to the Irish people (as it says in the Novus Ordo prayer), but to the *heathens*, whom we know fiercely resisted him. The Collect for

---

[15] Fiedrowicz, *Traditional Mass*, 244.

St. Augustine of Canterbury praises him not only for leading the English peoples to the gospel (as the Novus Ordo says), but also for "shedding upon the English people the light of the true faith," that is, casting out the darkness of pagan error. For St. Irenaeus of Lyons, the great second-century opponent of the heresy of Gnosticism, the Novus Ordo Collect says:

> O God, who called the Bishop Saint Irenaeus to confirm true doctrine and the peace of the Church, grant, we pray, through his intercession, that, being renewed in faith and charity, we may always be intent on fostering unity and concord.

The Latin Mass, on the other hand, uses this Collect:

> O God, who didst vouchsafe unto blessed Irenaeus, Thy martyr and bishop, by his strenuous teaching of the truth, utterly to confute heresies, and happily to establish peace in Thy Church: grant unto us Thy people, we beseech Thee, to be steadfast in the practice of our holy religion, and in all our days to enjoy that peace which is from Thee.

The entire *tone* and much of the *content* of these prayers is so different! Thus, for St. Robert Bellarmine, the old Collect pulls no punches:

> O God, who didst adorn blessed Robert Thy Bishop and Doctor with wondrous learning and virtue that he might lay bare the snares of error and maintain the rights of the Apostolic See: grant by his merits and intercession that we may grow in love of the truth, and that the hearts of the wayward may return to the unity of Thy Church.

In contrast, the new Collect says nothing about the snares of error, the rights of the Apostolic See, love of the truth, or wayward hearts returning to the Church.

Its Catholic content has been sucked out of it. Michael Fiedrowicz argues:

> This [older version of the] prayer does not lessen the charism of this saint, but rather increases it. It was precisely his astute refutation of the Protestant errors that made Cardinal Bellarmine the Catholic theological controversialist most feared by the Protestant Reformers, and to whose refutation several *"cathedrae anti-Bellarminianae"* were established. Furthermore, it is only the traditional prayer that speaks of the necessity of a return of heretics to the true religion of the Catholic Faith. The classical missal opposes an abandonment of the so-called ecumenism of return, the conviction of the Church of all ages that all confessions are in no way equally on the path to truth. The traditional orations recall in an uncomfortable way that in questions of faith there are not only various opinions, but also errors that must be overcome, or at least fought against. An abandonment of this battle would amount to a victory of relativism.[16]

One of the votive Masses in the back of the preconciliar *Missale Romanum* is the "Mass for the defense of the Church," also known as the "Mass against the heathen"—something that would never have been allowed to exist in the Novus Ordo, and in fact does not exist. The Collect reads:

> Almighty, everlasting God, in whose hand are the power and the government of every nation: look to the help of the Christian people, that the heathen nations, who trust in their own fierceness, may be crushed by the power of Thy right arm. Through Our Lord Jesus Christ...

---

[16] Fiedrowicz, 245–46.

The Gradual prays: "O my God, make them like a wheel and as stubble before the face of the wind." The Alleluia verse adds: "Stir up Thy might, O Lord, and come: that Thou mayest save us." The Secret prays: "Look, O Lord, upon the sacrifice which we immolate, that Thou wouldst deliver Thy champions [*propugnatores tuos*] from all wickedness of the heathen, and keep them secure in Thy protection."

This virile spirit of the traditional prayers is found throughout the *Missale Romanum* handed down to us by our forefathers. In his book *Lost in Translation*, Michael Foley describes how the Church prays on the Twenty-First Sunday of Pentecost:

> In the foreground of the Mass is an array of different biblical texts involving some kind of conflict between two parties:
>
> The Introit is from the Book of Esther, when Mordecai and Esther plead with God to save the Jews from a new Babylonian law decreeing their extermination;
>
> The Alleluia, from Psalm 113, pits the Jews against the "barbarous" Egyptians — apparently, there is more to being civilized than impressive architecture, political stability, and mummification;
>
> The Epistle, from Ephesians 6, describes the Christian spiritual warrior and the armor that he needs to defeat the demons, who are especially active during the final days;
>
> The Gospel, the Parable of the Unforgiving Servant (Matt. 18:23–35), presents Christ the King as the Judge who will not forgive those who do not forgive others;
>
> The Offertory verse presents the miserable figure of Job who is beset with misfortune at the hands of Satan;
>
> The Communion verse, from Psalm 118, turns the fear of judgment, which is evident in the Gospel, into an appeal for judgment

against our enemies. A sharp distinction is drawn between wicked persecutors and innocent victims.[17]

The entire Mass of that day illustrates the spirit of Christian militancy—of recognizing our enemies for what they are, preparing for engagement with them, and begging for divine reinforcements. Perhaps the laity attending Mass that day won't immediately recognize this theme running through the day's texts, but continual exposure to them will certainly have an influence on their imagination, memory, understanding, and will.

THE VIRILE SPIRIT ILLUSTRATED

As a more complete illustration, let's take a look at the Mass of July 28, the feast of the martyrs Nazarius, Celsus, and Pope Victor I, and the confessor Pope Innocent I—four saints who were given the axe in 1969, in spite of being called upon by the Church for a good 800 years.[18] The Introit is taken from Psalm 78:

> Let the sighing of the prisoners come in before Thee, O Lord; render to our neighbors sevenfold in their bosom; revenge the blood of Thy saints, which hath been shed. O God, the heathens are come into Thy inheritance: they have defiled Thy holy temple: they have made Jerusalem as a place to keep fruit. Glory be to the Father... Let the sighing...

One of these verses was stigmatized as a "cursing" verse and therefore removed entirely from both the

---

[17] Foley, *Lost in Translation*, 191.
[18] The revisers of the calendar say that Nazarius and Celsus came into the Roman Rite in the twelfth century, Victor and Innocent in the thirteenth. In Van Dijk's edition of the ordinal of Pope Innocent III, which is the first ancestor of the Missal of St. Pius V, they are present on the calendar as a group from ca. 1200. In the *Ordo Officiorum Ecclesiae Lateranensis*, which was written by a certain Bernard who died in 1176, they are celebrated without St. Innocent.

postconciliar Lectionary and the Liturgy of the Hours, as were 121 other psalm verses that are nowhere prayed in the Novus Ordo.[19] In general, the more "spirited" or "militant" psalms have been minimized or excised, which corresponds to the generally effeminate presentation of Christianity in recent times. This effeminacy, though absent from the liturgy and clerical life before the last Council, was unfortunately already long present in the realms of art and devotion. Think of the doe-eyed Sacred Heart images from the nineteenth and twentieth centuries, where Our Lord is depicted as a saccharine, fragile, androgynous figure, as if He would flinch at a passing softball, or deflate when poked with a needle.

The Collect of the Mass is muscular: "May the confession of Thy saints Nazarius, Celsus, Victor, and Innocent fortify us, O Lord, and may it graciously win for us reinforcement in our weakness. Through Our Lord Jesus Christ..." The Lesson is from the Book of Wisdom:

> God rendered to the just the wages of their labors, and conducted them in a wonderful way; and He was to them for a covert by day, and for the light of stars by night; and He brought them through the Red Sea, and carried them over through a great water. But their enemies He drowned in the sea.... Therefore the just took the spoils of the wicked. And they sang to Thy holy name, O Lord, and they praised with one accord Thy victorious hand, O Lord, our God.[20]

The Gradual and Alleluia verses are taken from the Book of Exodus:

> God is glorious in His Saints, wonderful in majesty, doing wonders. Thy right hand, O Lord, is glorified in strength; Thy right hand

---

[19] See Kwasniewski, "The Omission of 'Difficult' Psalms."
[20] Wis 10:17–20.

hath broken the enemies. Alleluia, alleluia. The bodies of Thy Saints are buried in peace, and their name liveth unto generation and generation. Alleluia.[21]

The Gospel is taken from St. Luke:

At that time, Jesus said to His disciples: When you shall hear of wars and seditions, be not terrified: these things must first come to pass, but the end is not yet presently. Then He said to them: Nation shall rise against nation, and kingdom against kingdom. And there shall be great earthquakes in divers places, and pestilences, and famines and terrors from Heaven, and there shall be great signs. But before all these things, they will lay their hands on you and persecute you, delivering you up to the synagogues and into prisons, dragging you before kings and governors for My name's sake; and it shall happen unto you for a testimony.... And you shall be betrayed by your parents and brethren and kinsmen and friends, and some of you they will put to death: and you shall be hated by all men for My name's sake; but a hair of your head shall not perish. In your patience you shall possess your souls.[22]

Let us pause for a moment on this potent Gospel, so utterly relevant to our postmodern, post-Christian age of intensifying persecution. It is a Gospel read *four times* each year in the traditional Latin Mass (unless one of these dates happens to fall on a Sunday): on June 2, for Sts. Marcellinus, Peter, and Erasmus; on July 28, for Sts. Nazarius, Celsus, Victor, and Innocent; on September 16 for Sts. Cornelius, Cyprian, Euphemia, Lucy, and Geminian; and on January 22 for Sts. Vincent and Anastasius. In the postconciliar Lectionary, this

---

[21] Ex 15:11, 6; 44:14.
[22] Lk 21:9–19.

Gospel is read on the 33rd Sunday of Ordinary Time
every third year, and part of it is read on Wednesday
of the 34th week (Years I & II). I leave you to draw
your own conclusions.[23]

This proper Mass for July 28 — and it is only one
of so many that we could choose from the Church's
year — has within it a spiritedness, a realism, a strength
of character, massive and fortified as a Romanesque
church, tall and straight as a Gothic column, orderly
and graceful as a Renaissance façade, well-worn and
rugged as a pilgrimage route, with a note of subdued
triumph, as of soldiers assured of victory but prepared
for hardship. We encounter in the traditional liturgy
what we heard de Mattei calling the "militant conception of Christianity." We are engaged in battle against
our spiritual enemies: the seething world of unbelief,
the flesh or disordered concupiscence, the devil and
his minions. The old liturgy does not run away from
this reality but confronts it head on. As the mainstream
Church slides further into self-referential effeminacy and
comfort-seeking compromises with the world, does it
not become ever more apparent that what we need to
hear — and strive to *live* — is the truth embedded in the
great ancient rite of the Church of Rome?

THE HOLY ANGELS

According to the classic saying, we battle against
three enemies: the visible enemy *around* us, "the world,"
meaning fallen humanity insofar as it has turned against
God by sin; the enemy *within* us, "the flesh," which

---

[23] The Communion verse for July 28 from the Book of Wisdom
(3:4–6) is also striking, inasmuch as it reminds us that the true
holocaust, the "whole burnt offering" that is pleasing to God,
is Christ Jesus in His Passion on the Cross, and His saints who
have emulated Him in their own passions and their unswerving
fidelity to mission. "And though in the sight of men they suffered
torments, God hath tried them; as gold in the furnace He hath
proved them, and as a victim of a holocaust He hath received them."

refers to the ravages of sin in our nature; and the invisible enemy *above* us in stature, namely, the devil and his fallen angels, who strive to lead us into sin. Against these enemies we have the help of the saints of the Church Triumphant, among whom stand the mighty armies of holy angels, about whom we read in a story from the Desert Fathers:

> While still a neophyte in monastic life, Moses the Black was warring against carnal desire. So he went, in a state of turbulence, to confess to Abba Isidoros. The elder listened to him sympathetically and, when he had given him words of appropriate counsel, told him to return to his cell. However, inasmuch as Abba Moses was still hesitant, for fear of the flame of evil desires rekindling during his return, Abba Isidoros took him by the hand and led him to a small roof atop his cell. "Look here," he told him, directing him towards the West. Thereupon Moses saw an entire army of wicked spirits with drawn bows, ready for warfare, and was terrified. "Look towards the East now," the elder told him once more. Myriads of angels in military formation were standing ready to confront the enemy. "All of these," Abba Isidoros told him, "are assigned by God to help the struggler. Do you see how our defenders are many more and incomparably stronger than our enemies?" Moses thanked God with his heart for this revelation and, taking courage, returned to his cell to continue his struggle.[24]

It is not difficult to see that the angels are much more frequently acknowledged in the traditional Mass and sacramental rites. The prayer at the end of the Asperges asks the Lord to "vouchsafe to send Thy holy angel from heaven, to guard, cherish, protect, visit,

---

[24] Translated by the V. Rev. Chrysostomos, www.goarch.org/-/the-ancient-fathers-of-the-desert-section-1.

and defend all that are assembled in this place." The centuries-old version of the Confiteor calls twice upon St. Michael the Archangel, prince of the heavenly host and the weigher of souls at the divine judgment, and does so three times each Mass. St. Michael is also called upon during the Offertory incensation of the gifts at High Mass, or in the Leonine Prayers at the end of Low Mass. That means he will be invoked a total of seven times each Mass.[25]

The traditional calendar generously makes room for five feasts in honor of the angels: St. Michael on September 29 and again on May 8, St. Gabriel on March 24, St. Raphael on October 24, and the Guardian Angels on October 2. The Novus Ordo collapsed all these feasts into only two, namely, September 29 and October 2, and abolished nearly all of the mentions of the angels in the Mass. That was a mistake. It's rather obvious that in this period of ever-heightening spiritual warfare, we need to cultivate a strong devotion to the angels, and the traditional liturgy helps us to do exactly that.

ASCETICISM AND MORTIFICATION

What is our help against the waywardness of the flesh? The answer is complex, because human nature is complicated. We can boil it down to a *via negativa* and a *via positiva*, a way of negation and a way of affirmation. The way of affirmation is the corporal and spiritual works of mercy, in which we occupy ourselves with worthwhile activities, involving alike the body and the soul, done for love of God and neighbor. The way of negation is asceticism, mortification, and penance. This was the original meaning and spirit of the season of Lent, a meaning and spirit that have now almost entirely disappeared from the consciousness of Catholics (and that's no exaggeration).

[25] See Kwasniewski, "Angels: Fellow Worshipers in the Liturgy of Heaven."

No one really wants to hear that we need to remove pleasure or add suffering to our lives. But the Church understands that we must do so.[26] As even the pagan philosophers Plato and Aristotle saw, human beings are prone to excess in their appetites, and they need to "bend the stick in the opposite direction" by choosing to deny themselves legitimate goods in order to gain self-mastery and grow in strength for endurance. Beyond that, we are sinners in need of repentance, and we have debts of punishment to pay. Moreover, because of the solidarity of the Mystical Body, we can make reparation for the sins of others, and this, we know, is pleasing to the Lord and meritorious for eternal life.

The traditional Mass itself places ascetical demands on us. The faithful are typically kneeling for long stretches, from the prayers at the foot of the altar to the Gospel, and from the Sanctus to the last Gospel. This demanding discipline keeps us mindful that we are in a special sacred place, taking part in a sacrifice to which we must unite ourselves, giving a small sacrifice of our own. At a High Mass, there will be a combination of standing, genuflecting, kneeling, and sitting, which, together with the signs of the cross, the beating of the breast, the bowing of the head, and the chanting of responses, immerses us in the act of worship, so that the Faith can enter into our bones, our muscles, our knees, our hands, as well as our ears, eyes, and noses. Catholic worship is physical through and through. Tragically, the Novus Ordo dropped a lot of these "muscular" and "sensuous" elements in favor of verbal comprehension and response, which, by themselves, constitute a fairly impoverished form of participation—in one ear and out the other.

If "the spirit is willing but the flesh is weak,"[27] then

---

[26] See Kwasniewski, "Should We 'Despise Earthly Goods and Love Heavenly Ones'?"

[27] Mt 26:41.

our effort must be directed to strengthening the flesh as support for the spirit. This is perhaps the greatest gap or oversight in modern Christianity, which has become altogether too "spiritualized," too abstract, conceptual, "in the head." If we want to be soldiers for Christ, we should be thinking as much of an army bootcamp as we do of getting more education. Obviously asceticism and learning belong together and we need both, but our knowledge will benefit us the most when we confirm it and support it with a regimen of prudent physical asceticism.

There is a lot we can start doing immediately, instead of putting it off for a future month or year when we are "more holy." We will not become holy until we embrace discipline. I mentioned fasting and abstinence. A fast is traditionally understood to be not eating until the evening of the day, when we take one meal. However, for those who are not ready to try that (or whose close relatives will not allow them to...), an effective and more manageable fast is to refrain from eating until noon, and then to eat nothing after 8pm. The sixteen hours of not eating, between 8pm and 12pm, will still be penitential, but you will probably not be as much of a burden to the people around you, and in any case, you'll be asleep for half of the time. It is a good "middle option" for the season of Lent, for Ember and Rogation Days, and for Vigils of great feasts.[28] As those who fast regularly have experienced, after initial difficulties we arrive at a better place, where we are not so dependent on our bodily urges and experience heightened mental clarity and spiritual alertness.

A major form of asceticism for modern people is to go to bed at an hour early enough to make possible a consistent early rising for a morning prayer routine,

---

[28] A similar idea is to eat in the morning and early afternoon (8am–2pm for an 18:6 ratio or 9am–1pm for a 20:4 ratio), and then to have nothing the rest of the day.

which might, for example, take the form of reciting the Office of Prime and spending fifteen minutes in quiet prayer, with or without a Bible. If we do not pray first thing in the morning, our day will almost certainly not go as well as it could have.[29] St. Alphonsus Liguori famously said: "He who prays is saved; he who does not pray is lost." If we want to pray, we need to get up; if we want to get up, we need to go to bed; if we want to be strong and not sluggish, we should adopt some fasting and abstinence. This advice is common to all of the saints who talk about the spiritual life.

A last thought about mortification: not everyone can do everything recommended by the saints, and some people are in a situation where they cannot handle any more challenges than life has already given them. For example, a mother with a nursing baby should not even dream about fasting. What God is asking of us is to take whatever steps we can, big or small, in order to pray more, to deny ourselves, and to order our lives more fully to the Lord. The traditional liturgy gives us tools for this lifelong work because its calendar, prayers, and customs continually remind us of the spirit of detachment and self-abnegation preached and practiced by Christ our King and His servants—always for the sake of more perfect love.

THE BOOK OF PSALMS

As a Benedictine oblate, every morning I pray the Office of Prime, the shorter of the two morning hours.[30] In the monastic use, Psalm 17 is divided between Friday and Saturday mornings. This Psalm is one of the most vigorous expressions in the Bible of the militant spirituality of the sons of God living in this land of exile and tribulation. I would like to quote some verses from it,

---

[29] See Kwasniewski, "The Best and Most Necessary First Thing."
[30] See Kwasniewski, "The Office of Workers and Fighters." The other morning hour is Lauds.

to show how profoundly this message permeates the revealed Word of God. In the Psalter He is teaching us *what to pray for* and *how to pray for it*. We must take Him at His word; we must make His words our own, week after week. King David begins:

> I will love thee, O Lord, my strength: the Lord is my firmament, my refuge, and my deliverer. My God is my helper, and in him will I put my trust. My protector and the horn of my salvation, and my support.

Then come the words spoken at every Mass by the priest as he takes up the chalice, ready to drink the Precious Blood of His Lord and God: *Laudans invocabo Dominum: et ab inimicis meis salvus ero.* "Praising I will call upon the Lord: and I shall be saved from my enemies." Skipping some verses, we come back to our theme:

> He delivered me from my strongest enemies, and from them that hated me: for they were too strong for me....
> For who is God but the Lord? or who is God but our God?
> God who hath girt me with strength; and made my way blameless.
> Who hath made my feet like the feet of harts: and who setteth me upon high places.
> Who traineth my hands to battle: and thou hast made my arms like a brazen bow....
> I will pursue after my enemies, and overtake them: and I will not turn again till they are consumed.
> I will break them, and they shall not be able to stand: they shall fall under my feet.
> And thou hast girded me with strength unto battle; and hast subdued under me them that rose up against me.
> And thou hast made my enemies turn their back upon me, and hast destroyed them that hated me....

> And I shall beat them as small as the dust
> before the wind; I shall bring them to
> nought, like the dirt in the streets....
> The Lord liveth, and blessed be my God, and
> let the God of my salvation be exalted:
> O God, who avengest me, and subduest the
> people under me, my deliverer from my
> enemies.
> And thou wilt lift me up above them that rise
> up against me: from the unjust man thou
> wilt deliver me.

The enemies against whom we are praying in this psalm are not, let's say, the people we happen to dislike or despise. The enemies are, first of all, our own evil passions and vicious habits; the primary battlefield is our own soul. Second, these enemies are the demons who truly hate God and hate us, and who therefore seek our ruination. Against them we are to wage an implacable war, never showing mercy. Third, the enemies of Psalm 17 are the sworn human adversaries of the Church, not insofar as they are persons, but insofar as they are adversaries—such as communists, Freemasons, Planned Parenthood, and, sad to say, many bishops in the episcopacy.

What's more, the "I" in this psalm—the one who is saying "*I* will break them, *I* shall beat them, *I* shall bring them to nought"—is Christ our King, the Head of the Church, for *He alone* has the authority to speak this way and to use us as His instruments. If we want *Him* to be the one who fights in us and through us so that we may share His triumph, we must remain united to Him in faith, strong in hope, ardent in charity, as living members of His Body. *Only He* can successfully defeat our enemies within and without; and He *will* defeat them for those who stay close to Him. He will defeat them for His Bride, the Church, immaculate in her heavenly glory. We have every reason to be

confident and not to lose heart. For was it not our
blessed Lord who said:

> My sheep hear my voice, and I know them,
> and they follow me; and I give them eternal
> life, and they shall never perish, and no one
> shall snatch them out of my hand. My Father,
> who has given them to me, is greater than all,
> and no one is able to snatch them out of the
> Father's hand.[31]

In the traditional Latin Mass, God is called "omnip-
otent" sixteen times. He is all-mighty, having power
to do all things...and He is at work in you and in
me. *Deus Pater Omnipotens.* That is why St. Paul can
exclaim to the Ephesians:

> Now to Him who is able to do all things
> more abundantly than we desire or under-
> stand, according to the power that worketh
> in us—to Him be glory in the Church, and
> in Christ Jesus, unto all generations, world
> without end. Amen.[32]

¡Viva
Cristo
Rey!

---

[31] Jn 10:27-29.
[32] Eph 3:20-21.

A SYNOPSIS OF THE
TEACHING OF LEO XIII

BORN MARCH 2, 1810, AT CARPINETO, Gioacchino Vincenzo Raffaele Luigi—the future Leo XIII—was the sixth of seven sons of Count Lodovico Pecci and Anna Prosperi Buzi. From the ages of eight to fourteen he received intensive training in Latin, Italian, and other standard subjects. After further courses in humanities, Vincenzo commenced studies in theology as well as civil and canon law.

His first appointment to ecclesiastical office, that of domestic prelate, came at the hands of Gregory XVI in 1837, when the young man was still in minor orders; he was ordained to the priesthood on December 31 of that year. After three adventurous years of service as civil governor of Benevento, a city belonging to the papal states but full of Neapolitan anticlericals, Mgr. Pecci was sent by Gregory XVI to pacify Perugia, a breeding-ground of antipapal revolutionaries. As before in Benevento he had used his influence to eradicate crime, so here Pecci instituted reforms to help the common people—road improvements, a low-interest bank, better schools.

These early assignments revealed features that would characterize the later pope: a diplomatic handling of explosive situations, ingenuity in finding solutions, and solicitude for the working poor, coupled with a growing awareness of the rampant spread of vice among the masses, the philosophical errors driving modern political developments, and the need to formulate a thorough Catholic response. His future pontificate was forged in the crucible of these harrowing years of Italian nationalist and anti-Catholic radicalism.

Early in 1843, Pecci was appointed nuncio to Brussels, a city rife with dissensions; again he managed to unite the opposing parties, liberal and Catholic, around a common platform. When the see of Perugia became vacant, Gregory XVI called back Pecci to fill the post, destined to be his longest-held office (1846–1877). Gregory had intended to make him a cardinal, but that pope's death, and the troubled opening of Pius IX's reign, postponed this distinction until December 1853.

As bishop, Pecci sought above all to improve the education and pastoral zeal of his clergy. When the Piedmontese invasion and subsequent suppression of religious orders badly reduced the number of ministers, Pecci set up an organization of diocesan missionaries ready to go wherever needed, and later a society for the relief of impoverished clergy. In Perugia's seminary he reintroduced the study of St. Thomas Aquinas, at that time something of a novelty. To the social uprisings, bloody conflicts, and natural disasters that occurred during his more than thirty-year tenure, Pecci responded with courage, compassion, and prompt remedies. Although he forcefully upheld the Holy See's prerogatives and opposed the aggressive secularism of the Piedmontese, he was left unmolested by the usurpers, for his popularity was feared and his integrity respected.

Pecci was elected supreme pontiff in the conclave of 1878, receiving 44 votes out of 61. Prior to Leo XIII, the Catholic Church in the nineteenth century was under siege and on the defensive. In many ways she was marginalized and held in contempt; the "enlightened" liberals who ran the show in Europe (as they do today) belittled her "medieval" words and ways, and predicted her disappearance as a matter of course. Her supreme leader was left little choice, it seemed, but to hurl protests and anathemas at a heedless world. Secularists would simply not have thought it possible that the Church would rally and boldly respond to the challenges of the day, gaining the moral high ground where she had lost physical territory or political support.

Yet this is precisely what happened thanks to Leo's surprising pontificate, which lasted 25½ years—exceeded only by that of Bd. Pius IX (almost 31½ years) and John Paul II (26½ years). Leo XIII's landmark interventions on political and economic issues created a fully consistent and well-articulated body of social doctrine, tying together loose strands of Scripture, Church Fathers and Doctors, and earlier interventions of the magisterium into a coherent social ethics. Considering that he wrote nearly one hundred encyclicals addressing a wide variety of subjects and audiences, it may seem a daunting task to recommend a modest number of "must-reads." Fortunately, it is not difficult to do, because Leo XIII himself told us near the end of his pontificate, in the retrospective letter *Annum Ingressi Sumus* of 1902, which of the social encyclicals he considered the most important.

There are five encyclicals that, taken together, make up a "crash course" in the fundamentals of Catholic Social Teaching: *Diuturnum Illud* of 1881, on the origin of civil authority; *Immortale Dei* of 1885, on the Christian constitution of states; *Libertas Praestantissimum* of 1888, on true and false freedom; *Sapientiae Christianae* of 1890, on the duties of Christian citizens toward the state; and *Rerum Novarum* of 1891, on labor and capital, i.e., the rights and duties of owners and workers. These documents and others akin to them are contained in *A Reader in Catholic Social Teaching*, which I edited for Cluny Media, and which has become the basis for university courses, book clubs, and parish classes. The texts contained in this volume have been purged of their typos (plentiful in online sources) and, in some cases, corrected against the Latin originals.

In *Diuturnum Illud*, Leo XIII demonstrates why God is and must be the source of all political societies as well as of any authority their rulers wield. Notably, the people who may have elected the rulers are *not* the source of their powers, nor are those rulers beholden to the people so much as they are to Almighty God, who will judge them all the more severely for the weight of their responsibility. Correcting numerous Enlightenment-derived errors held by modern Westerners about the origin and purpose of political power, this encyclical also presents an excellent account of what is called "civil disobedience" but is, in reality, consistent obedience to God's higher law.

In *Immortale Dei*, Leo XIII unfolds in some detail the ideal Christian constitution of a state and why it is impossible to maintain that states have no obligations to God or the Church and no obligation to form their citizens in moral virtue. As before, Leo argues against "the principles and foundation of a new conception of law"—he has in mind the "social contract" theory—that, contradicting both divine law and natural law, undermines the stability of the state, which depends on the successful profession of religion within it, the fulfillment of each citizen's primary duty to God. This encyclical also contains one of the best accounts ever penned of the likenesses and differences between civil or secular society and the society that is the Catholic Church; it depicts with exceptional clarity their propers spheres of authority as well as how they may overlap or come into conflict.

Closely connected to the foregoing is *Libertas Praestantissimum*, which remains the most comprehensive and acute analysis of the meaning of human freedom that has yet come to us from the Chair of St. Peter—which explains why this encyclical has been among the documents most frequently cited by a long line of Leo's successors. *Libertas* speaks of the human will's dependency on law, truth, and grace; how freedom when abused leads to slavery; how the eternal law, the natural law, and human law are interconnected; how modern political liberalism (meaning the doctrine of eighteenth-century philosophers like John Locke) "opens a way to universal corruption"; why the total separation of Church and state is a "manifest absurdity," and yet why toleration of false religions may be permissible in order to avoid greater evils.

Inserting another key component, Leo XIII issued *Sapientiae Christianae* on the rights and responsibilities of Christians as citizens in modern societies. As we might have expected, the pope speaks with wisdom and prudence about a host of questions that face the Catholic citizen: What is true patriotism or national piety, and how is it related to devotion to the Church? What is the mission of the laity and the Catholic family in the secular world, what are the rules that must govern a Catholic's political choices, and what kind of behavior of Christians in the public sphere is "base and insulting to God"? How are Church and state meant by divine Providence to work together such that citizens may achieve natural and supernatural perfection? In passing, Leo takes up a number of other questions such as what a layman's attitude should be toward erring bishops and why Christians who fail to live out their faith are guilty of a sin worse than that of the Jewish people in rejecting their Messiah. He spells out, with greater clarity than proponents of civil rights movements were able to do later on, the whys and wherefores of following one's conscience over against a government's immoral dictates.

Rerum Novarum is Leo XIII's most famous encyclical. Regrettably, many people have tried to find in it a comprehensive summary of Catholic social doctrine — something it surely neither contains nor sets out to offer. Pope Leo took pains to note, in the document itself, that he had written other encyclicals (such as the ones mentioned above) that supply the proper context for its predominantly economic considerations. These considerations include why socialism is "emphatically unjust" and guaranteed to make things worse rather than better; how the institution of private property, or possession of one's own goods, favors the welfare of individuals, families, and states; how the family is, in some sense, prior to the state, and yet why the state's role in promoting the common good of a larger group is most useful and necessary; why the state must protect and enforce the rights and duties of various classes. The employer's duties as well as the worker's are clearly spelled out; the "chief and most excellent rule for the right use of money" is laid down (doesn't that alone whet your appetite to read this document?); the influential concept of the "just wage" and the "family wage" are defined and defended against objections; and workingmen's unions or "guilds," along with the "right of association," are strenuously defended. Whenever I go back to this encyclical, I am amazed to see just how the mighty economic struggles and sufferings of the twentieth century (and indeed of the twenty-first) are anticipated therein, their causes exhibited, their solutions proposed.

So far, we have summarized Pope Leo XIII's chief social encyclicals, which he issued in order to offer guidance to the Church in her delicate and difficult dealings with modern nation-states and modern economic situations. Leo was grappling with the emergence of a thoroughly secularized way of life and worldview, severed from the Christian past and obsessed with the pursuit of worldly "progress." He was, arguably, the first pope to size up the full magnitude of the transformation that was under way as the Western world threw off the Redeemer's sweet yoke to run after fashionable "-isms" like liberalism, materialism, and consumerism, which promised ever-expanding freedom while achieving little more than the gradual destruction of the natural and supernatural institutions that console and delight man during his sojourn on earth. Thus, to fill out our portrait of Leo's teaching, we must mention several other documents that complete his response to the revolt of modernity against the divine order.

In his encyclical on Christian matrimony, *Arcanum Divinae* (1880), Leo XIII speaks of the Creator's original intention for marriage and the family and offers a forceful critique of the novel theories and liberal legislation that were just beginning to undermine the family at that time. Read from our vantage almost 150 years later, we can see how precisely accurate were the pope's predictions about the deleterious effects of such ideas and laws. More importantly, the pope beautifully develops the positive side of his subject.[1] *Arcanum* singlehandedly inaugurated modern Catholic teaching on marriage and family.

One of the first acts of Leo XIII's pontificate was the promulgation of "On the Restoration of Christian Philosophy," more familiarly known as *Aeterni Patris* (1879). The unfinished business of the First Vatican Council, which had been suspended late in 1870 by the outbreak of the Franco-Prussian War, included a thorough review and reform of Catholic studies in philosophy and theology. This Leo himself took up, drawing on his own experience of the systematic power, synthetic genius, and timeless relevance of St. Thomas Aquinas. *Aeterni Patris* was, as it were, the Magna Charta of the movement of Thomistic restoration, or better, invigoration. The encyclical is notable for its grand tour of Christian intellectual history and its balanced but decisive accolades for Aquinas.

---

[1] This positive presentation was to reach its apogee in Pius XI's *Casti Connubii*; for the text with commentary and study guide, see Lawler, *God Has No Grandchildren*.

Again, it was in keeping with the First Vatican Council's effort to articulate the harmony of faith and reason and to respond to the haughty spirit of historical-critical reductionism that Leo XIII issued his encyclical on the study of Holy Scripture, *Providentissimus Deus* (1893). Leo's encyclical robustly proclaims the divine inspiration, inerrancy, and infallibility of the sacred writings, reaffirming and explaining traditional Catholic doctrine on the dual authorship, divine and human, of the books of Scripture; the consequent guarantee of freedom from all error; the unbreakable connection between Scripture, Tradition, and magisterium; and the various senses of Scripture discerned by the Fathers of the Church.[2]

In 1896, Leo XIII brought out his encyclical *Satis Cognitum*, on the unity of the Church, which covers the fundamentals of ecclesiology so well that Pope Paul VI in his inaugural encyclical *Ecclesiam Suam* (1964) drew special attention to it as a key source for upcoming discussions at the Second Vatican Council. Leo's encyclical focuses squarely on the question: Did Jesus Christ really intend to found a *church*—a visible and hierarchically structured body of believers on earth, charged with the mission of carrying His gospel and extending the effects of His redemption to the ends of the earth? The pope succinctly marshals scriptural evidence, the testimony of tradition, and rational arguments to bring home his conclusions about the uniqueness and unicity of the Church of Christ with its episcopal structure. In all my years of studying ecclesiology and apologetics I have not seen any presentation of these themes that is as direct, uncluttered, elegant, and inspiring as Leo XIII's.

Although each of the nearly one hundred encyclicals promulgated by Leo XIII offers insightful commentary on the modern situation and good advice for Catholics,

---

[2] See Crean, *Letters from That City.*

there are three from around the turn of the twentieth century that have struck me for years as emblematic of this pope's acute theological vision, uplifting religious fervor, and bold cultural critique: *Annum Sacrum* on consecration to the Sacred Heart (1899), *Tametsi Futura* on Jesus Christ the Redeemer of mankind (1900), and *Mirae Caritatis* on the Holy Eucharist (1902).

Each speaks of the immense love of God given to us in Christ Jesus, the mercy extended to us castaways of Adam's shipwreck, the divine truth in which alone our minds can find peace amidst the storms of ever more bewildering and contradictory philosophies of life. The pope is not content merely to assert that such is our dire condition and such our salvation; he spells it out step by step: Here is where the false philosophies will lead you, Modern Man, and here is how God can rescue you from the pit of destruction that expands with your neglect and contempt of His Good News. I must say that it would have been very beneficial had the Fathers of the Second Vatican Council been asked to study these three texts prior to their arrival in Rome in 1962. It would have given them a much-needed dose of realism, a reinvigoration of their *sensus Catholicus*, and models of brevity and depth.

In this trio of encyclicals, Leo XIII issues an impassioned plea for conversion, beginning with the Church herself and moving outward in concentric circles to embrace all mankind. And, like all the popes before and after him, Leo beckons us to gather around the most sublime of all sacred mysteries on earth: the Holy Eucharist, the Body and Blood of our Redeemer, and to let It gather us into one Church, one Body, full of the lifeblood that heals the fallen sons of Adam.

Leo XIII, who died in 1903 and was succeeded by Pius X, gave to the Church a systematic and well-rounded plan for engaging the modern world—a plan he pursued energetically and without deviation for a

quarter of a century. While Pope Leo was deeply critical of and pessimistic about the direction the Western
world was going in and knew that its secular philosophies were mortal poison, he was animated above all
by an intensely positive vision of what Christ and the
Church can do for modern men, who need to be saved
from the idols their own hands have fashioned.

HUMAN FRATERNITY
AND WORLD PEACE

I N OUR TIMES, THE PHRASES "WORLD peace" and "human fraternity" are constantly on people's lips. One often has a sinking feeling that the phrases have not only lost their original meaning, which was once either Christian or compatible with Christianity, but have also become codewords for widespread errors to which the Church is and ought to be opposed. Worse still, it seems that it is most often members of the Church hierarchy who misuse these slogans as they sign agreements and shake hands (or perhaps bump elbows) with globalist hegemons who wear invisible crowns of enormous financial power and behind-the-scenes political influence.

There was once a time when the popes thought, spoke, and acted more independently, drawing upon three millennia of Christian, Jewish, and pagan thought, giving voice to natural law and divine law.

Beholding the precarious peace of Europe shattered as dictatorships of Left and Right hurled their armies into battle, Pope Pius XII (1939–1958) used the occasion of his inaugural encyclical *Summi Pontificatus*, promulgated October 20, 1939, to set forth the Catholic vision of the principles of unity that bind together men and nations, and to implore the world, for love of peace, to return to the Church's salutary teaching on political realities. After an introduction in which the pope, recalling Leo XIII's consecration of mankind to Christ the King forty years earlier, states his intention of consecrating his pontificate

to advancing the reign of Christ in the world, the
principal motif is stated:

> At the head of the road which leads to the
> spiritual and moral bankruptcy of the present
> day stands the nefarious efforts of not a few
> to dethrone Christ.... In the recognition of
> the royal prerogatives of Christ and in the
> return of individuals and of society to the law
> of His truth and of His love lies the only way
> to salvation. (21–22; cf. 103).

Right from the start Pius XII makes it clear that he
sees Christ's kingship as pertaining not only to individuals but also to societies, as his predecessor Pius XI
had emphasized in his encyclical *Quas Primas* of 1925.
Summi Pontificatus proceeds to a critique of "popular
modern errors" (25):

> The radical and ultimate cause of the evils
> which we deplore in modern society is the
> denial and rejection of a universal norm of
> morality as well for individual and social life
> as for international relations; we mean the
> disregard, so common nowadays, and the for-
> getfulness of the natural law itself, which has
> its foundation in God, Almighty Creator and
> Father of all. (28)

The pope regards the "darkness over the whole earth"
that accompanied the death of Jesus (Mt 27:45) as a
"terrifying symbol" of the effects of banishing Christ
from public life (30).

The peace of nations is disturbed above all by two
errors: "forgetfulness of that law of human solidarity and charity which is dictated and imposed by our
common origin and by the equality of rational nature
in all men...and by the redeeming Sacrifice offered
by Jesus Christ" (cf. 35–51), and "those ideas which do
not hesitate to divorce civil authority from every kind

of dependence upon the Supreme Being—First Source and absolute Master of man and of society—and from every restraint of a Higher Law derived from God as from its First Source" (52ff.).

In the first portion, Pius XII identifies the sources of the objective unity of the human race (36–43). In Adam and Eve, the triune God created mankind after His own image and likeness; from this first couple the human race is descended. All members of this race have the same metaphysical nature, composed of material, perishable body and spiritual, immortal soul. All live together on the same earth, enjoying the same rights of dominion over it; all share the same end and mission within the world; all are called to the same ultimate end, divine happiness, by the same means, the Church and her sacraments. In the Son of God all men were created, by His blood redeemed, by His grace sanctified, by His love empowered to love. "In the light of this unity of all mankind, which exists in law and in fact, individuals do not feel themselves isolated units, like grains of sand, but united by the very force of their nature and by their internal destiny, into an organic, harmonious mutual relationship" (42). Only in the Catholic Church and the civilization inspired by her can different nations, races, and cultures work peacefully together, sharing their diverse gifts for the building up of the human race; apart from the Church, pluralism turns into antagonism (44–49). Wherever the Church has gone, she has sown peace by spreading the knowledge and love of God. The "corrupt and corrupting paganism" (30) of modern times does the opposite: by denying to God and His law a reigning, regulative place in social life, it chokes noble aspirations, nurtures egoism, provokes conflict.

This brings us to the second error, which is the object of the pope's most vehement condemnation: totalitarianism.

> Once the authority of God and the sway of His
> law are denied in this way, the civil authority
> as an inevitable result tends to attribute to
> itself that absolute autonomy which belongs
> exclusively to the Supreme Maker. It puts itself
> in the place of the Almighty and elevates the
> state or group into the last end of life, the
> supreme criterion of the moral and juridical
> order, and therefore forbids every appeal to
> the principles of natural reason and of the
> Christian conscience. (53)

No one in 1939 could have failed to see that Pius
XII was speaking chiefly of the National Socialists of
Germany, the fascists of Italy, and the militant communism of the Soviet Union, and his position was never
misunderstood by these regimes, which did everything
in their power to thwart the pope's efforts.

Pius XII then invokes the teaching of Leo XIII on
the state's authentic purpose: to "facilitate the attainment in the temporal order, by individuals, of physical,
intellectual, and moral perfection" and to "aid them
to reach their supernatural end" (58). Accordingly,
"it is the noble prerogative and function of the state
to control, aid, and direct the private and individual activities of national life so that they converge
harmoniously towards the common good" (59). To
ward off faulty notions of the common good, the
pope continues: "That good can neither be defined
according to arbitrary ideas nor can it accept for its
standard primarily the material prosperity of society,
but rather it should be defined according to the harmonious development and the natural perfection of
man" (ibid.). Against totalitarianism the pope reaffirms
that "man and the family are by nature anterior to
the state" (61) and that the family has rights peculiar
to itself (63ff.), such as the parents' right to educate
their own children (66).

Having proved that it harms the internal life of nations, Pius XII then shows why totalitarianism, being a sort of voluntarism or egoism writ large, inevitably leads to international discord, breaking the "reciprocal ties, moral and juridical" that bind the human race "into a great commonwealth" (72).

> To tear the law of nations from its anchor in Divine law, to base it on the autonomous will of states . . . would [leave international law] abandoned to the fatal drive of private interest and collective selfishness exclusively intent on the assertion of its own rights and ignoring those of others. (76)

After this analysis of the situation in 1939 at the very outset of the Second World War, Pius XII, in a powerful rhetorical move, imagines a hard-won cessation of hostilities and then asks of this post-War period: "Will that future be really different; above all, will it be better?. . . Or will there be a lamentable repetition of ancient and of recent errors?" (79). "Safety does not come to peoples from external means, from the sword which can impose conditions of peace but does not create peace. Forces that are to renew the face of the earth should proceed from within, from the spirit" (81). The "new order" emerging after the war, if it is to prove any better than the interbellum order, "must rest on the unshakable foundation, on the solid rock of natural law and of divine revelation" (82).

Echoing the teaching of Pius XI before him, Pius XII insists that the problems of the modern world are not due principally to economic factors:

> Their root is deeper and more intrinsic, belonging to the sphere of religious belief and moral convictions which have been perverted by the progressive alienation of the peoples from that unity of doctrine, faith, customs, and morals

> which once was promoted by the tireless and
> beneficent work of the Church. (83)

Anticipating Vatican II's accent on the role of the laity, the pope underlines that every baptized Christian has the mission of preaching the gospel to the world, "the most noble and most fruitful work for peace" (84; cf. 84–91). The "first and essential duty" of the lay apostle is "individual sanctification," especially in these times, when "obstacles and oppositions [are] vast and deep and minutely organized as never before" and "the conflict between Christianity and anti-Christianism grows intense" (85–86). In this combat "the family has a special mission, for it is the spirit of the family that exercises the most powerful influence on that of the rising generation" (90).

In his closing observations, Pius XII returns to a charge often leveled against the Church, viz., that she interferes with worldly progress and civil authority. In reality, "there is no opposition between the laws that govern the life of faithful Christians and the postulates of a genuinely humane humanitarianism, but rather unity and mutual support" (93). He prays that the

> present difficulties may open the eyes of many
> to see our Lord Jesus Christ and the mission
> of His Church on this earth in their true light,
> and that all those who are in power may decide
> to allow the Church a free course to work for
> the formation of the rising generation accord-
> ing to the principles of justice and peace.

Here the pope is stipulating the minimum *negative* duty of states toward the Church—allowing her *freedom of action and education* (94). The Church in no way usurps the rights of civil authority; on the contrary, she preaches submission to earthly rulers as long as they strive to exercise their offices justly (102). The Church is moving in a different sphere and has different aims: "Glory to God in the highest; on earth, peace to men of good will" (102). She is "the City of God, whose King is Truth, whose law is love, and whose measure is eternity" (110, quoting St. Augustine). If only today's successors of the apostles would awaken to the fact that they have an indestructible God-given right *and duty* to pursue the Church's supernatural mission above and beyond anything that the state says or does to the contrary!

Beautifully the encyclical draws to a close with an appeal to children to pray for peace: "In this way you will put into practice the sublime precept of the Divine Master, the most sacred testament of His Heart, 'That they all may be one'" (115, Jn 17:21).

Summi Pontificatus is a permanent record of sound Catholic teaching on the unity of the human family, the duty of men and nations towards one another, and the role of the one true religion in bringing about those goods that secularists *say* they want but can never obtain by their own methods.

APPENDIX 3

······················

SHOULD WE APOLOGIZE
FOR THE INQUISITION?

I AM ALL IN FAVOR OF MAKING APOL-
ogies when wrongs have been committed. It is
not just a very Christian thing to do; it is the
core of the gospel. We are sinners who deserve judgment and we ask the merciful Lord to forgive us. Jesus
was sent into the world "not to condemn the world,
but so that the world might be saved through Him."[1]
To prove the connection between Christianity, confession of sins, and forgiveness would be to copy out
the New Testament.

One should not have any problem, then, with prom-
inent leaders of the Catholic Church, above all the
pope, making public apologies for past errors, mistakes,
and yes, crimes. The Church is made up of sinners,
and sinners do one thing best—they sin. The Church
ought to be filled with repentant sinners, and penitents
do one thing best—they repent. The more public and
heartfelt the repentance, the better. In the ancient
Church, serious sins were confessed publicly, and public
penances were portioned out, the severity of which
would make today's parishioners faint in the pews.

There was, accordingly, no reason to be troubled by
John Paul II's *mea* (or *nostra*) *culpa* on the Day of Pardon, March 12, 2000, the First Sunday of Lent during
that Jubilee Year. Or rather, there was *every* reason to
be troubled in spirit and groan heavenwards for mercy
when the pope recalled the seemingly endless catalog of
sins committed by men and women over the centuries

---

[1] Jn 3:16.

who were (and are) supposed to be "fellow citizens with the saints, and the domestics of God."[2] He never once said *the Church* herself sinned; indeed, he insisted that the Church as the immaculate bride of Christ could never sin. He only ever said baptized *Christians* had sinned—men and women trying, more or less, to live the gospel, and failing, more or less, to do so—and he begged forgiveness of God and of mankind for those lukewarm and errant faithful. And he did not spare himself or any member of the Church today. It was a heroic gesture of humility, contrition, magnanimity, of a pure and childlike love of God.[3]

The problem is when history begins to be rewritten to favor slandering the Church, to support the Hollywood image of a huge, dark behemoth stalking human history, dominating the Middle Ages with threats and punishments. Such a thing happened at the "International Symposium 'The Inquisition,'" held in Rome in October 1998, which attracted considerable attention at the time, and will attract even more in the future, because its proceedings—all 783 pages' worth—were subsequently published.

Is there anyone who has ever doubted that evils were committed during the Inquisition? No, not really, any more than people have doubted the evils committed by secular courts in every age and place. Yet no subject of history has been as routinely exaggerated, and as commonly brought forward by Protestants and atheists alike, for discrediting and vilifying the Catholic Church, as

---

[2] Eph 2:19.
[3] And it was an act long prepared for by the soundest of theologians: Cardinal Journet comes to mind (see his *Theology of the Church*, 207–32; cf. Maritain, *On the Church of Christ*, 6–14, 40–44, *et passim*). In December 1999, to prepare for the Day of Pardon, the International Theological Commission prepared a document *Memory and Reconciliation: The Church and the Faults of the Past*, which also demonstrates the legitimacy of an act such as the pope's on the Day of Pardon.

"the Inquisition."[4] The Proceedings of the Symposium bid fair to outdo all prior publications in the extent to which they pillory the popes, cutlass the Cardinals, and disembowel the Dominicans, among others, for their unspeakable crimes against humanity. Here's a tasty morsel: "Because of the Roman Inquisition, Pius V has more legal murders staining his record than any other sixteenth-century pope, including Paul IV and Sixtus V. Nevertheless, he has become the only one of this group to be canonized, while the other two remain bywords for bigoted ferocity."[5] "That the wisest and saintliest among the Fathers and Doctors of the Church, through their personal authority, gave credence to this 'communal doctrine' [of torture and death] to the point of seeming to imbue it with a quasi-Magisterial authority, necessitates that the authentic magisterium of the Church make honorable amends."[6]

All this is tediously tendentious. Pius V was in truth a mighty saint whose support of the Roman Inquisition can be easily defended. To speak of the deaths of convicted criminals, as Pius and others of his day understood them, as "legal murders" is lurid, journalistic prose. Moreover, to pit an "authentic magisterium" of today against a "quasi-magisterium" of the past reveals an almost childish understanding of how the Tradition of the Church works.

Let's adopt a realistic perspective. First of all, it isn't as if the Inquisition has never been studied by reputable, sober, and gifted historians. The disclosure of certain Vatican documents and the opening of hidden archives did not alter in any significant way the major historical facts that had already been digested and reflected

---

[4] As the Symposium volume itself acknowledges, while one may speak of "the Inquisition" in the singular for convenience, it is not really a single thing; there were several distinct inquisitions set up in various regions at different times for different purposes.
[5] *Proceedings*, 545.
[6] *Proceedings*, 767.

upon. Many fine books have been written, and most of them were able to show that the Inquisition was not as bad as it might have been, and certainly not as bad as authors who let their imaginations get carried away have pretended. An excellent book with no axe to grind is Henry Kamen's *The Spanish Inquisition—A Historical Revision* (Yale University Press, 1998). Kamen's goal is to correct, with accurate evidence, the badly exaggerated stories of the Spanish Inquisition, and to put the whole in perspective. At a generous estimate, only 1% of the persons tried by the Inquisition were burnt at the stake. Most of the guilty were punished with a flogging and required spiritual exercises. A reviewer of this book, Samuel Nigro,[7] made some interesting comparisons: Moses had more people put to death *in one day* for worshiping the Golden Calf[8] than Torquemada and his companions during many decades. The number of Catholics who were murdered in Protestant countries far outnumbered all who were executed as a result of the Inquisition; for example, during her almost forty-five-year reign, Queen Elizabeth I was responsible for more executions on religious grounds (i.e., the martyrdom of Catholics) than were the Spanish and Roman Inquisitions *combined* over a period of *three centuries*! Such observations do not necessarily *justify* anything; but they do put things very much in perspective. Some might say that the Inquisition was worse than other political crimes because it claimed to be a defense of the rights of God, who is above all interested in mercy and human dignity. I would reply that God Himself, according to the Bible, is responsible for starting and finishing many inquisitions more severe than the Church's, and that the Church claims to act with a divine authority that imitates not only God's perfection of mercy but also His perfection of justice.

---

[7] *Social Justice Review*, March-April 1999.
[8] See Ex 32:27-28.

In many places the Inquisition's court acted with considerably greater justice *and leniency* than its secular equivalents, which were habitually draconian and ruthless. The Inquisition introduced in many places for the first time a systematic procedure of evidence-gathering, a transparent juridical process, a requirement of eyewitness testimony subjected to cross-examination, and other features we have come to associate with democratic court justice.[9] A set of clear and honest rules had to be followed so that Church authorities could monitor the system; for instance, careful transcripts of the judicial proceedings had to be kept and periodically submitted. These records constitute a goldmine for later researchers, given that practically nothing like them is to be found among the often arbitrary and secretive proceedings of secular courts. These and many similar features were utterly novel at the time. People who were found to be falsely accused were quickly released, and the punishments allotted to people convicted of heresy, blasphemy, or what have you, were in many instances *less* than what had been customary prior to the establishment of the Inquisition.

It bears mentioning too that revisionist historians, under the lurid word "torture," heap together a whole range of medieval practices that include what we would call "trials" or "tests" or "pressure tactics" *as well as*, in a minority of cases, what can accurately be called physical torture. While it does not justify church leaders having recourse to secular approaches, knowledge of the universal severity of criminal justice throughout European history until modern times will tend to have

---

[9] As Fr. William Most writes: "Persons accused by the Inquisition were not allowed to know the accusers, to protect the accusers—this sort of thing happens in protection of witnesses in U.S. courts today. But the person arrested was to make a list of his personal enemies and none of their testimony would be used against him. What modern court allows such a thing?" (Most, "Inquisition").

a softening effect on one's view of ecclesiastical courts. And only a fool could fail to see that the great modern empires which derisively repudiated the leadership of the Church in order to (as they proclaimed in their propaganda) emancipate and exalt Man for Man's Sake, outrageously violated human rights in ways that could never have entered the minds of all the Torquemadas and Savonarolas of Christendom put together.

A historian brandishing the sword of historical judgment should find many reasons to exercise self-restraint, as well as other virtues of the discipline—a balanced perspective nourished by sources pro and contra, examination of one's own hidden motivations, the ability to be detached from one's own age and alert to its hypocrisies. Most historians seem to lack this restraint and all these virtues when it comes to bashing the Catholic Church, a fact that has often been noted, but evidently not often enough to have reached those who were involved in writing the papers of this Symposium.

Moreover—and this is perhaps the point most worth pondering—it seems bizarre that modern people are so dull to the social dangers of religious error. Anyone acquainted with medieval history is aware of the massive civil disorders caused by heretical bodies such as the Cathars, Albigensians, and Waldensians.[10] The problems at hand were not, as modern newspaper-readers too readily imagine, mere differences of opinion quietly expressed in polite publications. They were dissensions that tore apart the fabric of society, undermined the family, the political order, individual moral responsibility. The Church, or better, Christendom with the Church's encouragement, was right to act swiftly and, when necessary, severely. Summarizing Warren Carroll's account, Fr. William Most brings before our eyes two typical medieval situations:

---

[10] See Wakefield and Evans, *Heresies of the High Middle Ages.*

In France and Spain especially, the Cathar heretics were a danger not just to the Church,
but to the state, and to all.... The Cathars
then were as dangerous as terrorists today, and
brought fear, cruelty, bloodshed and war wherever they had sufficient numbers. In southern
France it took the full armed power of the
King of France to overcome them.... In 1242
the Cathars murdered ten of the Inquisitors.

As to the Spanish episode, the Turks in
1480 attacked the south Italian city of Otranto.
12,000 people were killed, the rest made slaves.
The sacred book of Islam does call for killing all "infidels"; the *Koran* says: "When ye
encounter unbelievers, strike off their heads
until ye have made a great slaughter among
them, and bind them in bonds" (cited from
B. Palmer, *Understanding the Islamic Explo-
sion*, Horizon Books, 1980, p. 36). The Turks
killed every cleric in the city and sawed the
archbishop in two. So Queen Isabel sent a
fleet to Italy. In September of 1480, when it
was clear the Turks might do the same to any
coastal city, Isabel established the Inquisition.
It dealt with the special problem of those who
pretended to become Christian, but were not
really converted, and might open the gates of
the city to the Turks.[11]

Medieval Christendom reacted in *two* ways to such
large-scale crises: with earnest prayer, and with a
sharp sword. Not just with prayer, nor only with the
sword; recourse was had to both, in due season. Modern churchmen condemn this "pragmatic" approach to
problem-solving not so much because they have thought
through the issues carefully, but because of the domi-
nance of a type of idealism that occasions irreparable

---

[11] See Most, "Inquisition," referencing Carroll, *History of Christendom,* vol. 3.

harm. I refer to the attitude that "All that has ever been necessary in Christianity is that we believe, pray, and suffer. Anything beyond this is sinful." Rarely is it stated so bluntly, but it underlies a lot of what our prelates are saying.[12]

So: the Europeans should not have fought the Turks when they tried to break into Europe again and again? We should have let them just pour in, rape the women and pillage the towns, desecrate the sanctuary and burn down the church; in due course, erect their mosques? The "counter-attack" should have been simply Christian meekness, forgiveness, and preaching, where preaching was practicable? Or: we should have let the Manichaean heretics of southern France promote their views and hold their peculiar forms of worship, regardless of the harm it caused—the loss of faith (and loss of salvation) of thousands of souls? Freedom and rights for all!

The popes of the nineteenth century were much more realistic: they saw that, in practice, this slogan almost always ends up meaning freedom and rights for everybody *but* the Church, placing Catholics at a disadvantage. True, Christian realism becomes pagan self-assertion if detached from the exercise of charity and forgiveness; but these latter, for their part, become dreamy nonentities if they are not rooted in a daily, tightly-knit community and way of life. In modern times we have almost abandoned the *worldly reality of Christian faith.* We are living in our heads and our faith seems to make no demands on the temporal order. What happened to the renewal of the face of the earth?

This leads us to a deeper problem, easily forgotten in our days of widespread relativism, indifferentism, and "value-free" democracy. Serious religious error does not stay in the head; it burrows into the heart, and is circulated throughout the bloodstream until it affects

---

[12] See chapter 19.

every word and work of man, tweaking, misguiding, perverting. It was *with good reason* that the Church once took pains to prevent the dissemination of heresy and other crimes against faith; it was *with good reason* that civil governments once took seriously their responsibility to the truth of the gospel and to the protection of the rights of weaker members of society, the poor and uneducated who were not able, like the minority of educated clerics, to refute plausible and flattering errors. Societies are glued together by charity, and charity is nourished by truth—the truth about God, the truth about man. There is no more elementary lesson of CST, as can be seen in nearly every encyclical from Gregory XVI to Benedict XVI.

It therefore seems all the more ridiculous to me that the Inquisition should be called to task for attempting to rid certain areas of pernicious crimes against the Catholic faith—as if no sin could ever be committed in *thought* or *desire*, but only with sticks and stones. I think it was Chesterton who said that the children's rhyme "sticks and stones may break my bones, but names will never hurt me" is exactly wrong, for it is what we *name* things that gives us power over them or them power over us. Which *names* are to be given to which *things* is the central question of intelligence. Is this or that belief *true* or *false*? Is this or that god *true* or *false*? From this vantage, it isn't sticks and stones that do the lasting damage to a person—it's error, vice, perversion.

Church leaders should have the courage to say that St. Thomas Aquinas was right in holding this, that the general conclusions he derives from it are equally right (civil government *does* have a solemn obligation to promote moral virtue, including the practice of religion, among the citizenry, and to take vigorous though prudent steps to limit errors and vices that undermine the common good), and that his particular social recommendations, though no longer desirable to us for a variety of reasons, are not intrinsically immoral (e.g., that notorious heretics may be handed over by the Church to the secular power to be punished). Aquinas was given the gift to articulate an understanding of Christian wisdom that unites charity and justice, freedom and order, at their highest pitch. To pretend that his articulation is no longer valid would simply indicate weak knees in front of (explicit or implicit) threats from liberalism's petty tyrants who run our modern Western governments. This would be truly shameful, when not so very long ago, popes and bishops and priests suffered unspeakably, in many cases to the point of martyrdom, precisely because they refused to compromise even a little with the Enlightenment's poisonous tenets.

There is much else that might be said to caution people against yielding themselves to wailings and lamentations over the Inquisition, which has long been a favorite target of attack, and is likely ever to remain so. But my main conclusions are four.

First, I recommend we not let ourselves be bullied into shame by conferences and symposiums that try to tell us how wicked we have been, and dazzle us with credentials, wads of footnotes, and official sanctions. History nearly always has two or three sides of a story to tell, all the more when it comes to the Middle Ages, an exceedingly complex period that contemporary authors frequently badly misunderstand and thus misrepresent. And the roots of this problem go very deep, all the way to the basic question of what the Christian faith alive in the Catholic Church *is* and *is to be in the world*—in other words, the social, cultural expression of the Mystical Body of Christ.

Second, there is no doubt that Christians, as individuals, have often badly lived the gospel; we need only look into the mirror of our own lives, no scholarly

degree required. Therefore it is not necessary to go
to the opposite extreme by indiscriminately glorifying
the Inquisition or denying the veracity of some of the
critiques presented. Nearly every critique has something
worthwhile to teach us. What is necessary is humility
and repentance in the face of proven sin, beginning in
my own breast and extending outward to embrace the
whole human race. This is what Our Lord did in His
flesh on the Cross, and He asks us to imitate Him with
co-redemptive sufferings.[13] Pondering human sin inside
us and around us can be spiritually fruitful only if it
leads to renewed faith in the Redeemer of mankind,
renewed pleading for His forgiveness, renewed sorrow
for having offended Him, and renewed joy in His superabundant gift of life. As a matter of fact, looking at sin
in any other way, to any other purpose, will distract,
discourage, and ultimately destroy us. Fr. Paul Murray
has written insightfully about this point:

> Perseus knows that he has to slay the evil Gor-
> gon, Medusa, and he has to do it by cutting off
> her head. But he also knows that anyone who
> stares directly into the face of the evil Gor-
> gon will at once be turned to stone. Perseus
> accepts as a gift from one of the gods a shining
> bronze shield...[and] instead of staring directly
> into the face of Medusa as he slays her, he
> looks only at the image of the Gorgon reflected
> in his shield.... If out of pride or curiosity I
> allow myself to contemplate evil directly, with-
> out seeking refuge in God, if I contemplate
> it, day after day, week after week, either in
> the ordinary realm of the public media or in
> private gossip, gradually it will rob me of all
> my energy and hope. But if, when I have to
> confront evil, I have the humility to look at
> it only in the light of Christ my shield, then
> my energy and my hope will not be taken

---

[13] Cf. Col 1:24.

> from me.... Learning to look directly at that
> mirror which is Christ my shield, learning to
> see the evil around me, and the evil within me,
> in the light of Christ, is the best way, in fact
> the only sure way, to prevent my heart from
> being hardened into stone by either fear or
> prejudice, despair or false judgment.[14]

Third, it is crucial for Catholics who seek a better
understanding of Church history to acquaint themselves with an extraordinary legacy of Catholic historical writing from the nineteenth and the first half
of the twentieth centuries. Much of this writing is
today forgotten, but rarely because it has been bettered,
mostly for reasons of fashion, and, alas, not always for
honest reasons. C.S. Lewis once urged modern people,
for their own good, to read at least one great old
book (and he meant notably old—an ancient Greek
poet or philosopher, a Father of the Church, a monk
or friar of the Middle Ages, that sort of author) for
every five modern books. I would urge an additional
principle: for every book that criticizes or attacks a
Catholic figure, event, period, etc., try to find out
the best book written from the opposite perspective.
It may take a bit of searching, but with the help of
well-read friends and the internet, it usually leads to
something worth the wait.[15] An example would be

---

[14] Murray, "Dominicans Drinking: A Neglected Image of the
'Holy Preaching,'" 279–81. For whatever reason, this passage was
not included in Murray's later version of this essay in his book
The New Wine of Dominican Spirituality: A Drink Called Happiness.
[15] For example, there are still many people who have not yet experienced the tremendous exhilaration of reading Hilaire Belloc's
magnificent biographies of some of the most important men and
women of European history—*Wolsey, Cranmer, Cromwell, Charles I,*
and on and on. When you read a biography like one of his, you
begin to appreciate the difference between a mere collector of
facts, and a penetrating mind with an eye for the decisive detail
(Belloc walked and studied with his own eyes every battlefield
he wrote about) as well as the vast sweep of the European drama
(where, again, Belloc is nearly unrivaled).

William Thomas Walsh's grand biography of Philip II of Spain, worth more than piles of other books on that ruler and his century, and corrective of countless anti-Catholic errors.[16] The same author's *Characters of the Inquisition*[17] ought to be read by everyone with an interest in the subject, and especially those who wish to learn many eye-opening facts about inquisitors and heretics alike that they are not likely to find in the aforementioned Symposium volume.

Fourth and finally, we should not allow to slip through our fingers the countless opportunities Our Lord is giving us every day to do our part for the restoration of Christian culture — and yes, of *Christendom*, which is no empty concept but was once a vibrant reality and can return among us if human freedom awakens from its secularist slumber to rejoice in the living God and worship on His holy mountain. Whether this happy reawakening will come in the years left before the Second Coming, no one can know but God, in whose hands are all times and seasons. Still, this much we can be certain of: Our Lord has overcome the world, and shares His triumph with all who remain loyal to Him. "Christendom" will rise from the dead at the sound of the last trumpet, when Christ the King returns to establish His kingdom forever, making the earth His footstool, the heavens His court, and our hearts His throne.

---

[16] Published by Sheed & Ward in 1937, reprinted by TAN Books in 1987. This book has some fine pages on the Spanish Inquisition. See also the aforementioned treatment in Carroll's *A History of Christendom*, vol. 3.

[17] Published by P. J. Kenedy & Sons in 1940, reprinted by TAN Books in 1987 and again in 2005. Another small book I can recommend is *The Medieval Inquisition* by Albert Clement Shannon (Augustinian College Press, 1983). This study restricts itself to a narrower period, the High Middle Ages.

FURTHER READING

What follows is a short list of particularly helpful works on CST that I recommend for readers who wish to continue their studies in this area. Some of these titles are also mentioned in the Bibliography but most are not.

Billot, Louis Cardinal. *Liberalism: A Critique of Its Basic Principles and Various Forms* [1922]. Translated by George Barry O'Tool and Thomas Storck. Arouca Press, 2019.

Bourmaud, Dominique. *An Introduction to Catholic Social Doctrine.* Angelus Press, 2019.

Cahill, E. *The Framework of a Christian State* [1932]. Roman Catholic Books/Catholic Media Apostolate, n.d.

Coulombe, Charles. *The Compleat Monarchist.* Os Justi Press, 2025.

Crean, Thomas, and Alan Fimister. *Integralism: A Manual of Political Philosophy.* editiones scholasticae, 2020.

Dillon, George F. *The War of the Antichrist with the Church and Christian Civilization* [1885]. Edited by Joshua Charles. TAN Books, 2023.

Dreher, Rod. *Live Not By Lies: A Manual for Christian Dissidents.* Sentinel, 2020.

Dubay, Thomas. *Happy Are You Poor: The Simple Life and Spiritual Freedom.* Second edition. Ignatius Press, 2003.

Esolen, Anthony. *Reclaiming Catholic Social Teaching: A Defense of the Church's True Teachings on Marriage, Family, and the State.* Sophia Institute Press, 2014.

Fanfani, Amintore. *Catholicism, Protestantism, and Capitalism* [1934]. IHS Press, 2003.

Ferrara, Christopher A. *Liberty, the God That Failed: Policing the Sacred and Constructing the Myths of the Secular State, from Locke to Obama.* Angelico Press, 2012.

Gilson, Etienne, ed. *The Church Speaks to the Modern World: The Social Teachings of Leo XIII.* With a Foreword by Thomas Storck. Arouca Press, 2021.

Hahn, Scott, and Brandon McGinley. *It Is Right and Just: Why the Future of Civilization Depends on True Religion.* Emmaus Road, 2020.

Hajduk, David C. *Healing the Culture and the Family According to John Paul II*. Arouca Press, 2022.

Husslein, Joseph. *The Reign of Christ, the Immortal King of Ages* [1928]. XIII Books, 2024.

Jones, Andrew Willard. *Before Church and State: A Study of Social Order in the Sacramental Kingdom of St. Louis IX*. Emmaus Academic, 2017.

Kalb, James. *The Decomposition of Man: Identity, Technocracy, and the Church*. Angelico Press, 2023.

Kwasniewski, Peter, and P. Edmund Waldstein, eds. *Integralism and the Common Good: Selected Essays from* The Josias. Volume 1: *Family, City, and State*. Angelico Press, 2021.

Maistre, Joseph de, Juan Donoso Cortes, and Hilaire Belloc. *To Restore All Things: Essays of Catholic Political Thought*. Edited by Austin L. Lambert. Stabat Mater Press, 2025.

Médaille, John C. *Toward a Truly Free Market: A Distributist Perspective on the Role of Government, Taxes, Health Care, Deficits, and More*. ISI Books, 2010.

Morello, Sebastian. *Unto the Ages of Ages: Essays on Political Traditionalism*. Arouca Press, 2025.

Mullady, Brian Thomas Becket. *The Roots of a Christian Civilization: First Principles of a Just and Ordered Society*. EWTN Publishing, 2023.

Ousset, Jean. *Action: A Manual for the Reconstruction of Christendom*. Translated by Arthur E. Slater and R. A. Hickey. IHS Press, 2002.

Rao, John. *Catholic Christendom versus Revolutionary Disorder*. For the Whole Christ: The Collected Works of Dr. John Rao, vol. 1. Arouca Press, 2023.

———. *Removing the Blindfold: Nineteenth-Century Catholics and the Myth of Modern Freedom*. Angelus Press, 2014.

Ravasi, Javier P. Olivera. *The Cristero Counterrevolution and the Battle for the Soul of Mexico*. Os Justi Press, 2025.

Storck, Thomas. *Economics: An Alternative Introduction*. XIII Books, 2024.

———. *Foundations of a Catholic Political Order*. Second edition. Arouca Press, 2022.

———. *From Christendom to Americanism and Beyond: The Long, Jagged Trail to a Postmodern Void*. Angelico Press, 2015.

———. *Seeing the World with Catholic Eyes: A Conversation with Thomas Storck*. Around Press, 2021.

Waldstein, Edmund, ed. *Integralism and the Common Good: Selected Essays from "The Josias."* Volume 2: *The Two Powers*. Angelico Press, 2022.

Welty, Eberhard. *A Handbook of Christian Social Ethics*. Two volumes. Herder/Nelson, 1960.

Williams, Thomas D. *Who Is My Neighbor? Personalism and the Foundations of Human Rights*. The Catholic University of America Press, 2005.

BIBLIOGRAPHY

MAGISTERIAL AND QUASI-MAGISTERIAL DOCUMENTS

Benedict XV. Allocution to the Roman Patriciate and Nobility. January 5, 1920.

Boniface VIII. Bull *Unam Sanctam*. November 18, 1302.

Congregation for the Doctrine of the Faith. Decree *Cum Sanctissima*. February 22, 2020.

——. *Doctrinal Note on Some Questions Regarding the Participation of Catholics in Political Life*. November 24, 2002.

Dicastery for the Doctrine of the Faith. Declaration *Dignitas Infinita*. April 2, 2024.

Francis. Apostolic Exhortation *Laudate Deum*. October 4, 2023.

——. Homily for the Feast of the Epiphany. January 6, 2022.

——. Udienza al Corpo Diplomatico accreditato presso la Santa Sede per la presentazione degli auguri per il nuovo anno. January 9, 2023.

Gelasius. *Famuli Vestrae Pietatis* or *Duo Sunt*. 494.

Gregory VII. *Letter to Bishop Hermann of Metz*. March 15, 1081.

Gregory XVI. Encyclical Letter *Mirari Vos*. August 15, 1832.

International Theological Commission. *Memory and Reconciliation: The Church and the Faults of the Past*. December 1999.

John Paul II. Address to Members of the Pontifical Council for Culture. January 12, 1990

——. Address to Members of the Pontifical Council for Culture. January 16, 1984.

——. Address to Members of the Pontifical Council for Culture, January 10, 1992.

——. Address to the Italian National Congress of the Ecclesial Movement for Cultural Commitment. January 16, 1982.

——. Apostolic Letter *Dies Domini*. May 31, 1998.

——. Encyclical Letter *Centesimus Annus*. May 1, 1991.

——. Encyclical Letter *Dominum et Vivificantem*. May 18, 1986.

——. Encyclical Letter *Evangelium Vitae*. March 25, 1995.

——. Encyclical Letter *Laborem Exercens*. September 14, 1981.

——. Encyclical Letter *Sollicitudo Rei Socialis*. December 30, 1987.

——. Encyclical Letter *Veritatis Splendor*. August 6, 1993.

———. Homily in Perth, Australia. November 30, 1986.

———. Post-Synodal Apostolic Exhortation *Ecclesia in Oceania*. November 22, 2001.

John XXIII. Encyclical Letter *Mater et Magistra*. May 15, 1961.

———. Encyclical Letter *Pacem in Terris*. April 11, 1963.

Leo XIII. Encyclical Letter *Aeterni Patris*. August 4, 1879.

———. Encyclical Letter *Annum Ingressi Sumus*. March 19, 1902.

———. Encyclical Letter *Annum Sacrum*. May 25, 1899.

———. Encyclical Letter *Arcanum Divinae*. February 10, 1880.

———. Encyclical Letter *Au Milieu des Sollicitudes*. February 16, 1892.

———. Encyclical Letter *Diuturnum Illud*. June 29, 1881.

———. Encyclical Letter *Graves de Communi Re*. January 18, 1901.

———. Encyclical Letter *Humanum Genus*. April 20, 1884.

———. Encyclical Letter *Libertas Praestantissimum*. June 20, 1888.

———. Encyclical Letter *Longinqua Oceani*. January 6, 1895.

———. Encyclical Letter *Mirae Caritatis*. May 28, 1902.

———. Encyclical Letter *Permoti Nos*. July 10, 1895.

———. Encyclical Letter *Providentissimus Deus*. November 18, 1893.

———. Encyclical Letter *Quod Apostolici Muneris*. December 28, 1878.

———. Encyclical Letter *Rerum Novarum*. May 15, 1891.

———. Encyclical Letter *Sapientiae Christianae*. January 10, 1890.

———. Encyclical letter *Satis Cognitum*. June 29, 1896.

———. Encyclical Letter *Tametsi Futura*. November 1, 1900.

Paul VI. Encyclical Letter *Ecclesiam Suam*. August 6, 1964.

———. Encyclical Letter *Humanae Vitae*. July 25, 1968.

———. Encyclical Letter *Populorum Progressio*. March 26, 1967.

Pius IX. Encyclical Letter *Quanta Cura*, with *Syllabus of Errors*. December 8, 1864.

Pius X. Encyclical Letter *E Supremi*. October 4, 1903.

———. Encyclical Letter *Singulari Quadam*. September 24, 1912.

———. Encyclical Letter *Vehementer Nos*. February 11, 1906.

Pius XI. Encyclical Letter *Casti Connubii*. December 31, 1930.

———. Encyclical Letter *Divini Redemptoris*. March 19, 1937.

———. Encyclical Letter *Ingravescentibus Malis*. September 29, 1937.

———. Encyclical Letter *Quadragesimo Anno*. May 15, 1931.

——. Encyclical Letter *Quas Primas*. December 11, 1925.

Pius XII. Allocution *Ci Riesce*. December 6, 1953.

——. Christmas Message of 1942.

——. Christmas Message of 1944.

——. Encyclical Letter *Summi Pontificatus*. October 20, 1939.

——. Message for Italian Catholic Action Family Day. March 23, 1952.

Second Vatican Ecumenical Council. Constitution on the Sacred Liturgy *Sacrosanctum Concilium*. December 4, 1963.

——. Declaration on Religious Freedom *Dignitatis Humanae*. December 7, 1965.

——. Decree on the Apostolate of the Laity *Apostolicam Actuositatem*. November 18, 1965.

——. Dogmatic Constitution on the Church *Lumen Gentium*. November 21, 1964.

——. Pastoral Constitution on the Church in the Modern World *Gaudium et Spes*. December 7, 1965.

OTHER SOURCES[1]

"*Dignitas infinita*: Rethinking Human Dignity." *Voice of the Family*, April 10, 2024. https://voiceofthefamily.com/dignitas-infinita-rethinking-human-dignity/.

"Love and the Message of the Mystics: Interview With Carmelite Father Maximilian Herraiz." *Zenit*, October 29, 2004. https://zenit.org/2004/10/29/love-and-the-message-of-the-mystics/.

Adams, Samuel. *The Rights of the Colonists (The Report of the Committee of Correspondence to the Boston Town Meeting, Nov. 20, 1772)*. *Old South Leaflets* no. 173. Directors of the Old South Work, 1906. Document at https://history.hanover.edu/texts/adamss.html.

Adolphe, Jane. "Reading *Laudate Deum* through the Lens of the World Economic Forum in Light of the Synod on Synodality." *Crisis Magazine*, October 18, 2023. https://crisis-magazine.com/opinion/reading-laudate-deum-through-the-lens-of-the-world-economic-forum-in-light-of-the-synod-on-synodality.

André Marie. "For Christ the King." *Catholicism.org*, March 10, 2008. https://catholicism.org/for-christ-the-king.html.

---

[1] In addition to Aristotle and St. Thomas Aquinas.

Aubert, Roger. "Religious Liberty from *Mirari Vos* to the *Syllabus*." In *Concilium*, vol. 7: *Historical Problems of Church Renewal*. Paulist Press, 1965.

Birzer, Bradley J. *Beyond Tenebrae: Christian Humanism in the Twilight of the West*. Angelico Press, 2019.

Bourne, Lisa. "US bishops follow Pope in calling death penalty 'inadmissible,' admit they don't know what it means." *LifeSiteNews*, June 21, 2019. www.lifesitenews.com/news/us-bishops-vote-to-follow-pope-francis-teaching-on-death-penalty/.

Brankin, Anthony. "Homosexual Immorality Pointed Out by Martyr Charles Lwanga and Companions." *CatholicCulture. org*. https://www.catholicculture.org/culture/library/view.cfm?recnum=9667.

Bulgakov, Sergius. *Spiritual Diary*. Edited by Mark Roosien and Roberto J. De La Noval. Angelico Press, 2022.

Cahill, E. *The Framework of a Christian State* [1932]. Roman Catholic Books/Catholic Media Apostolate, n.d.

Campbell, Phillip. *Power from on High: Theocratic Kingship from Constantine to the Reformation*. Cruachan Hill Press, 2021.

Carroll, Warren. *A History of Christendom*. Volume 3: *The Glory of Christendom, 1100–1517*. Christendom Press, 1993.

Chaput, Charles. "The Vocation of Christians in American Public Life." Lecture given on March 1, 2010 at Houston Baptist University. https://archive.wf-f.org/Chaput_2010PublicLife.html.

Charles, Rodger. *Christian Social Witness and Teaching*. Volume 2: *The Modern Social Teaching: Contexts, Summaries, Analysis*. Gracewing, 1998.

Chiron, Yves. *Paul VI: The Divided Pope*. Translated by James Walther. Angelico Press, 2022.

Corrêa de Oliveira, Plinio. *Nobility and Analogous Traditional Elites in the Allocutions of Pius XII: A Theme Illuminating American Social History*. Hamilton Press, 1993.

Coulombe, Charles. *The Compleat Monarchist*. Os Justi Press, 2025.

Crean, Thomas, and Alan Fimister. *Integralism: A Manual of Political Philosophy*. editiones scholasticae, 2020.

Crean, Thomas. "The Nine Choirs of Politics." *Tradition & Sanity* Substack, September 15, 2025. https://www.traditionsanity.com/p/the-nine-choirs-of-politics.

———. *Letters from That City: A Guide to Holy Scripture for Students of Theology*. Os Justi Press, 2023.

d'Eypernon, Taymans. *The Blessed Trinity and the Sacraments* [1961]. Os Justi Press, 2024.

Davies, Michael. *The Second Vatican Council and Religious Liberty*. The Neumann Press, 1992.

De Koninck, Charles. *On the Primacy of the Common Good*. Translated by Ralph McInerny. *The Writings of Charles De Koninck*, vol. 2. University of Notre Dame Press, 2009.

de Mattei, Roberto. *Love for the Papacy and Filial Resistance to the Pope in the History of the Church*. Angelico Press, 2019.

———. *The Paths of Evil: Conspiracies, Plots, and Secret Societies*. Translated by Nicholas Reitzug. Sophia Institute Press, 2023.

Desmond, Joan Frawley. "Catechism's New Text on Death Penalty Draws Praise and Concern." *National Catholic Register*, August 6, 2018. www.ncregister.com/news/catechism-s-new-text-on-death-penalty-draws-praise-and-concern.

Dignitatis Humanae Colloquium. Dialogos Institute, 2017.

Dubay, Thomas. *Happy Are You Poor: The Simple Life and Spiritual Freedom*. Second edition. Ignatius Press, 2003.

Duffy, Eamon. *The Stripping of the Altars: Traditional Religion in England, 1400–1580*. Yale University Press, 2005.

Dumortier, François-Xavier. "Totalitarianism." In *The New Dictionary of Catholic Social Thought*, ed. Judith A. Dwyer, 955–59. The Liturgical Press, 1994.

Ehler, Sidney, and John B. Morrall, eds. *Church and State Through the Centuries: A Collection of Historic Documents with Commentaries*. The Newman Press, 1954.

Elliott, Walter. *The Life of Father Hecker*. New York: The Columbus Press, 1891.

Feser, Edward, and Joseph Bessette. *By Man Shall His Blood Be Shed: A Catholic Defense of Capital Punishment*. Ignatius Press, 2017.

———. "Two problems with *Dignitas Infinita*." April 11, 2024. https://edwardfeser.blogspot.com/2024/04/two-problems-with-dignitas-infinita.html.

Fiedrowicz, Michael. *The Traditional Mass: History, Form, and Theology of the Classical Roman Rite*. Angelico Press, 2020.

Finley, John DeSilva, et al. *Sexual Identity: The Harmony of Philosophy, Science, and Revelation*. Emmaus Road Publishing, 2022.

Flanders, Timothy S. "*Dignitas Infinita*: the Good, the Bad, and the Ugly." *OnePeterFive*, April 9, 2024. https://onepeterfive. com/dignitas-infinita-the-good-the-bad-and-the-ugly/.

———. "It's Time to Purchase Your Sacred Heart Flag for June." *OnePeterFive*, May 13, 2025. https://onepeterfive.com/ its-time-to-purchase-your-sacred-heart-flag-for-june/.

Foley, Michael P. *Lost in Translation: Meditating on the Orations of the Traditional Roman Rite*. Angelico Press, 2023.

———. "The Orations of the Feast of Christ the King." *New Liturgical Movement*, October 23, 2020. www.newliturgicalmove ment.org/2020/10/the-orations-of-feast-of-christ-king.html.

———. "A Reflection on the Fate of the Feast of Christ the King." *New Liturgical Movement*, October 21, 2020, www. newliturgicalmovement.org/2020/10/a-reflection-on-fate- of-feast-of-christ.html.

Green, James R. "The Crisis in the Church Is an LSD Trip." *Grain of Wheat* Substack, August 23, 2025. https://grainof- wheat.substack.com/p/lsd-caused-the-crisis.

Gruber, Hermann. "Freemasonry." *The Catholic Encyclopedia*. Appleton, 1910. www.newadvent.org/cathen/09771a.htm.

Halecki, Oscar, and James F. Murray. *Pius XII*. Weidenfeld and Nicolson, 1954.

Hales, E.E.Y. *Pio Nono. A Study in European Politics and Religion in the Nineteenth Century*. Eyre & Spottiswoode, 1954.

Harrison, Brian W. "Is John Courtney Murray a Reliable Interpreter of *Dignitatis Humanae*?" www.rtforum.org/ lt/lt33.html.

———. *Religious Liberty and Contraception*. John XXIII Fellowship Co-op, 1988.

Haynes, Michael. "Cardinal Fernández calls for change to Catholic condemnation of homosexuality as 'intrinsically disordered.'" *LifeSiteNews*, April 8, 2024. www.lifesitenews.com/ news/cardinal-fernandez-homosexuality-intrinsically-evil/.

———. "Fr. James Martin urges Catholics to celebrate LGBT 'Pride Month,'" *LifeSiteNews*, June 2, 2025. www.lifesitenews. com/news/fr-james-martin-urges-catholics-to-celebrate- lgbt-pride-month/.

Hilgefort, Tate. "Parish Priests Are the Cure to the Crisis." *Crisis Magazine*, July 7, 2025. https://crisismagazine.com/ opinion/parish-priests-are-the-cure-to-the-crisis.

Hittinger, Russell. "How to Read *Dignitatis Humanae* on Establishment of Religion." Available at www.secondspring.co.uk/articles/hittinger.htm.

Hoffman, Matthew Cullinan. "Vatican II's Lost Condemnations of Communism Revealed to Public for First Time." *LifeSiteNews*, January 11, 2024, www.lifesitenews.com/news/vatican-iis-lost-condemnations-of-communism-revealed-to-public-for-first-ti.

Holböck, Ferdinand. *Married Saints and Blesseds Through the Centuries*. Translated by Michael J. Miller. Ignatius Press, 2002.

Holmes, J. Derek. *The Papacy in the Modern World, 1914–1978*. Crossroad, 1981.

——. *The Triumph of the Holy See. A Short History of the Papacy in the Nineteenth Century*. Burns & Oates, 1978.

Hunt, David. *Something for Nothing? An Explanation and Defense of the Scholastic Position on Usury*. Os Justi Press, 2024.

Jay, William. "Americanism—A Phantom Heresy?" *Catholicism. org*, May 16, 2005. https://catholicism.org/americanism-heresy.html.

Jefferson, Thomas. *Notes on the State of Virginia*. Richmond: J.W. Randolph, 1853.

Journet, Charles. *The Church of the Word Incarnate: An Essay in Speculative Theology*. Volume 1: The Apostolic Hierarchy. Translated by A.H.C. Downes. Sheed and Ward, 1955.

——. *The Theology of the Church*. Translated by Victor Szczurek. Ignatius Press, 2004.

Joy, John P. *Disputed Questions on Papal Infallibility*. Os Justi Press, 2022.

——. *On the Ordinary and Extraordinary Magisterium*. Arouca Press, 2023.

Kengor, Paul. "Vatican II's Unpublished Condemnations of Communism." *Crisis Magazine*, November 30, 2017. https://crisismagazine.com/opinion/vatican-iis-unpublished-condemnations-communism.

Koppelman, Alex. "Alan Keyes' letter from Notre Dame jail." *Salon*, May 8, 2009. www.salon.com/2009/05/08/keyes_arrest/.

Kwasniewski, Peter, and P. Edmund Waldstein, eds. *Integralism and the Common Good: Selected Essays from* The Josias. Volume 1: *Family, City, and State*. Angelico Press, 2021.

Kwasniewski, Peter. "Angels: Fellow Worshipers in the Liturgy of Heaven." *Tradition & Sanity* Substack, September 29, 2025. https://www.traditionsanity.com/p/angels-fellow-worshipers-in-the-liturgy.

———. "The Best and Most Necessary First Thing." *Tradition & Sanity* Substack, March 31, 2025. https://www.tradition-sanity.com/p/the-best-and-most-necessary-first.

———. *Bound by Truth: Authority, Obedience, Tradition, and the Common Good.* Angelico Press, 2023.

———. "Coincidences During the Reign of Pius XII? Political Background to Vatican II and Liturgical Changes." *LifeSiteNews,* May 25, 2021. www.lifesitenews.com/blogs/coincidences-during-the-reign-of-pius-xii-political-background-to-vatican-ii-and-liturgical-changes.

———. "Damned Lies: On the Destiny of Judas Iscariot." *Rorate Caeli,* March 30, 2015. https://rorate-caeli.blogspot.com/2015/03/damned-lies-on-destiny-of-judas-iscariot.html.

———. "Fiddling with the Collects of Ss Henry II and Louis IX: Wokeness Avant la Lettre." *New Liturgical Movement,* July 15, 2024. www.newliturgicalmovement.org/2024/07/fiddling-with-collects-of-ss-henry-ii.html.

———. "Five ways Catholic laity can powerfully influence Church for good from within." *LifeSiteNews,* November 8, 2018. www.lifesitenews.com/blogs/five-ways-catholic-laity-can-powerfully-influence-church-for-good-from-with/.

———. "God as Fire." *New Liturgical Movement,* March 15, 2021. www.newliturgicalmovement.org/2021/03/god-as-fire.html.

———. "The Great Cloud of Witnesses in the Roman Martyrology." *OnePeterFive,* February 12, 2020. https://onepeterfive.com/witnesses-martyrology/.

———. "How a False Unification of Nature and Grace Led to Their Divorce." *Tradition & Sanity* Substack, January 29, 2024. https://www.traditionsanity.com/p/how-a-false-unification-of-nature.

———, ed. *Illusions of Reform: Responses to Cavadini, Healy, and Weinandy in Defense of the Traditional Mass and the Faithful Who Attend It.* Os Justi Press, 2023.

———. "Lights and Shadows in the Pontificate of Pius XII." *OnePeterFive,* September 22, 2021. https://onepeterfive.com/lights-and-shadows-in-the-pontificate-of-pius-xii/.

———. *Ministers of Christ: Recovering the Roles of Clergy and Laity in an Age of Confusion*. Crisis Publications, 2021.

———. "The Office of Workers and Fighters: Praying Prime." *OnePeterFive*, February 5, 2020. https://onepeterfive.com/workers-fighters-prime/.

———. "The Omission of 'Difficult' Psalms and the Spreading-Thin of the Psalter." *Rorate Caeli*, November 15, 2016. https://rorate-caeli.blogspot.com/2016/11/the-omission-of-difficult-psalms-and.html.

———. *Resurgent in the Midst of Crisis: Sacred Liturgy, the Traditional Latin Mass, and Renewal in the Church*. Angelico Press, 2014.

———. "Should the Feast of Christ the King Be Celebrated in October or November?" *Rorate Caeli*, October 22, 2014. https://rorate-caeli.blogspot.com/2014/10/should-feast-of-christ-king-be.html.

———. "Should We 'Despise Earthly Goods and Love Heavenly Ones'? A Liturgical Lesson for Lent." *OnePeterFive*, March 2, 2022. https://onepeterfive.com/despise-earthly-goods/.

———, ed. *Sixty Years After: Catholics Writers Assess the Legacy of Vatican II*. Angelico Press, 2022.

———. "These condemned criminals accepted 'inadmissible' death penalty and became saints." *LifeSiteNews*, August 11, 2020. www.lifesitenews.com/blogs/these-condemned-criminals-accepted-inadmissible-death-penalty-and-became-saints/.

———. *Treasuring the Goods of Marriage in a Throwaway Society*. Sophia Institute Press, 2023.

———. *True Obedience in the Church: A Guide to Discernment in Challenging Times*. Sophia Institute Press, 2021.

———. *Turned Around: Replying to Common Objections Against the Traditional Latin Mass*. TAN Books, 2024.

———. "What Good is a Changing Catechism? Revisiting the Purpose and Limits of a Book." In idem, *The Road from Hyperpapalism to Catholicism*, vol. 2. Arouca Press, 2022.

———. "What Is the Catholic Intellectual Tradition?" *OnePeterFive*, February 10, 2021.

Lamb, Matt. "Target removes some LGBT merchandise linked to 'transgender' satanist designer after backlash." *LifeSiteNews*, May 24, 2023. www.lifesitenews.com/news/target-removes-some-lgbt-merchandise-linked-to-transgender-satanist-designer-after-backlash/.

Lamont, John, and Claudio Pierantoni, eds. *Defending the Faith Against Present Heresies: Letters and statements addressed to Pope Francis, the Cardinals, and the Bishops with a collection of related articles and interviews*. Arouca Press, 2021.

Lawler, Leila Marie. *God Has No Grandchildren: A Guided Reading of Pius XI's Encyclical* Casti Connubii, *On Chaste Marriage*. Arouca Press, 2021.

Lerhinan, John Patrick. *A Sociological Commentary on* Divini Redemptoris. Studies in Sociology 17. The Catholic University of America Press, 1946.

Lucien, Bernard. *Religious Liberty: Continuity or Contradiction?* Arouca Press, 2025.

MacDonald, Matthew. "A Tale of Two Religious." *Crisis*, September 16, 2020. www.crisismagazine.com/2020/a-tale-of-two-religious.

Manent, Pierre. *An Intellectual History of Liberalism*. Translated by Rebecca Balinski. Princeton University Press, 1994.

Marco, Rob. "'A Sign of Contradiction': Life Beyond the Smartphone—An Interview with Dr. Peter Kwasniewski." Edward Pentin's Substack, July 5, 2025. https://edwardpentin.substack.com/p/a-sign-of-contradiction-life-beyond.

Maritain, Jacques. *On the Church of Christ*. Translated by Joseph W. Evans. University of Notre Dame Press, 1973.

Marshner, William. "*Dignitatis humanae* and Traditional Teaching on Church and State." *Faith & Reason* (1983). Republished at www.catholicculture.org/culture/library/view.cfm?id=8778.

Martin, Regis. "Configuring All Things to Christ." *Crisis Magazine*, July 5, 2025. https://crisismagazine.com/opinion/configuring-all-things-to-christ.

——. "Cultivating the Soil." *Crisis Magazine*, June 21, 2025. https://crisismagazine.com/opinion/cultivating-the-soil.

——. "Living an Integrated Life." *Crisis Magazine*, August 30, 2025. https://crisismagazine.com/opinion/living-an-integrated-life.

——. "Rediscovering Our Roots." *Crisis Magazine*, July 19, 2025. https://crisismagazine.com/opinion/rediscovering-our-roots.

McCann, Catherine. "Pope Francis's non-judgmental style influenced abortion Yes vote." *The Irish Times*, July 17, 2018. www.irishtimes.com/opinion/pope-francis-s-non-judgmental-style-influenced-abortion-yes-vote-1.3566955.

Morello, Sebastian. *Mysticism, Magic, and Monasteries: Recovering the Sacred Mystery at the Heart of Reality*. Os Justi Press, 2024.

———. *Unto the Ages of Ages: Essays on Political Traditionalism*. Arouca Press, 2025.

Most, William. "Inquisition." www.catholicculture.org/culture/library/most/getwork.cfm?worknum=92.

Murray, John Courtney. "The Construction of a Christian Culture." In Published and Unpublished Works by John Courtney Murray. Woodstock Jesuit Theological Library, Georgetown University. https://library.georgetown.edu/woodstock/murray/1940a.

Murray, Paul. "Dominicans Drinking: A Neglected Image of the 'Holy Preaching.'" *Religious Life Review* 41 (Sep./Oct. 2002): 272–83.

Newman, John Henry. *Callista: A Tale of the Third Century*. Longmans, Green, and Co., 1901.

Pentin, Edward. "Why Did Vatican II Ignore Communism?" *Catholic World Report*, December 10, 2012. www.catholicworldreport.com/2012/12/10/why-did-vatican-ii-ignore-communism/.

Pieper, Josef. *Happiness and Contemplation*. Translated by Richard and Clara Winston. Pantheon, 1958.

Ratzinger, Joseph. *Salt of the Earth*. Translated by Adrian Walker. Ignatius Press, 1997.

———. "Truth and Freedom." In idem, *Communio*, vol. 2: *Anthropology and Culture*. Edited by David L. Schindler and Nicholas J. Healy. William B. Eerdmans, 2013.

———. "Worthiness to Receive Holy Communion: General Principles." 2004. www.ewtn.com/catholicism/library/worthiness-to-receive-holy-communion-general-principles-2153.

Ravasi, Javier P. Olivera. *The Cristero Counterrevolution and the Battle for the Soul of Mexico*. Os Justi Press, 2025.

Ruse, Austin. "Lighting a Candle to Rainbow Zeus." *Crisis Magazine*, May 26, 2023. https://crisismagazine.com/opinion/lighting-a-candle-to-rainbow-zeus.

Sadler, Ashley. "Bud Light sales crash 26% as boycott over Dylan Mulvaney partnership rages on." *LifeSiteNews*, May 2, 2023. www.lifesitenews.com/news/bud-light-sales-crash-26-as-boycott-over-dylan-mulvaney-partnership-rages-on/.

———. "Designer for Target's pro-LGBT 'pride' collection promotes satanism, violence against 'transphobes.'" *LifeSiteNews*, May 23, 2023. www.lifesitenews.com/news/designer-of-targets-pro-lgbt-pride-collection-promotes-satanism-violence-against-transphobes/

———. "Uganda's tough anti-sodomy bill heads to president's desk for final approval." *LifeSiteNews*, May 15, 2023. www.lifesitenews.com/news/ugandas-tough-anti-sodomy-bill-heads-to-presidents-desk-for-final-approval/.

Schneider, Athanasius. *Credo: Compendium of the Catholic Faith*. Sophia Institute Press, 2023.

———. "The True Face of Freemasonry." *LifeSiteNews*, May 8, 2020. www.lifesitenews.com/blogs/bishop-schneider-explains-true-face-of-freemasonry.

Schrader, Dylan. "The Revision of the Feast of Christ the King." *Antiphon* 18 (2014): 227–53.

Sedgh, Gilda, et al. "Abortion incidence between 1990 and 2014: global, regional, and subregional levels and trends." *The Lancet*, vol. 388, issue 10041, 258–67. www.thelancet.com/journals/lancet/article/PIIS0140-6736(16)30380-4/abstract.

Shannon, Albert Clement. *The Medieval Inquisition*. Augustinian College Press, 1983.

Sire, H. J. A. *Phoenix from the Ashes: The Making, Unmaking, and Restoration of Catholic Tradition*. Angelico Press, 2015.

Smith, P. J. "The Possibility of a Catholic Social Order." *First Things*, December 18, 2017. https://firstthings.com/the-possibility-of-a-catholic-social-order/.

Smits, Jeanne. "*Dignitas Infinita* as a Naturalistic Vision of Mankind." *Rorate Caeli*, April 11, 2024. https://rorate-caeli.blogspot.com/2024/04/counterpoint-dignitas-infinita-as.html.

Staudt, R. Jared. *The Primacy of God: The Virtue of Religion in Catholic Theology*. Emmaus Academic, 2021.

Stevenson, David. *The Origins of Freemasonry. Scotland's Century, 1590–1710*. Cambridge University Press, 1988.

Storck, Thomas. *Economics: An Alternative Introduction*. XIII Books, 2024.

———. *Foundations of a Catholic Political Order*. Second edition. Arouca Press, 2022.

Tate, Jacob. "*Dignitas Infinita*: Lowering the Bar." *OnePeterFive*, April 10, 2024. https://onepeterfive.com/dignitas-infinita-lowering-the-bar/.

Trabbic, Joseph. "Some Responses to Pope Francis's Revision of CCC 2267." *Thomistica*, August 6, 2018. https://thomistica.net/posts/2018/8/4/thomist-responses-to-pope-franciss-revision-of-ccc-2267.

Vree, Pieter, and Thomas Storck, eds. *Catholics and the American Polity: Approaches and Contestations.* Arouca Press, 2025.

Wailzer, Andreas. "Burkina Faso votes to ban homosexual acts." *LifeSiteNews*, September 10, 2025. www.lifesitenews.com/news/burkina-faso-votes-to-ban-homosexual-acts/.

Wakefield, Walter L., and Austin P. Evans. *Heresies of the High Middle Ages.* Columbia University Press.

Waldstein, Edmund, ed. *Integralism and the Common Good: Selected Essays from "The Josias."* Volume 2: *The Two Powers.* Angelico Press, 2022.

Walsh, William Thomas. *Characters of the Inquisition* [1940]. TAN Books, 2005.

——. *Philip II* [1937]. TAN Books, 1987.

Weigel, George. "The Ostpolitik Failed. Get Over It." *First Things*, July 19, 2016. https://firstthings.com/the-ostpolitik-failed-get-over-it/.

Whalen, William J. *Christianity and American Freemasonry.* Third edition. Ignatius Press, 1998.

INDEX

ABOUT THE AUTHOR

PETER A. KWASNIEWSKI holds a BA in Liberal Arts from Thomas Aquinas College and an MA and PhD in Philosophy from the Catholic University of America, with a specialization in the thought of St. Thomas Aquinas. After teaching at the International Theological Institute in Austria, he joined the founding team of Wyoming Catholic College, where he taught theology, philosophy, music, and art history and directed the choir and schola until 2018. Today, Kwasniewski is a full-time writer and lecturer known especially for his work in the areas of liturgy and music; his writings have been translated into over twenty languages, and his sacred music compositions have been performed around the world. He is a cofounder of the Pelican+ Catholic media platform where he writes for *Tradition and Sanity*; he also runs a publishing house, Os Justi Press.

Visit his sites:

www.peterkwasniewski.com

www.CantaboDomino.com

www.osjustipress.com

www.traditionsanity.com

https://app.pelicanplus.com

XIII BOOKS is dedicated to publishing new and vintage works centered around politics, the economy, and the family. Named after Pope Leo XIII—the pope of the "working man," whose pontificate was the first to comprehensively engage in the Church's relationship with the modern world—our imprint was born out of the conviction that we cannot separate the Catholic faith from our involvement with the world around us, and that the social doctrine of the Church, whether explicitly or implicitly, requires a commitment by Catholics to transform every aspect of the social order in conformity to the will of God. We aspire to earn a reputation amongst our readers as a reliable provider of the best the social tradition has to offer, which is rooted in our allegiance to Christ the King and passion for sharing with others the teachings of the Church.

www.ingramcontent.com/pod-product-compliance
Lightning Source LLC
Chambersburg PA
CBHW030907120626
46554CB00001B/47